T0345244

Shaping
the Wild

Shaping the Wild

David Elias

Text © David Elias, 2023
Illustrations and map © Peter Hanauer, 2023

www.uwp.co.uk

British Library Cataloguing-in-Publication Data
A catalogue record for this book is available from the British Library.

ISBN: 978-1-915279-34-7

Cover design by Andy Ward Design
Typeset by Agnes Graves
Printed by CPI Group (UK) Ltd, Croydon CR0 4YY

The publisher acknowledges the financial support of
the Books Council of Wales

Table of Contents

For Gethin,
who lives and breathes this life

Everybody needs beauty as well as bread
John Muir

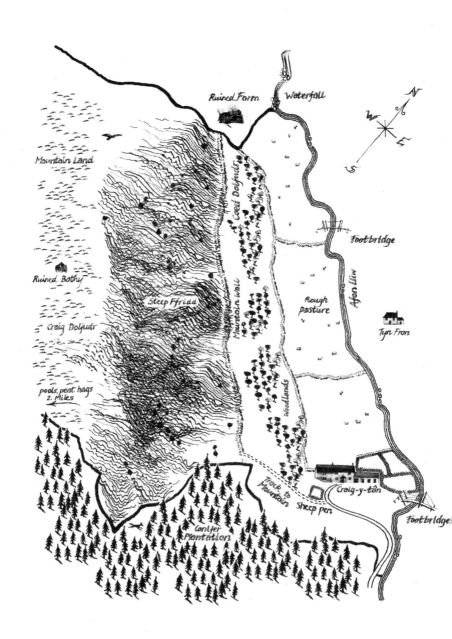

Foreword

by Iolo Williams

For thousands of years, humans have continuously struggled to transform the Welsh landscape. Generations of farmers have shed blood, sweat and tears to turn a largely forested country into an intricate mosaic of habitats rich in wildlife. It is only over the past 150 years, a blink of an eye in historical terms, that agriculture and wildlife have come into conflict due to the demands that we as consumers have thrust upon our land managers.

In these pages, David Elias tells the story of Craig-y-tân, a family farm situated near Bala at the southern end of the Eryri (Snowdonia) National Park. It is a beautiful area, but, as any farmer will tell you, beauty does not pay the bills. Successive agri-environment schemes have undoubtedly helped ensure that some wildlife can live alongside modern farming techniques but so many once familiar species, from curlew and corncrake to lapwing and linnet, have fallen by the wayside.

This book takes us through the seasons and across the many landscapes within the farm boundary. With its wild bogs, crystal-clear streams and scattered woodlands, Craig-y-tân is not a typical farm and yet it represents a microcosm of events unfolding throughout rural Wales. The future for our wildlife and farming is an uncertain one, particularly in this post-Brexit era. Throw into this mix the precarious nature of the language and culture of a proud nation and you have a potentially volatile canvas that forms the backdrop to this book.

David Elias is a craftsman, a man who paints vivid pictures with words, and a worthy addition to the pantheon of rural Welsh writing greats such as Bill Condry and Jim Perrin. It is his background, however, that makes him the ideal person to write this story. During his time as warden for the Nature Conservancy Council (later the Countryside Council for Wales) on the Berwyn Mountains, he was also my line manager and mentor for one memorable year in the mid-1980s. His ability to communicate and understand both sides of the potential conservation/farming conflict is one of his greatest assets, as is his eye for detail. Whilst I was spending six glorious months monitoring some of Wales's most threatened wildlife, David was uncomplainingly dealing with the minutiae of landowner management agreements whilst yearning for a day on the open hills with his green, enthusiastic assistant.

Reading this book transports me back to my carefree days on the open moorland of the Berwyn and the valuable lessons learned in David's company. The most fundamental was the realisation that not one of our seemingly wild landscapes here in Wales is untouched by humankind. Beautiful and rich in wildlife some may be, but they have been manipulated and transformed, often by families forced to eke out a living in the harshest of circumstances.

Shaping the Wild also looks at the future of farming and conservation, both at Craig-y-tân and in a wider context. With wholesale changes planned for the agri-environment schemes that have provided a lifeline for many of the small upland farms in Wales, will we witness a mass exodus from the Welsh countryside in the near future? Will family farms be replaced by huge sheep ranches and large-scale tree planting backed by huge corporations as a means of offsetting carbon emissions? As a Welsh-speaking conservationist with farming roots who has lived in the countryside all my life, I certainly hope not.

I highly recommend this book to anyone who enjoys nature and the outdoors, has an interest in farming and conservation, or any reader who revels in beautifully written prose. I would also recommend that any relevant politician or decision maker should read this book from cover to cover.

Iolo Williams

Chapter 1

Craig-y-tân

In a North Wales village huddled under the 3,000-foot bulk of Aran Benllyn, about fifty of us stood singing hymns around an open grave. We had come to bury Marged Jones of Craig-y-tân, aged ninety-one years. This warm-hearted, sharp-witted woman had been totally devoted to the community in which she lived all her long life, so it was fitting that so many people had turned out to her funeral service in Yr Hen Gapel, an hour or so before. Marged, along with her five sisters and one brother, was born not three miles away from here in a hill farm called Craig-y-tân and she and her brother, Hywel, both unmarried, never left. They farmed Craig-y-tân for the rest of their working lives.

As I stood amongst the mourners, one of the many thoughts going through my head was that Marged had been a link with an era that has almost passed from direct memory, a time before the countryside changed forever with the coming of mechanisation. Marged's life represents much of what this book is about: how the wildlife and landscape of upland Wales has been, and continues to be, shaped by a very particular human community and culture. Historically, this shaping has been driven mostly by farming and, to a lesser extent, forestry and game shooting, but now the biodiversity and climate crisis demand that the land is also managed for nature, flood prevention, carbon capture and other 'ecosystem services'. At its heart this book is searching for the reconciliation of hill farming, the tradition that Marged understood, and nature conservation, the discipline from which I have come. Beyond the strident headlines and bland policy statements I want to understand what it really takes to bring these two together, and to properly answer that you need to consider the 'full catastrophe' of life, as Zorba the Greek would have had it.[1] If human activity has shaped the wild, and continues to do so, then we need to embrace the 'full catastrophe' and understand the people who do the shaping as well as the wildlife and wild land that inhabit it. How they complement or collide with one another is crucial. With this perspective, it is vital not only to gather information but also to acknowledge how we are affected by wild land and life. What moves us is so often what drives us to action.

In an attempt to address all of this, I have chosen to focus this book on one very particular hill farm, Craig-y-tân, as a lens through which to view the whole rich and ragged picture. With Hywel's blessing I visited the farm repeatedly over a period of nearly seven years between 2015–21, getting to know him, the farming and the wildlife at all seasons in order to grasp a multidimensional picture of hill farming in these times of deep environmental concern and Brexit-induced agricultural upheaval.[2]

On an early spring day in 2015, I climb up into the steep woodland on the valley side in Craig-y-tân; this wood has always fascinated me: it seems somehow outside of time, as if no one has ever set foot in it. I sit high up near the top of the wood with my back to a small cliff, in a kind of *cwtch* in the rocks, so they fit round me keeping off the worst of the cold wind. It's likely people and animals have sheltered here for centuries. Fallen bracken the colour of dried tobacco is folded over the rocks; dotted amongst them are patches of crystalline snow. I can hear Hywel whistling to his dogs lower down the valley. A raven croaks overhead. Half a mile away, and one hundred feet below me, the river sounds like distant motor traffic, dispersed white noise I could easily not hear. Underneath this is a silence, a stillness that is always there. It is that which takes this place out of time.

I understand why I like this spot: I have my back against the wall, and I can see all the territory below me. If I don't move, I am unlikely to be seen amongst the trees. It gives me a sense of both safety and advantage, which could be hardwired in the brain from when we were predator or prey. I also have a sense of expectancy, waiting and watching for something. It is early March, light by 6.30 a.m., and the birds are beginning to sing again; the pregnant ewes will be back here from their away-wintering in three weeks and lambing will begin almost immediately. I realise that what I am looking for are the first signs of spring in the hills – but there is little to encourage me. These woods seem unrelenting; the expectation is only mine.

Where I am sitting at the base of the cliff a series of rocky outcrops tumble down 200 feet in a series of steps to the woodland at Craig-y-tân.

The great bulk of this farm is above and behind me, a huge expanse of bog and heather-covered peat about two miles across; one of the wildest and most inaccessible places I know in Wales. The ground in front of me slopes steeply, a chaos of boulders ranging in size, from a bucket to a garden shed, and trees that have somehow elbowed their way amongst them are bent and twisted, festooned with moss and lichen. Mosses also carpet the boulders wall-to-wall, concealing all manner of fissures and holes. This is a treacherous place to walk and I'm mindful that there is no phone signal here. Across the river, on the opposite side of the valley, I can see a mixture of moorland and blocks of conifers fringed with birch trees, which are turning a deep aubergine colour before bud-burst. To my left Moel Llyfnant, covered with snow, looks like a huge cone of sugar and beside it the flank of Arenig Fawr disappears into low cloud, its summit at nearly 3,000 feet lost from view. The farmhouse and outbuildings of Craig-y-tân are about half a mile away down the valley to my right, clustered around them are several small fields enclosed by stone walls – the only land here you could call good grazing. Far to the right, perhaps ten miles away, is the rounded profile of the Berwyn Mountains, where I spent a good chunk of my working life. Looking out from here I feel content; there is nowhere I would rather be. Perhaps this is what Thoreau meant by 'the tonic of wildness'.[3]

Looking back at Marged's life, it is important to acknowledge that there was nowhere she also would rather have been: Craig-y-tân, and Pennant-Lliw, the valley and community in which it is set, were everything to her; it was the whole world in which her life was expressed. Marged saw life through the prism of her warm-hearted sociable personality; she was surprisingly tactile, often taking my hand and holding on to it. She was also a considerable presence: I remember seeing her at a distance down one of those interminable hospital corridors in Wrexham and I immediately knew her confident, straight-backed walk and trademark dangly earrings. I also remember her telling a sixty-year-old local man very clearly what she expected him to do, to which he meekly agreed. When I related this to my wife, Elen, she said, 'That is because she used to be his Sunday school teach-er!' Her Christian faith was pivotal in her pervading gratitude for a happy and fulfilling life; sometimes, when telling me some anecdote, she was so lit up with joy at her good fortune she would clap her hands exclaiming 'Happy, happy times!'

The first time I went to visit Marged at Graig Wen, her retirement bungalow in the village, it was exactly as I expected: furniture polished, brasses gleaming – not a speck of dust anywhere. She was as well turned out as her front room and greeted me with her usual shiny-eyed enthusiasm. After settling me by the window, she went to prepare some tea, leaving me surrounded by beautiful old furniture that had come from Craig-y-tân, including an enormous oak dresser, glossy from generations of polishing, for which there was scarcely enough room in her modest bungalow. Marged came back with tea, Welsh cakes and *bara brith* (traditional fruit loaf), then settled herself opposite me, straight backed and attentive. Although nearly ninety, she was sharp and eager to talk, but our conversations took a bit of managing as Marged rarely spoke *Saesneg* (English) and would often struggle for a word whilst I tried to fill in with my inadequate Welsh. What is more she sometimes misunderstood me, as she didn't often hear English either – Welsh language radio was her staple. But what we lacked in ease of communication was overcome by our mutual enthusiasm. Our conversations (coupled with two reminiscences she wrote for a local publication) gave me a vivid picture of her early life and farming before the Second World War.

Marged was born at Craig-y-tân in 1926 and lived there for the next seventy years – a period of tumultuous change even in the hills of North Wales. She was the eldest of seven: six girls and one boy, Hywel, who was the youngest. Their small house huddled under the mountainside in what was a remote valley, approachable only on foot or by horse and cart along a rough and winding track. Motor vehicles were uncommon in the district, and it was some years before they had a van or tractor on the farm. Lighting was by paraffin lamps and candles; heating from open fires burning wood or peat. Craig-y-tân is a wet, cold place in winter with more snow then than now, so keeping warm and dry was a preoccupation, but, as Marged was keen to point out, they walked everywhere and work was by hand, so exercise helped keep them warm (and fit), in stark contrast to our sedentary lifestyle today. From the age of six, Marged walked the three miles to school each morning and back again in the afternoon. Along the way, she would pick up with other children waiting, but if they weren't there as expected she would leave a white stone on the gatepost to show she had passed. Today, a small girl walking on her own could seem risky, but she would have been known to every person in the valley and strangers were few and far between. That sense of localness is still tangible today, a comfort that enfolds people and sometimes makes them slow to warm to strangers.

The habit of walking everywhere never left Marged: well into her seventies she would trudge several miles to the village and back with her bags of shopping. Even as a ninety-year-old she would walk two or three miles round her beloved Pennant-Lliw picking blackberries. When I asked her why she went so far for them, she replied conspiratorially, 'Because I know where the best ones are.' The necessity of walking everywhere was exemplified by the postmen (they seem always to have been men), who did their deliveries on foot, thus establishing paths from farm to farm, many of which are the foundation of our current network of rights of way. The postman in Pennant-Lliw at that time, John Ellis Roberts, lived in Tyn y Fron, just across the river from Craig-y-tân where he had a small farm. He delivered to the middle valley in the morning starting early and then went home for his lunch, but it was his misfortune that the man in Blaen Lliw, right at the top of the valley, took a newspaper, which had to be delivered each day: a steep round trip of 5 miles or so every afternoon. At Blaen Lliw they would give him *siot* (butter milk with oat cakes crumbled into it), which helped a bit. Marged said if they needed urgent help in those early days they would hang a white cloth over the hedge so that anybody passing along the road on the other side of the valley, including the postman, would send word or come to their aid. At that time the road must have only been a track, albeit an important one, leading over the mountain and down to Trawsfynydd; even today it is only a single-track road with five gates to open and close.

When it was time for Marged and her brother to retire in the mid-

1990s, the running of the farm passed to their nephew Hywel. After leaving school, he had been packed off to Shrewsbury by his parents to do an apprenticeship with Rolls-Royce, rather than go to agricultural college as he would have preferred. He told me that when he drove over the hills to Shrewsbury he would see farmers working their sheep and think 'I would much rather be doing that.' So after six years he came back home and worked as a milkman and then a postman, gradually acquiring a network of part-time farm work that kept his farming dream alive. Taking on Craig-y-tân was a wonderful opportunity for him.

Hywel and I first got to know each other when he was our postman; many hill farmers have a day job to make ends meet and Hywel went on delivering the post for years after he took over at Craig-y-tân. We would talk farming and nature when he delivered the letters.

Early on in my explorations of Craig-y-tân, back in 2015, I arranged to meet Hywel to go through the farming calendar with him so I could understand his work better. We met in the yard muffled against a strong wind and a smattering of sleet coming straight off the mountain. He is always bigger than I expect; in my mind he is slight but he is taller than me and has the lean, rugged look of somebody who has been exposed to the weather all his life, though with fair curly hair and bright blue eyes, he looks younger than his sixty-odd years.

'Will you come in, David?' he asked politely. Clambering out of our waterproofs in the porch, we sat round the table in his spacious modern kitchen, drinking tea and talking farming. Hywel is reserved, self-contained and not given to hyperbole. Like most hill farmers, he likes to convey an air of independence, or more particularly non-dependence. Two hours later, he was still spelling out the farming year at Craig-y-tân, keen for me to understand the constraints and limitations of making farming work here. Each time we talk, I see the particularities of this place a little more clearly. Hywel is thoughtful and articulate about farming and countryside matters, and I am grateful that he is willing to speak to me about these things in English. He speaks Welsh almost exclusively with his family, other farmers and in our community, but he knows my Welsh isn't up to it. A deep sense of identity, of Welshness, only some of which is conscious, is nourished by the language and it binds people to the land. Although I have lived in this valley for more than thirty-five years, that will never be mine.

I first came to live here in 1983, when the Nature Conservancy Council (later the Countryside Council for Wales) offered me the job of warden on the Berwyn Mountains, an enormous expanse of rolling moorland centred near Bala. The Berwyn was in uproar at the time because the interests of agriculture and nature conservation had come sharply into conflict: farmers were being grant aided by government to convert moorland into improved pasture, as well as being subsidised to maintain very high sheep numbers. At the same time, the government's own nature conservation agency was seeking to protect the best moorland sites principally by preventing agricultural improvement and reducing sheep numbers. Conflict was inevitable and passions ran high, there was open hostility from the farming community towards the Nature Conservancy Council and its staff.[4] Over the next thirteen years, I experienced at first hand the views of both sides and what it takes to reach the degree of understanding and compromise necessary to create long-term harmony.

The friction between agriculture and conservation is still pivotal to the fate of wildlife in Britain today. I have often heard it said, including by Hywel, that 'farmers get blamed for everything' but the facts are unavoidable: agriculture, incentivised by governments and the European Union, has been the principal cause of the decline of our wildlife over the last sixty years. The authoritative 2016 *State of Nature* report published by the UK Centre for Ecology and Hydrology stated unambiguously that 'the intensification of agriculture has had the biggest impact on wildlife, and that has been overwhelmingly negative over the period of our study (40 years)'.[5] A rural country like Wales has inevitably felt that impact. Depending on whose statistics you believe, eighty to ninety per cent of Wales is devoted to agriculture and managed by just two per cent of the population: farmers are a small, but critically influential group of people for the future of our wildlife.[6] If conservation fails to influence that two per cent, then there is no hope of biodiversity recovering here.

When I come to leave, Hywel takes me round the back of the barn to admire his new dog kennels. 'I put them here so they don't get off barking every time someone comes,' he says. He has eight sheepdogs and he speaks softly to them, using their names. The kennels have been carefully designed and look as though they work well – like everything else at Craig-y-tân. This is the only farm I have ever been on where every gate swings and fastens as it should.

From my perch at the base of the cliff I can see how little 'bottom land' there is here. If you want to rear a lot of profitable sheep, you need rich grassland sown with ryegrass and boosted with artificial fertiliser. That's the norm on most farms, at least on the lower land, but not here. Even the three or four small fields round the house are traditional 'unimproved' pastures. The rest is rough grazing: wild and rugged, some of it boggy, rocks are everywhere, scattered with ancient hawthorns and crab apples. You might think it barely tamed, but it has been farmed for centuries and that has fundamentally shaped it, despite its wild appearance. Hywel regrets the lack of good grazing at Craig-y-tân; 'every farmer wants to farm,' he is fond of saying, which for him means producing good quality lamb for market. Part of the reason the land here is so unproductive is the intractable nature of the terrain, but that wouldn't be an insurmountable obstacle to modern machinery on the grazing land between the wood and the river.

A more recent constraint is that Craig-y-tân, besides being in the National Park, is part of a large Site of Special Scientific Interest (SSSI) that stretches for miles across the moors and mountains around here. SSSIs are designated by the national conservation agencies to identify and protect our best wildlife sites. All my adult life I have been agonising over wildlife habitats eroding and diminishing. In truth, the UK's wildlife stock has probably been in decline since the start of the Industrial Revolution, a trend that has only accelerated over the last fifty to sixty years, so working to protect ever diminishing populations of plants and animals can be painful and demoralising. It can make conservationists defensive, determined to cling on to every scrap and sometimes self-righteous about the justness of their cause. Consequently, unlike Hywel, I am relieved that Craig-y-tân is protected in this way. Agriculture has undoubtedly been the single most destructive force in the impoverishment of British wildlife over the last sixty years, although paradoxically prior to that it was farming that created much of the beauty and richness in the countryside, giving rise to our celebrated 'cultural landscapes'. Farmers didn't set out to create or destroy any of this; it was an unintended consequence of their work, although I haven't heard many of them express regret about it. Conservationists, who often come from somewhere other, talk (in the language of their trade) about these areas as 'sites' and they 'designate' them. Hywel doesn't call Craig-y-tân anything other than 'here'; he isn't separate from it – he is of this place. He doesn't think in terms of the UK's wildlife stock but of 'around here'. Inevitably there is friction between these two cultures. SSSIs bring specific constraints, so Hywel couldn't 'improve' most of his land even if he wanted to. Like many farmers he resents the imposition, which brings nothing but restriction to his business: it's a bit like living in a Grade 1 listed building. But importantly his farm is also in a Glastir agri-environment scheme (more details about this in Chapter 3), which further limits how he can farm but, crucially to him, is voluntary and an important source of income. He gets compensated for complying with the constraints of the scheme.

On the other side of the river I can see the small unoccupied farmhouse and outbuildings of Tyn y Fron. The focus of Marged's reminiscences were mostly from the time when she was young, in the 1930s and 40s, but by great good fortune there is also another very local account that predates Marged's era. E. D. Rowlands (Edward David) was born in Tyn y Fron in 1880. One of nine children, born to Ellis and Catrin, E. D. spent his childhood there in the 1880s and 1890s; he did well at school and eventually became a head teacher of a primary school in Llandudno Junction. In later life he wrote *Atgofion am Llanuwchllyn* (*Remembering Llanuwchllyn*), a memoir that is partly about his early life in Tyn y Fron, giving us a picture of life in the valley a generation or more before Marged.[7]

Craig-y-tân and Tyn y Fron were at that time part of the Watkin Williams Wynn estate, which covered an enormous area in North and Mid Wales. Consequently, the Williams Wynn family were highly influential, and E. D. remembered the fuss when the 'old Sir Watkin' died in 1885 and 'Sir Watkin *bach*' inherited the estate. The local irreverent nicknames for them amongst their tenants were 'Swatkin' and 'Swatkin *bach*'. The former apparently had a terrible temper but would respect a man who stood up to him. He liked to work hard with his tenants, unlike his son, whom it was said ran up £60,000 in gambling debts, which his father had to clear.[8] However, from the time the younger Sir Watkin took over, many of the old single-storey long-houses like Tyn y Fron began to be replaced with 'modern' two-storey houses, which improved the living standards of their tenants considerably. E. D. remembered the stonemason coming to build their new house with the Glanllyn horse-drawn waggon arriving with wood and lime for the construction. When they moved in, the nine-year-old E. D. was impressed by the fine new kitchen, the range and an outside building with a bread oven. Equally impressive were the fireplaces in the bedrooms and the light flooding in through the big windows.

Farming is weather dependent under the best of circumstances, but before mechanisation it was critical. When E. D. says 'we prayed for better weather' in his memoir he was being literal, remembering a special service in Capel Carmel when it had been persistently wet at harvest time. He also remembered vividly his first visit as a six-year-old to the Hen Gapel, the large chapel nearer to the village. It was his first wide-eyed walk down the valley and he recalled feeling 'suffocated' by the high hedges and big trees, which grew in the comparative fertility of the lower valley. There was a 'strange and unpleasant smell' as they passed the cottages along the road, which his mother told him was burning coal; he had only ever smelled peat or wood from the fires at home. Although Tyn y Fron was only three miles up the valley, to this six-year-old boy it was as if he had entered another world.

Tyn y Fron is now uninhabited; the last people to live there were John Ellis Roberts and his family – he was the postman when Marged was a girl. There is still a small area of grazing round the house and down to the river, but the rest of the land has grown over with gorse and bracken. This is a common story in the uplands of Wales – many people left small farms like Tyn y Fron during the last century – but the core of those who remain in farming are indigenous; very few from outside come into farming in this area. Hywel's son Rhys, who farms with him some of the time, will take over from him when he retires, as has happened in an unbroken chain for generations before them. One way or another that's a lot of continuity: an unconscious investment of labour, heartache and satisfaction, in this obdurate and beautiful place.

And I do find it beautiful – Richard Jefferies wrote 'the heart from the moment of its first beat instinctively longs for beauty'.[9] How we express that is another matter. Many farmers and others who have worked on the land all their lives probably wouldn't split off something they called beautiful but rather take satisfaction in the place 'looking well' or there being 'a good show of bluebells this year'. I once walked with a farmer into a narrowing valley on the western escarpment of the Berwyn. It was a glorious spring day, the birds were singing and a waterfall poured over the towering cliff at the head of the valley in front of us. I stood in wonder. He looked at me appraisingly:

'I suppose you think this is beautiful?'

'I do, don't you?'

'It's just the place where I work.'

Perhaps he was winding me up or, more likely, making a point that this was not just a 'playground for nature' but a place of hard and sometimes brutal work. But it seems to me that embracing both these viewpoints – the beautiful and the brutal, if you like – is essential to understanding such places and our relationship with them. I acknowledge that if it were my garden, my nature reserve, I would see the problems, the work that needs to be done, which often obscures appreciation. Recently, I was walking with my son Gethin, who is a warden for the RSPB, in a beautiful place in Eryri (Snowdonia). After a while, I realised we had talked almost exclusively about the work required to maintain or enhance it: rhododendron and conifer removal, path maintenance, grazing levels, heather burning and so on; we had hardly mentioned the beauty. I think perhaps that was the point the farmer on the Berwyn was trying to make to me. Even naturalists don't often acknowledge the beauty of the organisms that fascinate them, or the wild places where they are found; usually preoccupied with the technicalities of taxonomy, distribution, or biology, the place remains a scenic backdrop.

Another element in this cultural friction can be that of the outsider coming in and viewing the land through an aesthetic that is not rooted in that place. There is a long tradition of literary people (usually men) making excursions into wild countryside and describing it in a way that can be seen as alien or exclusive. The poet Kathleen Jamie referred scathingly to this as 'the lone enraptured male' – of which I fervently hope I am not one.[10] Few would deny the validity of Wordsworth's poetry about the Lake District, but perhaps the distinction is, as the farmer James Rebanks acknowledges in his book *The Shepherd's Life*, that Wordsworth had an understanding and affinity with the people who worked there, because that is where he was born and brought up.

Despite the cold beginning to get to me, I am reluctant to leave my perch in the woods. Since I was a child, nature has been a 'safe place' for me – so it is not surprising I became a naturalist and conservationist. The solace, joy and fascination it offers me has been an unbreakable thread throughout my life. And I am not alone: in Michael McCarthy's wonderful book *The Moth Snowstorm* he suggests that the joy and sense of connection that nature brings is innate and could be the antidote to our suicidal destructiveness of the natural world.[11] Suicidal, because nature will just go on; battered and distorted perhaps, but ultimately indestructible; we cannot say the same for ourselves – unless we wake up very soon. I recognise that this is far away from Hywel lugging bales of hay out to his sheep in the mud and winter rain, but if we are to under-stand through contact and joy then we have to reconcile the beauty and brutality – the pretty with the gritty – that Craig-y-tân has in abundance.

Even here farmers are a breed apart, a tribe within, somewhat separate from the rest of Welsh life. They often have a sense of being misunder-stood by the rest of us, especially those from the various countryside agencies who are often perceived as having come straight from college with maps, classifications and computerised systems. While working on the Berwyn, I once met with a farmer whom I knew well and got on with. We were negotiating a management agreement over his mountain land and all was going well until I produced some aerial photographs to support my contention that the extent of heather cover on his land had declined, rather than increased as he claimed – and he walked out, considering this to be unethical, 'spy in the sky' tactics. As previously mentioned, the conservationists (of which I am one) frequently refer to the farm as 'the site' and they often only speak English, although that has changed for the better recently. To the farmer it is *his* farm expressed with the unconscious weight of generations of labour. There is also a fatalism about being here that can seem counter-cultural to the restless global village, where people move to better themselves and may know little of the people around them, but have multiple distant and on-line relationships. Farmers here are sometimes still living out their grandfather's favours and feuds. If this land has always been your family's livelihood, you expect to hand that on, and it is not yours to sell even if, as sometimes, it is a millstone round your neck. In recent years, speculators have been investing in land, without knowledge or care for the work done there, so prices are now very high. Some hill farmers are rich men on paper and keeping the continuity going can be a burden, but selling up is still rarely seen as an option.

Reflecting on these things seems to emphasise my differentness. My early life was the opposite of rooted; my father was in the Forces, so we moved every two or three years. When I arrived here in my late thirties, I came with almost no sense of community or family. I am an only child of two only children and the few relatives we had remained unseen and unvisited in our ever-shifting geography. Before moving here, Elen and I were living and working in a national park in Malawi. I came because the conservation agency I worked for had a new and politically sensitive job on the Berwyn Mountains and they wanted an experienced, Welsh-speaking person for the post – and couldn't find one. I was the next best thing as I had the experience and had married into a local family; they hoped that would get my feet under the table, and to some extent I think it did. Perhaps it made me seem less of a 'here today, gone tomorrow' type of character; the sort that, if all else fails, farmers just decide to outlive. But in all other ways I felt different. I came steeped in concepts of habitats, species and conservation management at a time when none of that was common currency locally. I had had precious little to do with farmers and I am English – not necessarily a neutral condition. I could have seemed like the classic interfering outsider, and perhaps to some I was.[12]

Thirty-five years on, Welsh-speaking children reared, I have come to respect and value a sense of continuity and community, even if I still view the latter from a little way off. I am also aware that thirty-five years is nothing. If your family have worked a piece of land for generations, then I have only just arrived. Perhaps this weakness is also a strength in that I can now tell something of an inside story from an outsider viewpoint. I do know about wildlife and wild places from the perspective of a lifetime of appreciation and conservation knowledge; I can see the bigger picture. Deep in my bones I feel inclusive: that both positions, the beauty and the brutal, are valid and what interests me is how they can be reconciled. Looking out from here I can see the whole story of what has shaped the uplands in the last several hundred years: moorlands, bogs, woodland, conifer plantations, pastureland and the river have all been moulded and reshaped by human activity. We have had a radical impact on the composition and appearance of wild land. This is as true of the uplands, which look so attractive and unchanged to the untrained eye, as the intensively managed and populated lowlands. Craig-y-tân is a beautiful microcosm of all of that: a place where the impacts can be understood from differing angles; where lessons can be learned, and future directions considered. Is this place an anachronism or is it the future? It is a farm and there is a living that must be made, one that also represents a way of life. Farmers want to maximise their productivity and manipulate their land and stock to do so; equally conservationists want to see the land manipulated to maximise 'productivity' for wildlife and landscape value. Can these two urges be reconciled, or will wildlife and beauty have to be confined to the ghettos of nature reserves set within an impoverished agri-scape surrounding them?

I have been sitting here for more than an hour and the cold is beginning to get into me. Reluctantly I pick my way between the trees and over the boulders towards the fence. It is then that I notice them: hundreds of stiffly pointed bluebell leaves pushing through the moss, a literal manifestation of Dylan Thomas's 'green fuse', through which the life force flows. It is beginning again. In six weeks, this place will be a carpet of blue – and I will call it beautiful.

Chapter 2

Lambing

Craig-y-tân is all about sheep – it is too rough and wet for much else – and over the centuries hundreds of thousands of them have, by their constant nibbling, gradually shaped the vegetation of the farm. Despite this long and seemingly unchanging context, there have been profound developments in upland farming over the last seventy years, which have significantly impacted the land and its wildlife. By studying Craig-y-tân, I want to try and understand these changes, and how they have affected the land and wildlife, as well as farming. Spring on a hill farm is all about lambing: not least because lambs reared through to sale are the farm's 'cash crop' – its profit (or not). Consequently for Hywel, and his son Rhys, the survival of lambs in spring is paramount – the fortunes of the farm's wildlife is bound to be peripheral. Yet if wildlife is ever going to thrive again on farmland, it will have to become more central for those who manage the land.

I'm back at Craig-y-tân in early April and, despite the wet and cold, there are a few signs of spring: two newly arrived swallows zip up the valley and I catch a snatch of a redstart's song, elusive amongst the hawthorns. A bumblebee blunders past, seemingly oblivious to the chilly wind. All around me, narrow-faced, thick-coated ewes, each with a lamb at foot, are moving slowly through the rough pasture, some rasping on the lumpy fodder beet scattered about to provide extra nutrition whilst they are lactating. Dozens of spindly lambs, some with brown collars, saddles or muzzles dot the landscape; their high-pitched bleats demand attention like a baby's cry and have me smiling widely. The pregnant ewes only returned to Craig-y-tân a fortnight ago from wintering away on a lower, more fertile farm, and already the place is a bedlam of lambs and their mothers.

Back near the house I come across Rhys, who has turned a ewe and twin lambs into one of the stone pens; his two dogs look on. Rhys is tall, slim and dark whilst his father is fair. He is typically unruffled, almost laconic, which belies his twenty-nine years. He tells me he is doing nine straight weeks of lambing on various farms, starting last month near Aberystwyth at his uncle's, which was all done indoors: 'Good lambs, but the wool is very thin so they couldn't survive outdoors.' He will finish here, at home on Craig-y-tân, in a few weeks' time – lambing is always later on hill farms due principally to the upland climate. 'It's fine; I'm only doing daylight hours here,' he says with a wry smile. 'These ewes are good at birthing and caring for their lambs.' That said, the ewe he has penned is butting one lamb aggressively, repeatedly knocking it over. It is pitiful to watch as the skinny little thing struggles to its feet only to be sent flying again. Rhys explains that there has been a mix-up in the chaos of lambing and that this lamb has probably been with another ewe for a few hours, so now it smells wrong and its mother will not have it. Despite its desperation there is no chance she will accept it now. Instead, Rhys says he has a dead lamb of hers which he will skin and then tie the pelt over the sad little reject and present it to the dead lamb's mother. All being well it will then smell right to her, and she will accept it and allow it to suckle.

Hywel arrives with some more ewes and twins, which he has gathered from where they have birthed; he likes to have the twins near the house where he can keep a close eye on them. One of the ewes is refusing to budge. Hywel positions one dog to cut off her escape route whilst another crouches flat to the ground, moving slowly forward like a crocodile. The ewe turns to face the dog, stamping her foot defiantly, but is gradually backing up, her lamb close at her side. Dog and lamb are nose to nose, no more than a foot apart. Hywel is calling to the dogs – a string of words, some soft, others harsh – to which they instantly respond. Leaning on his crook with a newborn lamb under one arm he looks totally at ease – a man in his element.

There seems to be so much to keep an eye on. A ewe trailing bloody afterbirth wanders off without one of her lambs, seemingly indifferent. Another newborn is left behind hunched and sleepy, its mother and sibling fifty yards away, until it bleats, and she hurries back towards the triggering sound. Reunited, she sniffs it carefully to be sure it is hers and then walks on with both. Hywel agrees they are mostly good mothers, but some are not, and that is when they must intervene.

Lambing started on the dot on 1 April, timed precisely from when they put the rams to the ewes in November. 'The ewes didn't look quite so good when they came back and the lambs are a bit small, but they are doing well, fewer losses that usual,' Rhys says. 'Getting them through the first week or so is important. These Welsh lambs have thicker fleeces and skins, so stand the weather better than most other breeds – if you skin one you can feel the difference.' The weather is also critical: yesterday was so wet Hywel worried lambs might fall in the swollen streams and drown.

The steep pasture in front of the house is relatively safe for lambs – close at hand, dry and with only one stream – so this is where they keep the ewes with twins. 'There is plenty of cover for them as they can get down behind stones or rushes. They are tough little buggers,' Hywel explains. Despite this they have been losing lambs on this dry pasture each night, probably to a fox. Hywel says that foxes seek out twin lambs as the ewe can't defend them both at once, then the fox can pick one off.

The management of sheep has always been central to this family's farming life. Marged's father, Ifan, and after him her brother, Hywel, were devoted to shepherding, each in their element up on the mountain with their dogs, caring for the sheep at lambing time. Marged's brother left school at fourteen, and from then worked full time on the farm until he retired sixty years or so later – his whole life was expressed through Craig-y-tân.

E. D. Rowlands seems to have been another boy who always wanted to be a shepherd. In spring, when the sheep were taken back to the mountain to relieve the lower, more fertile land for growing hay, he sometimes missed school for days because the sheep would pull back down, looking for the comfort of the lower ground. For three or four weeks, he would help drive them back up repeatedly until they became acclimatised again and reacquainted with their *cynefin* (habitat) on the unfenced mountain.

Although such close attention to the sheep is rarely necessary today, I still see this love of shepherding in Hywel; there is an extra edge of enthusiasm and depth of knowledge when he explains to me about earmarks, lambing, shearing and the like: a light carried forward from his grandfather and beyond.

Although the flock size has varied over the decades, Craig-y-tân has always been too harsh and with insufficient winter-keep for the bulk of the breeding ewes, not least because when they are pregnant they need good quality grazing. Even when Marged was a girl, most of the breeding flock spent the winter at a lower farm and, before motor transport, the only way to get them there was to walk. Marged recalled an occasion, when she was about eleven, that she and her father shepherded 200 sheep along the public roads to a farm at Betws Gwerful Goch, a village about twenty-four miles from Craig-y-tân. Marged walked at the front and her father at the back with dogs to keep the sheep together. Once they had settled the sheep into their new pastures, they stayed the night at the farm and then walked all the way back the following day. These days, using a lorry, the whole job would be done in two to three hours.

Farming in the UK has, at least until recently, been almost exclusively about producing food – and that is certainly what most farmers (and the public) see as their job. But in upland Britain that is a limited proposition as the soils are poor and the climate harsh; low temperatures mean that grass grows slowly, and steep terrain makes access and use of machinery difficult. Livestock farming is the only practical proposition in this district and, other than two dairy herds and a scatter of beef cattle, sheep are overwhelmingly the principal 'crop' here. But despite these constraints, high-quality lamb is produced both for the domestic market and export.

During and following the Second World War there was a government-incentivised drive to produce more food from British farmland, which kickstarted a period of agricultural intensification that continues to this day. Most of the wildlife found on the rich and much mythologised pre-war farmland was an unintended by-product of slower and less intensive farming systems, whether it was the corn buntings in the crops, orchids in the hay meadows, or marsh fritillary butterflies in the rough pasture. New strains of seeds, improved machinery, artificial fertilisers, pesticides and more – all propelled by government subsidies and guaranteed prices – had the desired effect of increasing agricultural productivity leading to a plentiful supply of cheaper food. Meanwhile farmland wildlife was quietly eviscerated.

Craig-y-tân is set within the spectacular landscape of the Eryri (Snowdonia) National Park, a place millions of people visit every year for its beauty and wildness. Because of this, it is often assumed that it has avoided the destructive aspects of agricultural intensification that have been so marked in the lowlands of Britain. It looks wild, so is assumed to be in good shape, but the impacts from farming have been significant.

Pasture improvement is prominent amongst these: ninety-seven per cent of the flower-and-insect-rich permanent pasture of pre-war Britain has gone.[13] Although the re-seeding of pastureland started well before the Second World War,[14] it really gathered pace after the 1947 Agricultural Act, which for the first time guaranteed farmers a price for their produce. By the late twentieth century most pastures had been drained, ploughed, re-seeded with a commercial mix – usually rye grass and clover – and then they are regularly boosted with artificial fertiliser. All of this results in a prolific, but monotonous, growth of grass that will support a much higher density of sheep. The other important change to our pastureland was the switch from hay to silage. Traditional hay meadows were rich in flowers and insects, but hay must be dried and turned in the sun before it can be baled, which is a difficult proposition in our climate. But the huge quantity of grass produced by the improved fields can be cut and wrapped when green, then left to ferment in plastic wrappers. The resulting silage is used as feed for the sheep and cattle in winter when grass is always in short supply. Silage is an earlier and more certain crop than hay and farmers can often get two, or even three, silage cuts in a season. Silage has massively reduced the likelihood of livestock going hungry in the winter but sadly, this means the few flowers, insects or birds found in these fields rarely complete their life cycle before being destroyed in the cut.

I despair at the blank monotony of this lush grass that farmers find so satisfying. The need to make the land *work* runs very deep and no doubt reflects an ethic that Marged would have relished in Sunday school. Reflecting on this urge in his book *Native*, Patrick Laurie describes how 'the whole lot will be reseeded, and the land will be rescued from idleness'.

We should not forget that the agricultural intensification of the last seventy years has brought much needed improvements in living standards for many small farmers, something to which, like the rest of us, they reasonably aspired. The urge to 'rescue the land from idleness' was part of the powerful post-war drive for improvement, but sadly policy makers gave little thought to the unintended consequences of this revolution.

A long, in-depth article about the Glanllyn estate from the *Farmers Weekly* in January 1949, written by Charles Topham, gives us some fascinating insights into the beginning of the post-war agricultural revolution locally. The estate was then a part of the enormous Williams Wynne holdings, which for 400 years had been the biggest estate in Wales. The Glanllyn section alone was 39,000 acres and contained 150 farms, one of which was Craig-y-tân. Within this there was, of course, a whole other level on which things operated apart from the near subsistence farming that Marged describes. Sir Watkin's mansion on the shores of Llyn Tegid (Bala Lake), about five miles away, was little more than a shooting lodge for him, his main residence being near Ruabon. Nonetheless, when the newly established railway wanted to buy land for their line on the opposite side of the lake, he sold it on the condition that he could have a request stop there. Thereafter, if he wanted to take the train to London, he would have a man row him across the lake to his personal station.

When the then-current Sir Watkin died in 1945 (Marged would have been nineteen), the Glanllyn estate was accepted by the Exchequer in lieu of death duties, a not uncommon arrangement at that time. More unusually, in June 1948, the Labour government took it into public ownership, in effect nationalising it. At that time, the estate contained some good quality lower land with numerous small dairy herds and a little small-scale arable, but the outer and higher parts were rough and difficult for agriculture. Craig-y-tân fell into this latter category. These hill farms had sheep flock and hardy Welsh Black cattle; what pastureland there was had been reclaimed from 'boulder, bracken and rush' by persistent hard work. It was a constant struggle to maintain this as better quality grazing and good enough for a hay crop, the latter being essential for winter feed.

The *Farmers Weekly* article emphasises the strong attachment to the land amongst the community on the estate farms. The industrial revolution had not yet penetrated these hills to change social and farming patterns as much as it had in some parts of England. People stuck to their farms despite hardship and poverty. The attachment to land and community meant more to them than comfortable living. Coupled with this was a strong nationalistic pride in culture and language and a suspicion of control from outside, which in many ways still holds true today amongst farming families.

The article sets a more sober and realistic tone than Marged, who was always keen to put things in the best possible light. For example, seventy-three per cent of the farms in the county in 1941 relied on streams for their water supply. Most of the farm buildings on the estate were in poor repair and unsuitable for modern agriculture. Many farmhouses were damp and leaking. And it was – is – wet: the annual rainfall on the mountain farms ranged between 80 and 120 inches. Only a few farms had electricity in 1945 – generated by individual water wheels or turbines – and most were approached by an often rutted and muddy track. The tone of the article reflects a time when agriculture was modernising rapidly and the Glanllyn farms were seen as 'backward', especially the hill farms. To quote Charles Topham:

> *Higher up farms become few and far between. One that can be seen from the track, standing out like a jungle clearing amongst the brown heath and giant rocks, is Craig-y-tân. This solitary farm, with no neighbours for miles, is farmed by sixty-five-year-old Evan Jones[15] with his five daughters and twelve-year-old son, whom Mr Jones says can handle sheep as well as any man.*

He went on to say that Evan Jones kept fifteen to eighteen cattle, 900 sheep, and ploughed about two acres a year. He also mentioned that Craig-y-tân 'followed the old custom' of keeping wild goats which, by occupying the crags, kept the sheep away from the most dangerous places.

Once in public ownership, the government's aim, in the spirit of the times, was to 'breathe new life into the hills' and run a profitable and modern estate. A programme of improvements to houses, buildings and roads ensued, and the installation of water and electricity supplies got under way. This involved major capital outlay, which meant the estate was unlikely to pay its way for a long time to come. In the event, a Conservative government, re-elected in 1951, decided to privatise the whole operation and the farms were offered for purchase to the incumbent families. Marged's father bought Craig-y-tân, Dolfudr and Tyn y Fron from the government in 1952.

The fields in this district are mostly divided by hedges which, up until the early twentieth century, were the only way of separating stock and keeping them out of crops and hay. The hedges were laid and re-laid to give them a thick stock proof base and trimmed occasionally by hand, to prevent them getting too tall and straggly. Then wire netting became cheap and widespread enough for farmers to use fencing as their stock barrier, and so hedges became less important. As it was no longer necessary to maintain them, hedges gradually became a line of bushes and eventually trees, with the sheep grazing between them from the un-fenced side. They no longer provided the refuge in which wildflowers, insects, birds and mammals could live and move through.

In the last twenty-five years, the agri-environment schemes available to farmers have had a provision to double fence and maintain hedges, which is a great boon as it reinstates the grazing-free hedge bottom, an important habitat for a wide variety of wild plants and animals. It also provides the connectivity, or desert highways if you like, across the improved fields, which is especially important for less mobile species that cannot run or fly to the next available cover. On many farms there is a tendency to mechanically trim the hedges annually, which means there is little chance for the hawthorn, blackthorn and other hedge-row species to flower and fruit, so depriving wildlife of food and us of beauty. The uptake of agri-environment schemes is by no means universal, so many hedges remain sad and ragged lines of bushes, but the current situation is a good deal better than it was twenty years ago.

The net result of pasture improvement and hedgerow neglect means that much of this 'green and pleasant land' is more or less a desert for wildlife; where once there were butterflies and grasshoppers, primroses and violets, curlews and yellowhammers, now there is next to nothing.

Although this is the agricultural context in which Craig-y-tân is set, it has been little affected by these changes. Dry-stone walls rather than hedges divide the fields and, remarkably, none of the pastures have been improved. The lack of pasture improvement was, I presume, due to choices made by Hywel's grandfather, and particularly his uncle, who farmed Craig-y-tân through the main period of intensification. It would have been difficult and expensive work as much of the ground is either rocky or wet, but not impossible with modern machinery and grant aid. Marged always emphasised that her brother was a shepherd and intensive farming was not for him – happily, this means the pastures are still populated by native flowers and grasses. But despite this the flock was twice the size in his day as farmers then received a government payment per head of sheep: it paid to keep a lot of animals. He also had more room, as he was able to graze the mountain throughout the year. This would have been a damaging period for the vegetation and its dependent wildlife at Craig-y-tân; the sheep numbers had probably never been so high. Twenty years ago, Hywel agreed to nearly halve the size of the flock to meet the requirements of his new agri-environment agreement, which also did not allow sheep on the mountain land between October and March, principally to protect the heather from overgrazing. This was a major adjustment in the farming system and extra wintering grounds had to be found for most of the sheep.

The fields around the house that were cut for hay when Marged was a girl are now lightly grazed all year round; Hywel doesn't have enough summer grazing to spare for hay making, but this, coupled with an overall lower density of sheep, means more flowers can bloom and insects thrive. In Marged's youth, and for centuries before that, the number of animals on a hill farm was limited by the amount of hay that could be grown in the summer, because this fed the animals during winter. It was therefore important to put as many sheep or cattle as possible on the mountain land in summer, to free up lower land for growing hay. Once mechanisation and motor transport arrived, it became possible to buy in hay from lowland farms and so hill farms, for the first time, were no longer restrained by the capacity of their own land. Also with the arrival of tractors they no longer needed to grow crops to feed to horses so more land became available for grazing. Hywel continues to buy in the hay he needs for winter-feed today. Conservation designations and the agri-environment scheme now prevent pasture improvement, the use of slurry or fertiliser, or an increase in sheep numbers – and Hywel is compensated financially. So, against the trend, grassland wildlife at Craig-y-tân has probably improved over the last twenty years. How good it is to be able to say that.

Despite the lack of intensification, it would be a mistake to think that the farm has been completely immune from the changes that have affected the surrounding countryside. There are no longer curlews or yellowhammers, let alone corncrakes, in the fields as there were locally in the early twentieth century.[16] One reason a seed eater like the yellowhammer may have gone is that sixty years ago a small farm like this would have grown some vegetables and cereals, particularly oats, for their own consumption and to feed the horses. Spilt grain and arable weed seeds were an important source of food for birds such as yellowhammers and tree sparrows.

I'm back at Craig-y-tân ten days later and the tree pipits are in full song in the gnarly thorns, sobbing for love and territory as they parachute from the topmost branches. There has been a frost every night this week and I am dressed in multiple layers plus a woolly hat. Across the pastures, pairs of ewes and lambs are repeated dozens of times, a lovely contenting sight in the weak sunshine, but they must be tough to get enough nourishment from this scant grass. As I plod up the steep track to the mountain, a harsh *chir* announces a wheatear: a handsome male, which flips from a rock and out of sight into a gully – my first of the year. Meadow pipits are towering up in hopeful song but otherwise there is no sense of spring up here. The lichen-encrusted rowan and hawthorn trees look impervious to the season; they might as well be made of stone. A chill wind cuts me as I top the slope and heavy grey clouds are beginning to drift eastwards, but still it's not raining, so we must call it a fine day. In the valley below, I can see a pair of crows cruising low over the ewes and lambs; the lambs shy a bit, but the ewes ignore them. No doubt the crows are looking for afterbirth, a good source of nutrition for them, and a useful clean-up service for the farm.

About five metres from the edge of the track, amongst some clumps of rushes, a ewe has just given birth, her hindquarters still bloody. The lamb is wobbly headed, with ears still folded back from entering into the wide world. I watch them for a long time. Occasionally the lamb tries to stand then collapses again; its mother is carefully licking it clean, making low maternal rumbling sounds in her throat. She seems completely absorbed, oblivious of my presence. By the time I came back down several hours later, the lamb was on its feet and suckling, tail shivering with pleasure.

I meet Hywel on the track; he had just pulled a lamb which had its head and one leg out but was resisting with the other foreleg – resisting the one thing it needed to do to survive. He tells me that, ironically, if they die in that position the leg relaxes and they are born easily.

Ten days later, it is early May and spring has truly arrived; Craig-y-tân is transformed, bursting with birdsong and new growth. Hywel has heard a cuckoo – he has been beating me to the first one for years. On the stout old crab apples down by the river, small green and bronze leaves are splayed out on a maze of twigs as dense and intricate as blood vessels. A redstart sings drowsily from the crown. Swallows tip and plane in twittering arcs over the rough fields, evoking the sappy vigour of spring, but also something altogether more languid and spent. A red kite above me starts to ease its way up on a thermal. Thirty years ago its presence here would have been remarkable.[17] Everywhere I look there are ewes with attendant lambs – feeding, sleeping, standing. The place has an overwhelming maternal feeling, like some gigantic mothers and toddlers' group; as a man I feel oddly out of place.

Sometimes Hywel asks me questions like, 'Do you think there are more swallows/less cuckoos than there used to be?' and I am often at a loss to give him a confident answer, which is odd considering British wildlife, and birds in particular, are some of the most closely monitored species in the world. Not unreasonably, Hywel is primarily interested in how these birds are doing locally, in this district. It is difficult to answer his questions mainly because nobody has been repeatedly mapping or counting birds locally over the last ten or twenty years, which is what would be needed to make informed comparisons.

Mapping lets us know where the birds are distributed and counting tells us how abundant they are. The most local and recent information on distribution is in *The Breeding Birds of North Wales* published in 2013.[18] Information regarding abundance, on the other hand, is only available at an all-Wales level and only for the most common species.[19] Hywel's questions are mostly about abundance, so disappointingly I cannot give him a more local answer.

However, provoked by his questions, I decide to try and get some idea, from the available information, about how birds may have fared on farmland here.[20] Even deciding what to include as 'farmland' proves to be a bit tricky: I decide to include pastures, farmsteads and what is known in Wales as *ffridd*,[21] but exclude woodland or moorland which, although a significant part of this farm, are not usually understood as farmland. Significantly I do not include birds primarily found in arable land because there isn't any in this district.[22] Consequently, it is important to acknowledge that, although the intensification of arable farming has played a significant part in wildlife declines in the UK, hill farmers often resent being blamed for problems caused by those they see (at best) as distant cousins.

Looking at the fortunes of those birds that breed in or around our kind of farmland in the all-Wales figures up to 2020,[23] there have inevitably been winners and losers over the last twenty-five years. Birds that have significantly increased (fifteen per cent or more) are stock dove, wood pigeon, red kite, wren, song thrush, blackbird, house sparrow, dunnock, stonechat, goldfinch and reed bunting. Those registering significant declines (as above) are curlew, buzzard, green woodpecker, magpie, rook, skylark, swallow, house martin, willow warbler, whitethroat, starling, wheatear, meadow pipit, tree pipit, chaffinch, greenfinch, linnet and yellowhammer. Other species that use farmland which we know have declined significantly, both locally and across Wales, over the last fifty years[24] but are not common enough to count in the standard way are: grey partridge, kestrel, lapwing, snipe, turtle dove, whinchat, tree sparrow and corn bunting. Both turtle dove and corn bunting are now extinct as breeding species in Wales, and grey partridge, lapwing and tree sparrow have disappeared from this district in my time. It is encouraging that there are some winners, but a closer look at these reveals that more than half are highly adaptable 'generalist' species (wood pigeon, wren, song thrush, blackbird, house sparrow, dunnock and goldfinch), which probably owe their increased abundance as much to our parks and gardens as farmland per se. Many of our birds and other wildlife are naturally adapted to live in edge or transition habitats such as hedgerows, copses and gardens. Sadly, despite the impressive effort of the mappers and counters, the information is not localised enough to be sure what is happening to birds in this valley. There may be more stock doves and fewer buzzards, as the Wales figures suggest, but I wouldn't bank on it.

When I sum all of this up and tell Hywel, 'There have been winners and losers, but we don't have enough information to be sure what is happening here,' I don't think he is very impressed. And of course attributing probable causes to probable declines seems even clumsier.

Agricultural intensification has not been as great here as in lowland area, so some of our bird populations may be doing better than the overall picture suggests. Also, none of the prodigious effort to map and count birds across Wales tells us directly why populations have gone down on farmland, but research usually points to the changes in agricultural practices over the last sixty years or so.[25] I am struck by the complexity and level of effort that is required to really know what is happening to our wildlife in the countryside. If this is as refined as we can get about a popular group like birds, it doesn't take much to imagine how little we know, for example, about beetles or mosses.

This is due less to bad organisation or lack of effort than the sheer complexity of the natural world. For this reason conservationists often put great emphasis on habitat, their assumption, or hope, being that if the place where insects or birds live is in good condition (whatever that might be) then the species should be doing all right. Sadly, this is far from being a universal truth. Some of these birds may use more than one habitat or, even more imponderable, migrate to other parts of the world for part of the year. So although our farming practices may impact on the abundance of wheatears, tree pipits, curlews or whinchats, it is difficult to disentangle this from what might be happening to these birds in Africa, en route or even in the coastal areas of Britain where, for example, lapwing and curlew over-winter. At a local level it might be that swallows and house martins can still find nest sites in farm buildings, but pasture improvement has meant that flying insects are less plentiful, so they have insufficient food to feed their young. A barn that loses its roof in a gale will no longer be suitable for barn owls to nest, so they may desert a farm despite a sufficient supply of voles in unimproved fields.

Of the farmland birds that have become extinct locally, the lapwing is one of the best loved and most distinctive and farmers often regret its disappearance. In the early twentieth century, it was common enough for 'plovers' eggs' to be for sale in Bala[26] just five miles from here. Agricultural intensification as well as increased fox and crow populations are likely important in the lapwing's demise. *The Birds of Wales* says that the decline of lapwings is 'closely linked to changes in farming policy and practices'[27] and goes on to discuss many of the aspects of agricultural intensification explored in this chapter. Many farmers I have spoken to prefer to put the blame squarely on the shoulders of the foxes and crows.

As I am leaving the farm at the end of the afternoon, I meet Hywel and Rhys by the sheep pens. Hywel tells me they are still losing lambs to a fox, although 'no more than usual'. One or two 'singles' had gone, which is worse because 'you have to feed the ewe for nothing' – was his rather matter of fact assessment. Overall, he cautiously agreed that the lambing had 'gone a bit better than usual'. Because they are no longer permitted to graze the mountain in winter, even these Welsh mountain sheep had gone 'a bit soft'. He says, 'If you had a lot more of them and let them lamb on the mountain without any help, as they did thirty years ago, the weaker ewes would die having difficult births and a stronger strain would gradually evolve – survival of the fittest.' To keep the flock strong and healthy, he will pick out about half the ewe lambs as replacement breeders and sell the rest along with the ram lambs and the three-to-four-year-old ewes. The latter will be sold to 'softer farms down-country' where they will get several more years' breeding from them under those easier conditions. This is no country for old ewes. Hywel buys in a couple of rams each year to mix the genes and he says it pays to get them from similar hill farms otherwise they don't do well.

Rhys is coming to the end of his long lambing stint; he will now go off to other farms for a spell of shepherding and then shearing. We talk about farming at Craig-y-tân and he says in his view there is not a lot else you could do here except keep sheep, and hardy ones at that. If it was unrestricted by conservation designations, you could 'improve' some fields, but he says it would be difficult and expensive. The present farming system at Craig-y-tân is 'extensive', that is a low density of animals spread over a wide area; consequently, there is less disease contagion, and they don't need handling or moving as often: consequently there is less work. If you kept cattle they would need feeding and wintering indoors, which would mean capital costs for a new barn. He doubted it would be cost effective. I wondered if it might be possible to keep some traditional breeds of cattle such as Highlands, Galloways or Welsh Blacks out of doors all the year round, but the difficulty of access to the mountain land at Craig-y-tân would make feeding and caring for such large and valuable animals impossible without creating a drivable track up to the top, which would not only be expensive but unlikely to be permitted under the SSSI regulations. Under these circumstances, it seems reasonable and obvious that farmers should be subsidised for providing the 'ecological services' the rest of us want from the countryside.

Chapter 3

Wild Woods

The woods at Craig-y-tân are, in many ways, the most mysterious and unfathomable part of the farm for me. Draped over the escarpment on the south side of the valley, they run for about a mile in a rumpled strip along the steep rocky slope beneath the crags. Situated between 290–380 metres, they are high and very wet – more than 2,000 millimetres of rain falls here each year, draining down through the woods in streams and seepages into the river in the valley bottom. The history of these woods is palpable yet somehow unknowable; that they are here at all in the face of hundreds of years of sheep grazing seems extraordinary. I am intrigued to try and understand how they have been shaped by human activity, especially farming, over the centuries and what the future might hold for them.

From where I am standing on a chilly spring day, the woods look like a black-and-white photograph that is gradually being hand-tinted, starting with a fresh green wash on the tips of the birches and hawthorns and the odd chalky dab of blackthorn blossom. I find myself trying to imagine the finished masterpiece, but these natural cycles are never finished, or started, but continuously emerging. The fresh green will soon be gone. As I let myself in through the gate at the bottom of the wood, the cascading song of willow warblers, freshly returned from Africa, still delights my ear, not yet consigned to the unheard, as new arrivals become more novel.

These woods have grown up on a litter of boulders split off from the cliff above by the action of ice in the deep cold that gripped this land 12,000 years ago. These are now heaped in a steep and chaotic jumble along the slope beneath the crags. Between the boulders, in pockets of deeper soil, are some mighty birches and rowans; others which seem to grow straight out of the rocks are as spindly as a whippet's leg, having been forced to live on a subsistence diet – but they may be just as old. Reflecting the gradients of light and moisture, each tree is mossed up to its knees and encrusted with lichens at its fingertips. An unbroken carpet of moss covers every plane and tilt of the boulders, muffling their hard identity; in places it hangs in sheets like some Louisiana swampland.

A jay bounds ahead of me screaming coarsely, which sets a wren off ticking amongst the boulders. Then all is quiet again and nothing moves save a wisp of grass drifting through the trees, wind-whipped from a tussock on the moorland above. It is as if every leaf that has ever fallen remains exactly where it landed. No humans come here. In places the branches are so low I have to duck or even crawl to pass underneath. I stumble across an ancient mossed-up stone wall running inside the lower edge of the wood; perhaps it is the old *ffridd* wall that divided the better grazing from the woodland; if so, the trees must have extended downhill since then, for it is well inside the wood by now. I wonder whom to ask, but probably there is no one left who would know. Whatever its purpose, it is now a ragged scribble through the trees, like a petroglyph from some forgotten culture.

For a long time I have assumed that these woods must be of recent origin; that they had got started on the rocky slopes sometime in the last 200 years when grazing pressure happened to be light – consequently the sheep didn't need to clamber up amongst the boulders as there was sufficient grazing lower down. The wood is dominated by birch and rowan with a scattered understorey of hazel and sallow. Birch and rowan are pioneer species, colonisers of open ground and often the forerunners of new woodlands, with longer-lived species such as oak and ash following on behind. The age limit for trees is difficult to arrive at as so much depends on specific environmental conditions, but these are short-lived species: birches rarely reach 100 years[28] and rowan sometimes 200.[29] However, trees on infertile soils and at higher altitude are often slow growing and live longer – the less bulk they accumulate each year, the longer they can keep going without falling apart. I had a chance to learn more about this when one of the biggest rowans at the top of the wood blew over in a gale, taking a fence with it. To repair the fence, Hywel had to clear the tree away and he offered to cut a section out for me so I could count the annual growth rings. This gnarly old tree was nearly two and a half feet in diameter with all manner of fissures and protuberances on its trunk, the sweet-smelling heartwood a deep, earthy red. In some years, there had been so little growth the rings were hard to distinguish, too tight to count with the rough finish made by the chainsaw. I took the section to a local wood turner who smoothed the surface, which clarified the rings. Much to my surprise the tree turned out to be only seventy-six years old; I had thought it might be twice that. It was hard to imagine many rowan trees in the wood being significantly older than this whiskery old senior, so if this is truly ancient woodland, the same cannot be said of the current crop of trees.

Whether or not woodland is of ancient origin is important to ecologists, especially where tree cover is known (or presumed) to have been continuous for a long period of time. This is because research has shown that such woods have a greater diversity of wildlife than younger ones and are, therefore, of greater nature conservation value.[30] I know these slopes have been wooded for a long time: Marged remembered them from when she was a girl ninety years ago and they are on the 1921/22 Ordnance Survey map in more or less the same configuration as now. I have seen an aerial photograph from 1948, which shows them in a similar shape, but the trees looked younger, less dense and the area nearest the farm seemed sparse, perhaps because it was cropped for firewood. Marged remembered chains being put round felled trees so a horse could pull them to the yard, where they were cut into firewood. Large logs were for the *popty mawr* (big bread oven) and small ones used in the house. She said the trees felled were chosen from places where the horse could be brought to them but much of Craig-y-tân's woodland is too steep and treacherous for a horse; consequently the steep and rocky places are less likely to have been cut over the years. Marged said her father favoured birch for firewood over rowan, which is the other dominant tree in these woods. The trees were felled using a two-handed crosscut with a man each side of the tree. I pressed her for memories of work in the woodlands because their history is such a puzzle to me, but she was much hazier around this than some other topics. She said 'hundreds' of trees had been cut for firewood over the years, but surprisingly she didn't remember them being used for anything other than firewood. At that time cutting wood for making gates, fence posts etc would have been commonplace and most villages had a wood mill for processing local timber.[31]

Importantly the northern part of these woods, known as Coed Dol-fudr, appears in the Wales Ancient Woodland Inventory. If this is an ancient wood then I am surprised it lacks the tree species associated with more mature woodlands: so far I have only found about half a dozen oaks, two small clumps of aspen and singles of ash, sycamore and beech in fifty acres. I haven't found any old stumps suggesting a previous generation of trees that had been felled. I began to think it was a case of arrested development, a pioneer wood whose natural succession had been frozen by the reintroduction or intensification of grazing, meaning any germinating seedlings would have been nipped off by the sheep.

Many of the oak woodlands on valley sides in Wales were heavily cropped or even clear-felled in the eighteenth and nineteenth centuries, when timber was in high demand for ship building, construction, tanning bark and charcoal. World War One also took a heavy toll on woodland because extra timber was needed for trenches and mines. Those woods that remain today have often grown back from the stumps of felled trees, but that clearly has not happened at Craig-y-tân as there are so few oaks. Acorns from oak trees are spread principally by jays, which bury them for later recovery as food but, despite being intelligent birds, they do not remember where they hide them all, and those forgotten give rise to new oak trees.

I see plenty of oak seedlings locally but had begun to wonder if it was just too high for them to grow at Craig-y-tân. However, not long ago, I visited two local woods that are fenced and free of sheep to see what I could find: Coed y Graig and Coed Gordderw, which are both within a mile of here. In Coed y Graig there was a scatter of oak seedlings up to about 330 metres and in Coed Gordderw, one of the highest woodlands in Wales, there was a seedling at 475 metres, so clearly Craig-y-tân is not too high for oak regeneration.

The nearest oaks, other than the handful in the wood, are only half a mile away as the jay flies, so perhaps this is not a frozen pioneer wood that, given freedom from grazing, would eventually develop into one of those regal oak woods that quilt the valley sides of Wales. I turned to the National Vegetation Classification,[32] which arranges all the habitats in Britain into characteristic botanical communities, and it turns out there are upland birch woods that are not transitional, especially in Scotland, but also scattered in northern England and North Wales. These are mostly a subset of the oak/birch woodlands but are without the oaks due to harsh environmental conditions, especially altitude. So perhaps the Craig-y-tân woods are the finished article, what ecologists call climax vegetation, an upland birch/rowan wood where the conditions are too harsh for it to be anything other.

If this is not a fairly recent pioneer wood stalled by sheep farming, the intriguing possibility is that it may have been here for a very long time indeed. About 8,000 years ago, northern and western Britain was emerging from the tundra-like conditions that followed the last Ice Age, and trees and shrubs began to colonise all but the highest, most exposed and wettest areas. The picture of this original wildwood that I grew up with was one of closed canopy high forest, like something out of Tolkien. As only about one per cent of Wales lies above 600 metres[33] which is thought to be the approximate limit of natural tree growth,[34] ninety-five per cent of Wales or more could have been covered in a sort of Mirkwood, according to this model. But in the year 2000 a Dutch ecologist called Frans Vera proposed a somewhat different model for our original wild vegetation.[35] He suggested that ecologists had previously underestimated the effects of grazing and browsing by the herds of native cattle (aurochs), horses, pigs and deer that were all present at the time, plus their attendant carnivores – wolves, lynx and bear, as well as fox. He postulated that the interaction between these animals and their environment would have created something more akin to savannah or parkland, with clumps of trees, thickets of scrub and areas of grassland dotted with individual trees. These ideas are somewhat controversial amongst ecologists, and we will never know for certain, but it is likely that the original wildwood varied on a spectrum between high forest and savannah.

It is possible that people were an earlier influence on the development of the wildwood than we have previously thought[36] but human modification would initially have been in the lower more equable areas and not until later in higher, colder places like Craig-y-tân, as the climate warmed. All we can say with some certainty is that thousands of years ago humans began clearing trees to create areas for shifting cultivation, building shelters and hunting herbivores for food – shaping the wild for the first time. As all of Craig-y-tân is below 600 metres, it is likely that, except for the most exposed and wettest areas, much of it was once covered in a mixture of forest and scrub, which was gradually cleared and suppressed from regrowing by humans and their stock, between then and now. If Hywel and his family were to walk away today, taking their sheep with them, much of the lower land would inexorably develop into something like a wildwood again and, in the absence of herbivores, eventually become a closed canopy forest. Exactly how that would be made up is impossible to predict as changed environmental conditions such as leached and compacted soils, natural and human-induced climate change, deposition of atmospheric nitrogen and introduced exotic species would likely affect its composition so, in detail, it would not be the same as the original wildwood.

Could it be that the woods at Craig-y-tân are an ancient relict derived from that original wildwood rather than more recent colonists? It is easy to imagine why people might never have completely cleared the trees from here: the boulders scree makes it awkward and sometimes treacherous to get around. It would have been a difficult place to fell trees and haul timber by hand, or later with horses, and if there were never many oaks there would have been little commercial incentive to cut timber in this inaccessible valley. I am not suggesting the wood is unaltered, still the same as it would have been thousands of years ago. It has certainly been cropped for firewood and no doubt timber for local building, gateposts and the like, probably by all four farms that existed in this part of the valley 200 years ago. But perhaps that was done at a rate that the wood could sustain, and so it was never completely cleared of trees. In this context it is also important to remember that a wood is not just a collection of trees: the soils, fungi, plants and invertebrates that have evolved together over the millennia, as well as the trees, are what truly constitute a woodland ecosystem. Many of these can persist over long periods of time despite the cutting and felling of timber, which is why conservationists value ancient woodlands so highly.

If this wood is a relic or descendant of the wildwood then, just to still be here, new trees must have grown up to replace dead ones – and fairly often, with these short-lived birch and rowans. There are trees here that are in their old age and beginning to fall over, but until a few years ago, sheep had been free to graze here for a very long time and consequently there are no young saplings to be the next recruits. Woods heavily grazed by sheep can persist for centuries if the trees are long lived, which has been the case in many Welsh oak woods over the last 200 years, but ultimately without new trees they are condemned to death by grazing. There must have been times in the last two or three hundred years when grazing was light enough at Craig-y-tân for young trees to become established, otherwise there would be no woodland here today.

Clearly the most important factor shaping these woods over the last several hundred years has been grazing by domestic stock, particularly sheep. Twenty years ago there was a game-changing moment when the woods were fenced out under Hywel's new agri-environment scheme. Four blocks of woodland were enclosed, leaving narrow corridors of open ground between them. Initially, the scheme allowed light summer-only grazing inside the woodland for a maximum of forty sheep. Hywel liked this arrangement as he is short of grass in the summer when his flock size is at its maximum, so the sheep were keen to graze in the woods; this probably held tree and bramble regeneration in check. Then in 2012 a new version of the scheme switched the woodland-grazing pattern to winter only, presumably so that tree seedlings would have a better chance to prosper in the growing season, and other plants could flower and set seed. Hywel was not pleased to lose his summer grazing in the woods, but the financial incentives made it worth staying in the scheme. However, this imposed switch made him cynical about the expertise of the scheme's officials. He said the staff have often changed and lacked experience of managing land, imposing a 'textbook' formula onto real situations that called for a holistic and flexible approach. He told me that when an officer from the agri-environment scheme first came to visit Craig-y-tân he declared it 'perfect', but then suggested a big reduction in sheep numbers. Hywel's sardonic response was, 'How did he think it got to be perfect if we have got far too many sheep?'

Perhaps forty sheep across fifty acres of woodland over the course of a winter is light enough for new trees to be recruited, where gaps in the canopy allow. It will depend to some extent how the sheep distribute themselves over time – animals never graze evenly across a wood, or anywhere else. Left to their own devices, sheep would probably only venture into these rocky woods in wintertime, when grass is in very short supply elsewhere, or for shelter, particularly in times of heavy snowfall, but if they are shut in, they will probably forage more extensively.

The money for these agri-environment schemes, which pay farmers to carry out environmental work, was made available through the EU's Common Agricultural Policy and channelled through the UK's devolved governments. Currently these payments are being maintained until post-Brexit schemes are finalised. In July 2022, the Welsh Government published its new proposals for agricultural support to be known as the Sustainable Farming Scheme,[37] which it hopes will deliver economic, environmental and social outcomes for farmers and the farmed landscape. Amongst many admirable aims it proposes to 'protect natural landscapes and promote resilient ecosystems, including benefits for biodiversity, species and habitats'. An important underpinning aim of the scheme is to keep farmers on the land and support the continuing use of the Welsh language in the farming community.

The scheme proposes a basic level of 'universal actions', which will be compulsory and give access to payments that will be seen as replacing the current Basic Payments. So far, the main concerns I have heard about from farmers is that at the 'universal' level there must be at least ten per cent tree cover on the farm, and that a further ten per cent must be managed as semi-natural habitat. That could be easy through to very difficult to deliver depending on the circumstances of your individual farm. In addition to 'universal' there are 'optional' and 'collaborative' levels; the former is likely to involve more specific habitat management, and perhaps bigger gains for nature, similar to those at Craig-y-tân designed to protect these woodlands.

This scheme could be revolutionary for nature on farmland in Wales – or it could be much less than that. Its final form, promised for 2023, will depend on the strength of the Welsh Government's resolve, in the face of strong lobbying from farming unions – whose first priority is the economic wellbeing of family farms. Beyond that, what the scheme actually delivers will be dependent on the effectiveness of incentives, monitoring and penalties, as well as the expertise of the staff involved in the scheme. For wildlife in Wales to recover the ground lost on farmland over the last fifty years the new scheme will need to be unusually effective.

If an acceptable scheme is not agreed between the Welsh Government and farming representatives, the prospects for wildlife will be very grim. In the case of woodlands like these, many farmers would probably just open the gates and allow the sheep to come and go as they please, so undoing years of progress for wildlife conservation. It would be easier for Hywel to manage Craig-y-tân without the woods fenced off; he could have his summer grazing back. He has now adapted his regime around these restrictions, and light winter grazing probably is the best prescription for wildlife, but only time will tell. What is essential is the continuity of financial support that allows him to go on doing this.

Unlike Craig-y-tân, many farms have little or no woodland, so farmers are currently being encouraged to plant trees on their land. Ironically, some current agri-environment schemes are not flexible enough to allow this, whilst other farmers are reluctant to set land aside permanently in case they are not compensated for it in future schemes. Many conservationists are wary of tree planting as so often it does not result in 'the right tree in the right place', but rather an unsuitable mixture of non-native or imported trees, that will be of little benefit to wildlife. Many would prefer to see natural regeneration, where all that is required is to fence out the stock and wait to see what happens: natural processes will inexorably give rise to trees in a place where they are fitted to grow. However, there are some situations where the seed sources for trees are now so distant that natural regeneration will not give rise to diversity of tree species; there is a limit to how far a jay will carry an acorn. A psychological hurdle to this approach appears to be that it frustrates the (mostly admirable) urge to 'do something'; tree planting has an aura of basic goodness that many people find satisfying – there is something elemental about planting a tree. However, it is important to re-state that a collection of trees does not constitute a woodland and it may be many years, or even centuries, before the full wildlife benefits of tree planting are realised. Meanwhile, at 'five minutes to midnight', the clock is ticking on all our net-zero and biodiversity aspirations.

In late May I am back at Craig-y-tân to see the bluebells at their most glorious. I thought they would peak about mid-May, but Hywel predicted it would be at the end of the month – and he was right. The bluebells are thickest at the woodland edge but plainer somehow in the bright light and mixed with last year's tawny bracken fronds. Under the trees, the swathes of blue alter in intensity according to the angle of view and there is a mysterious sub-marine quality, as if the air itself is green, which seems to amplify the intensity of the colour. White stars of greater stitchwort and an occasional pure white bluebell punctuate the blue. I find it impossible to walk without treading on them, and I am not the only one. Badgers have flattened a path to a place where they have been rolling or playing, crushing hundreds of them – such freedom not to care. The bluebells are not evenly spaced but in patches and pockets, presumably in the deeper soil, which sometimes coalesce. Arising out of them are moss-covered boulders, like green atolls in the Pacific Ocean.

Across the valley at Tyn y Fron, bluebells are revealed like blue-grey seams of bedrock along the sheep paths that wind through the dead bracken. This is their moment and there are millions of them, just as numerous in the rough pasture as in the woodlands. We often think of bluebells as a woodland plant but here, in the far west of Britain, they are just as happy growing in grassland, often in association with bracken, turning whole hillsides blue for a couple of glorious weeks before the ferns overtop them. Although widely distributed in Europe, it is only on the western fringes that bluebells occur in the carpets that are so familiar to us. These are as thrilling to visiting European naturalists as orchids in the Alps are to British botanists.

As I scramble further through the wood where small streams and springs bubble up along the slope, valerian and meadowsweet are beginning to poke up through the saturated ground. There are carpets of spongy bog-moss in waterlogged patches testifying to the high rainfall. Broken branches, uprooted fallen trees and randomly stacked boulders suggest chaos, and yet it is somehow immaculate – unmarked and unoccupied. A fallen rowan limb, as thick as a sprinter's thigh, stands propped between its trunk and a rock; it will probably stay like that for years until rot eventually collapses it. I am gratified to see how much dead wood there is lying about; nobody comes here, so it is never tidied up. It is easy to see a wood as a collection of trees decorated by birds in the foliage and flowers on the floor, but they are so much more complex than that. Where I am standing there is bark peeling back like skin exposing heartwood bleached as bone; pulpy limbs are gradually being engulfed by moss and bluebells; branch ends are fractured, and brittle nests of twigs are littered everywhere. From beneath my feet to thirty feet above me these provide living spaces for a multitude of invertebrates, fungi and lower plants which are largely unseen, their interdependent life cycles essential to the workings of this wood. Moving forward I slip on a boulder and find myself apologising out loud for leaving a mark. Then I'm tutting over a piece of polythene, the only litter I have ever found at Craig-y-tân, which turns out to be a deflated birthday balloon that has drifted in from another world. A twelve-foot-high flat-topped rock, like one of those Venezuelan lost worlds, has an out-of-reach capping of bilberry and rowan saplings, hinting at how this wood would look had it been out of the reach of sheep.

Sitting down on a mossy boulder, my hands sink into the coolness of bluebells; it is a relief that for once they seem to be an inexhaustible multitude, rather than some precious commodity. I am right under one of the few oaks that I have found in the wood and a male pied flycatcher is chuntering at me twenty yards away. Perhaps the oak has provided a nest hole; these are likely to be in short supply in a wood without big trees. A cuckoo is calling drowsily above me somewhere near the cliffs; it has a distant, matter-of-no-concern feeling to it even if only 400 yards away. At the base of the rock, two big chutes of debris indicate a badger's sett, with a regular highway leading off through the bluebells. But something else catches my attention: a bramble growing out of a crevice near the sett entrance. This is the first one I have seen and shows that, nearly twenty years on, fencing the woods out from intensive grazing is slowly having an effect. So far quite a lot of basal shoots have grown up, particularly on hazel stools, and there are birch saplings two to three feet high in some open areas around the woodland edge, and now a few brambles. That doesn't seem much over that time, but poor soils and harsh conditions mean these upland ecosystems move pretty slowly. Five-year plans are not much use here; fifty- to one-hundred-year plans would be more like it.

Brambles are more shade tolerant than most tree seedlings and may begin to spread if there are not enough sheep to nip them off when young. It is not uncommon to find a great tangle of brambles in ungrazed woodlands, which can smother bluebells. Consequently, if the winter grazing in these woods proves insufficient, there may no longer be a carpet of blue here twenty years from now. To get some further understanding of this process I head back to Coed y Graig, a steep birch wood about a mile away and a similar altitude to Craig-y-tân, from which the sheep have been excluded for more than thirty years. Back then I remember this as an open grassy wood, with abundant mosses and bluebells. It was so steep that the easiest way to get out of it was to slide down on your backside. Not anymore. It is now thick with young trees, mostly rowan and birch, with a ground cover of tall bilberry, bracken and brambles, the last two in an impenetrable combination, especially around the edges. Brambles have spread throughout the wood, and conifers – mostly Sitka spruce and western hemlock – having seeded in from an adjacent plantation. I find three oak seedlings, the oldest perhaps five to ten years old; mature oak trees are not present in the wood, so they must have been introduced by jays or squirrels carrying acorns. The effects of fencing the sheep out for thirty years are dramatic with the wood now full of vigorously regenerating saplings including exotic conifers, oak and holly, all of which are new arrivals. The proliferation of bracken and brambles is also shading and smothering the ground and the lower parts of the trees and boulders, which will be detrimental to the mosses and liverworts.

This is how the woods at Craig-y-tân would evolve over the years if sheep were to be totally excluded, although tree regeneration would probably be more limited due to the denser canopy. The carpet of bluebells would be smothered, but perhaps that doesn't matter from a strictly ecological viewpoint; it is important to remember that the bluebell carpet only arose and persisted due to the grazing of stock, which held back the succession of trees and shrubs. It would be a terrible loss of beauty but, like farming, aesthetics are usually seen as a by-product, rather than an aim, in science-based nature conservation. Conservationists are often obliged to decide what is most valued, as some species will have competing requirements. For example, if brambles and young trees begin to develop in the more open areas, this will benefit some species of wildlife and be a threat to others, and it is sometimes difficult to know where the balance lies.

But before you choose which species to favour, you must know what you have already got, or even might acquire through natural processes. This is not so difficult for well-studied organisms such as birds or butterflies but much harder, for example, with groups such as spiders or lichens which are difficult to find and identify, let alone evaluate what their needs might be, and specialists who can do this tend to be few and far between. Even once you know what you have got and have decided what is most valued, producing the conditions that suit them and ensuring these are stable over time can be very difficult. It is true that minimal or no grazing will allow for new trees and thus perpetuate the wood, but beyond that it is much more complicated.

Consequently, when Hywel asks me why it is good for wildlife to have the wood fenced out, I find myself prevaricating and qualifying until he looks increasingly sceptical. He knows what he wants for his sheep and unsurprisingly expects conservationists to be equally clear and consistent.

What I do know is that only fifteen per cent of Wales is wooded (and at least half of that is conifer plantation), and of those woodlands specially designated for nature many are not in good condition. Better ways of delivering management for conservation are needed if our woodland wildlife is to have a viable future; we badly need more people with knowledge and experience on the ground.

Chapter 4

Pastures

Approaching Craig-y-tân by car you follow a narrow road out of the village for a couple of miles, and then negotiate a further half a mile of rough track, pass through a gloomy conifer plantation, rattle over a cattle grid, and finally swing up round a big left-hand bend. This is a moment I love, because there it all is, spread out in front of me: a view straight up the valley to the rocky 2,000-foot summit of Moel Llyfnant, the river cascading towards me before crashing into the gorge below. On either side are rough rock-strewn, tree-scattered pastures, which rise steeply to the boggy mountain land above. Straight ahead, tucked under the woodland is the farmstead of Craig-y-tân: a solid stone farmhouse and outbuildings, ancient stone sheep pens in front, and two low-rise metal barns behind. Around the house are a few small fields enclosed by stone walls, and beyond them the rough and rocky *ffridd*; it is these half-tamed pastures that I have come to look at more closely. For Hywel they are his best grazing land, yet remarkably they are still rich in wildlife: understanding that balance is important in the debate around hill farming and wildlife.

It is early on a spring day when I park in my usual conspicuous place beside the track about fifty yards in front of the sheep pens, where I think Hywel will have the best chance of seeing the car. Reasonably enough, farmers like to know 'who is about' and I could be here all day and not encounter him.

There is nobody around as I pass the house and yard but the smell of creosoted posts and fresh washing snapping on the line reinforce the sense of all being well that I so often have here. It is a fine morning and I set off across the rough pasture in high spirits, following a sheep path diagonally down towards the river. The grasslands are scattered with aging rowans, hawthorns and crab apples, some of which look as though they are sitting on a tump, skirts spread, their arthritic roots clamped over a rock in a life or death embrace. A whinchat flitting between the bushes catches my eye, a bird I would love to find breeding here, but it is probably just passing through. From a boggy area a heron lumbers into the air, reptilian neck stretched out for take-off and squirting droppings as it goes – which feels like a comment on my intrusion.

Just in from the riverbank is a grove of spindly blackthorn bushes a week away from flowering, thousands of pale buds pushing up from the encrusting lichen. Their trunks are draped with wool scarves around polished necks where the sheep rub, burnishing them with lanolin. Three ewes and lambs are sheltering beneath them. Blackthorn is not common at Craig-y-tân but tends to occur in thickets due to its habit of throwing up suckers. I wonder what kept the sheep from nibbling these off when they were soft and delicate – perhaps sheltering bracken that has since been eradicated by Hywel. The history of vegetation in a place like this is always measured against the incessant nibbling of sheep.

This is neatly illustrated by the series of fields surrounded by rugged stone walls close to the house. Situated on better-drained, drier slopes, most have been cleared of rocks – which were used to make the walls, or have been simply piled up in corners. As these are the only rock-free pastures on the farm, they must be the ones that were cut for hay when Marged was a girl, although probably not in the seventy years since. Mostly they are too steep for mechanical cutting so hay may not have been harvested here since the era of the scythe. Probably some grew oats, potatoes or vegetables, but they do not appear to have been 'improved' and sown with rye grass in the modern era. Although prettily decked out at this time of year with characteristic plants such pignut and bulbous buttercup, they are not very diverse botanically: there are no vetches, knapweed or yellow rattle. They may be most interesting for fungi, which often prosper in lightly grazed permanent pastures; I have found several species of wax caps here in the autumn. Some of the fields are without bluebells, which is unusual at Craig-y-tân; this supports the idea that these are the fields that were once cultivated – the bulbs would not have survived the plough. Hywel considers these fields as his best grazing on the farm, and certainly the sheep favour them; at a distance you can often pick out the fields by the clusters of animals.

These fields no longer have the characteristics of flower-rich hay meadows, if they ever did; decades of sheep grazing will have reduced their diversity. Heath bedstraw and lesser stitchwort, as well as the pignut and bulbous buttercup, are abundant with plenty of tormentil and white clover; there are also bits of bracken and scattered marsh thistle. Such plants are characteristic of the species poor acid grassland that you would expect to find on drier pastures hereabouts. It is also why the sheep like it; this is palatable vegetation which they will preferentially graze in the summer, only turning to the adjacent heath and bog once grass has become scarce on the better ground.

To understand the history of these fields, it is worth turning to Marged's memories. Food was never far away in our conversations; she often wanted to tell me how diets had changed since her youth – and not for the better, in her opinion. In the early twentieth century, farming families in places like Craig-y-tân bought very little food, only tea and sugar were regularly purchased – Marged recalled how at one time there was a man who went round from house to house selling tea. Nearly everything else was grown or reared on the farm – although some home produce like butter and cheese was sold or bartered between neighbours. Of course, a few other necessities were bought: paraffin for the lamps, some clothing, footwear, and tobacco was widely smoked. They kept hens, which provided them with eggs, and several cows whose milk was turned into *llaeth enwyn* (buttermilk) and butter. There was always mutton available (rather than lamb it seems, perhaps because those were the farm's main source of income) and every farm kept a pig or two. Marged recounts the slaughter and butchering of the pig with great relish. Her attitude of earthy pragmatism conveys a sense of how much closer to the land people were back then:

> *Another old tradition was the slaughtering of the pig. The poor pig would be starved the day before having been well fattened for six weeks prior to this. We had to be sure everything was ready for the butcher by ten o'clock: a washing boiler full of boiling water to scald the pig, the stent and the gambrel to hang it on. After the butcher struck the pig, the sound of it squealing would resound across the valley. My mother would rush over to collect the blood and put it through a fine sieve while it was still warm. Then she would put it in the oven with onions, salt and pepper to make a blood pudding. When it was ready, she would break it up very finely and fry it in a frying pan. That was always our supper on pig slaughtering*

day. It was much tastier than the blood/black pudding that is for sale these days. After scrubbing the pig clean and removing every bristle from its body, it was hung beneath the llofft allan[38] *and its innards were removed. The following day, the butcher would come and cut the pig into six pieces: two shoulders, two middle pieces and two hams. Fat ribs and the small bits of meat and the liver were made into faggots and sausages and the head of course made brawn. The old folks used to say nothing of the pig was wasted except its squeal. On the third day, we would salt the pieces: rub them with salt, pepper, saltpetre and brown sugar and then put them in a tub in the cellar on the slate slab and cover them with salt. We would usually take out the two middle pieces after a fortnight, leaving the others for a month as there were big bones in them. There was a hook in the kitchen where the meat would be hung to dry, after which it was wrapped in a flour bag and buried in the oatmeal chest.*

The final process would be to boil the pig's head in the washing boiler with a piece of beef or even a hare, if we were lucky enough to have caught one. We'd boil it until the meat was off the bone, then chop it very finely and put it into a purpose-made tin with holes in the sides; we would put lots of weight on the top so the fat would come out through the hole. We, the children, would look forward to having a pig's head sandwich to take with us to school. We would also use the bladder, as it would make a football for us children, after drying it to begin with then pumping it full of air with a bicycle pump.

Each farm grew oats, which were important as animal feed, especially for horses, as well as for the family. Some of the oats were taken to the village for grinding at the mill and the flour was used mainly to make *bara ceirch*, a kind of oat biscuit that was a staple food. Marged remembered the delicious smell on baking days, especially if these were being baked on a skillet over a peat fire – which she considered superior to wood or coal. *Bara ceirch* were often broken up into buttermilk and allowed to stand to make a kind of porridge known as *siot*, which she would take to the men scything hay for their mid-morning break.

Marged said they milked about six cows in the summer and two in the winter. The dogs had the 'first milk' and the second was for churning. A water wheel turned the paddle inside the big square churn. Other than the butter eaten by the family, the rest was stored in a pot for wintertime or sold: two shillings a pound in summer, half a crown in winter.

Other than oats, each farm grew some potatoes and a few vegetables to vary their diet. These crops, plus the meat, eggs and milk from the farm, meant they were nearly self-sufficient in food. This was in great contrast to life in the towns and cities at the time. My own parents were of Marged's generation, but their contemporaneous stories of growing up in London with its motor transport, paved roads, telephone, electricity and shops seemed to be from another world altogether.

In Marged's early life, they had no motor transport at Craig-y-tân; later they had a series of vans, followed by a Land Rover and in about 1960 a tractor arrived – until then horses had done the heavy work. Marged said surprisingly little about horses on the farm, even though they would have pulled the plough, carts and the sledge that was used to haul various things, including peat, to and from the mountain.

Horses would have dominated the lives of farmers of her father's generation and before him, but Marged spanned the transition to mechanisation when the tractor replaced the horse. E. D. on the other hand is careful to point out how well the horses were looked after. The farmhand was up at 6 a.m. to feed them, they then had two hours to digest, followed by four hours working on the land. After that, they had two hours for their next feed and then a further four hours working, finishing at 6 p.m. Horses were the tractors of their day and they needed careful maintenance, which included the best hay, clean straw and bracken to sleep on.

Three weeks later and I am back at Craig-y-tân to take another look at the pastureland. I meet Hywel by the gate and he brings me up to date with his nature observations. He is puzzled as to why the bluebells don't grow above the mountain wall and we speculate unconvincingly about differing grazing levels over the years, but become no clearer.

Hywel is pleased to have a bird nesting in the stone wall by the house, which once we had sorted out what it was – *tingoch* – meaning red bum – in Welsh, redstart in English – we both took pleasure in. He also told me he had found a bluebell with an exceptional twenty-two bells on it. A dragonfly he had seen over one of the boggy areas he was less sure about; we concluded it was probably a golden-ringed hawker, a magnificent insect characteristic of our upland bogs. It is a delight to know such a well-informed and interested farmer.

Leaving Hywel, I set off up the valley across the rough pastureland at the back of the house. A striking thing about Craig-y-tân is that, other than the few small fields around the farmstead, there is no in-bye (enclosed pasture) to speak of; the *ffridd* runs right down to the river in a wild jumble of tussocky grass, bog and rush pasture, dotted with boulders and bushes and dissected by small streams.

Sheltering under the hawthorns and rowans are dozens of stocky thick-coated ewes with their pristine two-to-three-week-old lambs. The nearest ewe watches me carefully, occasionally answering the falsetto cries of her lamb with guttural bleats. When it runs to her, she sniffs it carefully: smell is as much the language of ewes as sound.

Millions of bluebell leaves, their tips trampled by sheep, carpet the ground – fields of blue unborn. Sheep don't find bluebells very palatable: they tend to only nibble the leaves when times are hard, but once the grass begins to grow they leave the bluebells alone. In a couple of weeks Hywel will be able to send many of these ewes and lambs up to the mountain, relieving the grazing pressure on these pastures. Then the bluebells will really take off.

Bluebells aren't the only plant about to take off: the unfurling fronds of bracken, known as croziers, are forcing their way through the soil now around the edges of the woodland. In a few weeks these will be five feet tall and all but impenetrable.

On a hot day with a cloud of flies round your head, forcing your way through dense bracken can be a misery. Hywel tells me that his grandmother's teasing advice to him and his siblings when pestered by flies was, 'If you catch one poke it in its left eye, then you won't have any more trouble.'

It seems that bracken was widespread and dominant over much of the drier pasture at Craig-y-tân until about twenty years ago when Hywel, under his Glastir agreement, had a helicopter spray herbicide all across the *ffridd* and some of the lower slopes of the mountain. Asulox, the herbicide used for bracken control, is poisonous to all ferns but few other plants. So, as long as it is kept away from watercourses (it is toxic to aquatic life), it is licensed for use, although some doubts seem to persist about its safety to wildlife or even humans. It has been extensively applied in hill country over the last fifty years. It is unusual that land managers regard a native plant like bracken as so much of a nuisance: conservationists as well as farmers frequently detest it. Bracken has a worldwide distribution in temperate situations, and I can remember feeling unpleasantly surprised when I went to work in a remote national park in Malawi and found valley-heads full of it.

Bracken seems to have originally been a fern of open woodland in Britain, which adapted to open ground as the wildwood was cleared. It prefers deep well-drained acidic or neutral soils and thins out the higher you go, as it cannot tolerate the increasing frosts or waterlogged peaty soils. There is a Welsh proverb which begins '*Aur dan y rhedyn*' (gold under bracken), meaning where bracken grows the soil is fertile. It is sometimes suggested that bracken reflects the distribution of richer soils laid down by long vanished woodlands – and where therefore they should be recreated. But the fertilising effect of increased atmospheric nitrogen may now enable bracken to spread into ground that has never been wooded, at least in historic times. Conditions suitable for bracken are often found on valley sides, on *ffridd*, where the intensity of agricultural use has advanced and contracted over the years; it often thrives and sometimes dominates when fields have been abandoned. In the past it was useful to farmers: Marged referred to it as the last crop of the year, describing how they cut it in the autumn, once it had turned red, and made it into a stack that was then used as winter bedding for the cows and horses. By spring it had been trodden in and mixed with manure, and would be put back on the land as fertiliser.

Cattle are not so commonly grazed in the Welsh uplands anymore and some people have suggested that increases in bracken are linked to the decline in cattle, which are good at trampling the brittle young bracken fronds when they first push through the ground. Farmers dislike bracken partly because it is toxic to livestock (although animals mostly avoid eating it), but mainly because it makes grazing unavailable. Sheep find dense fronds difficult to penetrate – and anyway, little grows under it due to its heavy shade and highly acidic litter. It supports a very limited invertebrate fauna and suppresses most flowering plants, so conservationists generally don't value it, except as a component of *ffridd* habitat. Whinchats will nest amongst bracken and the caterpillars of small pearl-bordered and high brown fritillary butterflies depend on violets which will grow underneath it if it is not too dense, but generally it is the *ffridd* habitat as a whole, rather than just the bracken, which is valued. Large areas of *ffridd* were ploughed and reseeded in the 1980s with financial incentives from government, much to the disgust of conservationists who were incensed by the destruction of this wildlife rich habitat. Many farmers saw it as useless bracken-infested land.

Large areas of hill land in Wales situated roughly between 200 and 450 m in altitude are dominated by bracken. Estimates of the total extent varies, but the Countryside Council for Wales estimated that between 1979–97 there were 63,000 hectares of dense bracken in Wales; this does not include scattered or woodland plants. They also concluded 'it is unlikely there has been a major bracken expansion (in Wales) in the last century'.[39] Many would find this contentious. Farmers and others consider bracken a scourge and will frequently claim it is spreading in the hills: although data to support this is hard to come by, it certainly seems to be true at a local level, at least. Perhaps we underestimate the effects of bracken harvesting no longer being commonplace; when every farm had horses the need for bracken as bedding would have been significant. Hywel says that bracken is closing in over the more open areas in his woodlands since they have been fenced out and grazing is now confined to winter, when bracken is dormant. Perhaps the sheep used to concentrate in these glades and incidentally trample or lie on the newly emerging fronds.

On a mountain farm near Yr Wyddfa (Snowdon), the National

Trust has reduced grazing to a minimum[40] to try and encourage the re-establishment of a natural treeline. Repeat photographic monitoring there has shown a marked expansion of bracken since they started this new regime.[41] This may be because there is now little trampling of young bracken fronds, but that seems unlikely to be the whole story. There is speculation that atmospheric nitrogen deposition may be encouraging the growth of bracken at the expense of less competitive plants, in the same way it does with nettles and hogweed on roadside verges, but as yet I have seen no data to support this. Our uplands get an unhealthy concentration of this atmospheric fertiliser due to the high rainfall.

The drier parts of the *ffridd* at Craig-y-tân are prime bracken land and, when Hywel took over the farm in 2000, he soon set about reducing it. He says the helicopter spraying did a good job and he has been typically assiduous in following up each year on any missed or recovering bracken – using a knapsack sprayer. This means the rough pasture, which I find so attractive and rich in wildlife, has changed significantly in the last twenty years. I am surprised to find myself concluding that the grassland plants and invertebrates have benefitted from this drastic herbicide treatment, and that the land is more beautiful because of it. Hywel has suggested a possible downside to the bracken eradication is that replacements for the now elderly hawthorns, rowans and crab apples are unlikely to arise, as the sheep would nibble them off in the open. It seems they won't be replaced for want of a bracken nursery. Once again landscape beauty and wildlife richness hinges on land use to shape it.

It is a sultry summer's afternoon and even the dogs barely stir as I walk through the yard, but two pups in the old pigsty-turned-temporary-dog-kennel are keen to greet me. The shine has gone off the green; only the magenta spears of foxgloves punctuate the dullness of the vegetation in the valley. The big sliding door on the barn is closed but swallows, taking food to a late brood, are whipping in and out of a six-inch square around the door handle with unerring accuracy. I can hear them nattering, the metal roof amplifying their conversation. Half a dozen fine-looking rams run ahead of me; one has impressive spirals in his horns, just right for getting stuck in a fence, I think ruefully. Some of the ewes have been shorn and marked with a lurid turquoise cross. The lambs, with thickening coats they will wear until next year's shearing, look portly and serious compared to the leggy playfulness of two months ago.

Ambling across the rough pasture, I seem to be contained in a cat's cradle of swallows; adults and newly fledged young weave and call to one another, as they work the grass tops. I realise that they are following me, as they would a cow, to pick off the insects I disturb from the long grass. There are lots of flowers now: buttercups, white clover, drifts of pignut and the stately candelabras of marsh thistles, their flowers just opening. Tormentil and heath bedstraw woven through the grassland are so characteristic they seem integral to its identity. I kick a molehill and the dusty soil blows away in the breeze; it hasn't rained in weeks. Bluebell heads, now parchment-like bladders full of hard black seeds, rattle against my boots like tiny maracas. On the drier grassland, I disturb dozens of grasshoppers – how good it is to be able to say that in these impoverished times. The tossing white filaments of cotton grass flag up a wet patch; getting down close I can see faded blue marsh forget-me-nots and the pink bells of cross-leaved heath amongst the structured architecture of sedges and rushes. Amongst the hummocks of green and red bog mosses are exotic-looking cranberry flowers with reflexed pink petals, their ripening berries as sour as scrumped apples. Along the edges of the rills, clumps of lemon-scented fern live up to its name and in the wettest part the yellow spikes of bog asphodel mingle with bottle sedge, its cylindrical fruits like miniature brushes. A slim powder-blue keeled skimmer dragonfly twitches along the tiny stream, patrolling its territory with hyperactive vigilance.

At this season invertebrates are everywhere in places like this, both underfoot and in the air: spiders, bugs, beetles, flies, grasshoppers, frog-hoppers, bees, moths, damselflies are all around me. I play grandmother's footsteps with the scurrying wolf spiders as I move forward. A million delicate stems of deer grass are each topped with a tiny rufous tuft: their time will come in late autumn when, by sheer weight of numbers, they will blush the bogs and flushes russet. Several heath spotted-orchids dotted across the bog are as delicate as aristocratic ladies, their broad pink lips fashionably traced and scribbled. I find a few, not many, sundews, their sticky rackets extended – a passive snare for minute flies. To have my boots in soggy bog moss surrounded by dragonflies and orchids is some kind of heaven for me.

These rough pastures and bogs are only lightly grazed, but even so I find myself wondering if they would be even better for wildlife with no grazing at this time of year. However, while some of the plants are nipped off before they set seed, or even flower, a good number seem to be surviving. I pacify the conservationist in me with a reminder that this is a farm and in that context it is wonderfully rich. Also leaving this ground un-grazed in the summer would risk the build-up of ranker vegetation that can choke the very plants you are trying to encourage. Grazing at conservation levels requires so few animals that it ceases to be farming, and even then, it might not work.

Inherent in this is that sheep are not native – they were introduced to Europe from the Middle East thousands of years ago and had no indigenous ancestors here. Our wild plants and animals evolved with the native ancestors of cattle, horses and pigs, and are better adapted to the effect of their grazing and browsing. With their small mouths, sheep graze very differently from cattle and horses, selecting more palatable species over coarser ones, which can lead to a decline in the more delicate plants and allow the tougher ones to dominate. From a purely ecological point of view, sheep have little to offer. Like most animals, they often distribute themselves unevenly, not only concentrating on the most palatable vegetation, but also the most sheltered areas or adjacent to where they receive supplementary feeding. Consequently, a theoretical formula of so many livestock units per hectare can produce unintended consequences. A farmer who knows his land and animals intimately through the seasons will factor such things into his stock management, in order to maximise meat production. Conservation management is a very new art (or science) so there is still much we don't know, but clearly in situations like this stock management skills are necessary to maximise wildlife 'productivity'. Establishing the best grazing regime for wildlife is a more trial-and-error than formulaic process, requiring flexibility from regulators and knowledge and commitment from land managers (farmers), neither of which are commonly found. Is the time coming when the definition of farming includes this, so that Hywel's dictum of 'every farmer wants to farm' could respectably include wildlife 'production'? There is now political urgency around these issues to meet the government's carbon reduction pledges, and 'nature-based solutions' are attractive because they also address the biodiversity crisis and are often relatively cheap. Approaches such as regenerative agriculture, agroecology and permaculture are attracting increased attention from farmers in both the arable and livestock sectors. These tend to overlap rather than being totally distinct, but in essence they are sustainable systems that give particular attention to soil health, recycling of nutrients and the water cycle. They are aimed not only at producing food but enhancing biodiversity, drawing down and storing atmospheric carbon, and erosion and flood prevention. They can range from simply no longer ploughing (a 'no-till' approach) to promote soil health, through to a fully integrated system of growing trees, mixed with cropping or livestock grazing in between. Relevant to pastureland like that at Craig-y-tân, regenerative agriculture includes the practice of 'pulse' or 'mob' grazing, which involves periods of intense grazing followed by periods of rest, which mimics the effects of wild herbivores.[42] This can contribute to any of the benefits above, including biodiversity. An important acknowledgement in all these approaches is that nature will not just 'get along fine' on the margins of agriculture but needs farming systems specifically designed to foster it.

I find Hywel in the yard on my way back and he says he has something to show me in the rough pasture down by the river. After a bit of searching in some tussocky grass we find what he is looking for: a patch of bright yellow slime around the lower stems of the grass. Up close I could see that it consisted of a clear gelatinous mass tightly covered with a network of chrome yellow granules. I thought it was probably a slime mould – which I was later able to confirm with a bit of research – but these organisms are difficult to identify; rather tentatively I decided it was probably *Fuligo septica*, sometimes known as 'dog's vomit slime mould'.

Slime moulds are extraordinary life forms: they are neither plants nor animals, although they can resemble fungi. One of their distinctive features is that they move about, purposely shifting from one place to another in search of the microbial organisms on which they feed. They do not move very fast but recorded times of 1 millimetre per second would be clearly visible. Much of the time, they live as tiny single-cell organisms on substrates of one kind or another, but if food becomes scarce they can aggregate in a bag of slime and start moving as a single body. Eventually this enters a more conspicuous reproductive stage, a bit like the mushroom stage of a fungus and, in this case, shows up as an acid yellow blob. Finding the slime mould is a wonderful example of the richness of wildlife that can occur in 'unimproved' pastures and it leaves us both feeling pleased as we walk back to the yard.

The story of the pastures at Craig-y-tân is a neat example of the interplay between native vegetation and sheep grazing; on many other farms you can add drainage and cutting, not to mention the universal problems of aerial pollution and climate change. If you put all that on top of the unique circumstances of aspect, topography, soils and historic land use, it is very hard to come up with a formula for what is best for wildlife and farming, as each is restrained by the other – even in a farm of such low intensity as Craig-y-tân.

Although many of us value nature for its intrinsic worth (and I say amen to that), there is another way of looking at it which may be helpful when considering how conservation like that at Craig-y-tân can be paid for in future. The Dasgupta Review commissioned by the UK government in 2021 argues that we should acknowledge that nature provides us with 'services' (food, water, nutrients, oxygen to breathe – the list seems endless) and we can therefore see it like health or education, as an asset that needs investment.[43] Paradoxically we, as asset managers, are embedded within the asset – which emphasises the existential importance of the task: our future depends on us ensuring that demand does not exceed supply. This viewpoint suggests nature should enter economic thinking in the same way as roads or skills, as a component of prosperity that has economic worth and requires financing for the ecosystem services that it provides. In this system of 'natural capital accounting' nature must be budgeted for. This kind of economic approach seems particularly relevant to large-scale sustainable land management projects such as Tir Canol in Mid Wales (see Chapter 12) or the innovative Mega Catchment scheme being promoted by Dŵr Cymru in the Brecon Beacons. At bottom this model treats nature not as an unprofitable loss but rather an essential asset requiring investment – an approach that is framing the devolved government's models for post-Brexit agricultural support. Looked at this way, the woods and bogs at Craig-y-tân are economic assets which should attract finance – private as well as public. It has to be said there is little access to private finance for ecological services at present, so most farmers are anxiously looking to the government.[44] This economic approach can seem a rather bloodless view of nature, but it is a useful perspective when working out where the money can come from. Without financial support, many hill farmers, including Hywel, would go out of business – and he is clearly worried. 'Anything you write might help,' he tells me. Even seemingly self-reliant hill farmers are subject to so many outside factors that they often feel that their livelihoods are dictated by those elsewhere.

Chapter 5

Conifers, Foxes and Crows

In 1947, when the *Farmers Weekly* published its article about the agricultural changes on the Glanllyn estate, another great change to land use was also taking place: the expansion of the Forestry Commission. As part of the post-war revival there was a push for the country to be more self-sufficient in timber, so the Commission was given funds to buy up land and plant trees, mostly monocultures of conifers: 'productivity' was the watchword then. Prior to this, there had only been a few small blocks of exotic conifers dotted about the district, planted by the Glanllyn estate as pheasant cover. The buying up of large areas of mountain land to plant trees was new, and farmers or their landlords were offered good prices; Marged's father Ifan was vehemently against it, saying, 'Once the mountain has gone, you will never get it back again.' However, several blocks of land adjacent to Craig-y-tân were sold for forestry and the southern tip of the farm is now surrounded by plantations.

As a devoted shepherd on a farm with very little good quality pasture, it was understandable that Ifan Jones would feel that way. Others, with better pastureland, sold their mountains and ploughed the money into intensifying lower down, leaving them with a farm that was easier to run and perhaps more profitable. Ironically, when the agri-environment schemes arrived in the 1990s, some who had sold their mountain land for forestry came to regret it, as the new schemes paid handsomely for farmers to go on grazing their mountains. Thus was the wisdom of Ifan Jones confirmed.

The very extensive areas of hill land planted with conifers in upland Wales right up until the1980s has had a profound and lasting impact on wildlife and landscape which needs to be fully understood, not least because it might just be starting to happen all over again.

The block of conifers behind our house owned by the then Forestry Commission (now Natural Resources Wales) used to be a sombre place: forty-year-old spruce trees creaking and knocking in the lifeless gloom, their pillowing needles suffocating the forest floor save for an occasional fern. Even when the sunlight did find a gap, it shone a light on nothing much at all. Only in the canopy was it ever-green, and robins, blackbirds and the like found a home there, along with a few siskins and an occasional crossbill.

Then one spring day, about fifteen years ago, a contractor turned up with a sexy-looking Finnish machine to harvest the trees. Within three weeks he had felled the lot – by himself. It was extraordinary to watch. From his cab, O. G. (as he is known locally) felled the trees with an automated chainsaw on the end of the machine's arm, stripped the branches by flossing the trunks through mechanical teeth and then cut the timber to length as slickly as slicing cucumber. He told me he had spent nine years 'on the saws' before learning to operate these voracious harvesters, which effectively replace a gang of men. Whilst we spoke, he was tinkering with the machine, which had broken down. He could do a bit mechanically but if it was the computerisation, he was stumped. I asked him what happened then. 'I'll phone Helsinki – they'll sort it out,' he said, tapping his mobile phone.

What he left behind was devastation: churned mud, broken limbs, amputated stumps, tangled brash. The place was trashed and left, like an abandoned battlefield, with newly exposed peat leaking stored carbon into the atmosphere like invisible smoke. To my surprise, I found it liberating. The landscape had been turned on its side from vertical to horizontal; I was no longer inside it but on top of it. Within days, fern fronds, now flooded with light, were uncurling in brilliant green. After three weeks, smashed birch trees were sprouting new growth and brambles had begun to feel their way across the turmoil. Dozens of swallows and house martins sliced back and forth in the new space liberated by the felling. A flock of a hundred meadow pipits joined them, combing through the wreckage for days on end, like a search party after some gigantic plane crash.

Fast forward two or three years and the place was transformed once again, softer and greener now as the replanted spruce began to win the growth race against the sallow, birch and rowans. All were waist-deep in a glorious tangle of bramble, brash, rushes and rotting stumps. This labyrinth of hiding places punctuated by song posts gifted us new birds: reed buntings, tree pipits, whitethroats and the purring invisibility of grasshopper warblers. Butterflies flicked back and forth and dragonflies patrolled the edges. There were frogs in the ditches. Along the rough forest road, the flood of warmth and light nurtured an annual burst of colour as drifts of rosebay, ragwort and thistles lined the roadside like a street market from which bees, wasps and flies gathered nectar and pollen. Less competitive flowers such as eyebright, fairy flax and trailing St John's wort had colonised the seedbed of the open gravel. Delicate pink bird's-foot, which probably arrived here on machinery tyres from some other forest road, is gradually taking hold on this one.

This is their moment in the sun: the young spruce trees are growing at a prodigious rate and the lifeless gloom is beckoning again. In fifteen years from now, the forest floor will be as dead as a doormat and the siskins and crossbills will be back in the canopy. But before then O. G., or somebody else, will be back with an even slicker machine to knock hell out of a different block of this forest, and it will all begin again as the light floods in, and the whitethroats begin to eye it up.

That cycle was in one small block of a much larger plantation, which was established about sixty years ago, on what was probably a mixture of rough grazing and boggy ground, not unlike the *ffridd* at Craig-y-tân. And that is the point about conifer forests in Britain: in ecological terms they have only just arrived – until recently they were something very different. The plantation close to our house was planted on peat up to a metre deep in places and, like ghosts, a few plants of cotton-grass and cross-leaved heath emerged from the seed bank after it was felled. Tecwyn Jones, who grew up in Eithin Fynydd on the other side of the plantation, told me that when he was a boy eighty years ago, they called this area the *mawn* (peat) and he could remember digging peat there to burn on the fire at home.

In 1997, there were approximately 170,000 hectares of conifer plantations in Wales, more than twice the area of native broadleaved woodland.[45] Most of these plantations were established in the mid-twentieth century on poor-grade agricultural land, much of which was on the fringes of the uplands. Nearly all this land was covered in native grasses, bilberry and heather: undervalued at the time (even by conservationists), it is now better appreciated for its fungal associations, long established soil structure, stored carbon and wildlife interest. In particular, it has potential to develop from overgrazed, species-poor pasture into something far richer for nature. But, once submerged under planted trees, that potential is effectively lost forever.

The dominant conifer planted in Wales has been Sitka spruce, a native of high rainfall areas on the west coast of North America;[46] it grows well in the climate and soils of upland Britain. In the old-growth forests of north-west America, Sitkas can apparently grow to be magnificent trees dripping with epiphytes, but we rarely see them in their pomp here. Despite their extent, the National Vegetation Classification, which is the most authoritative account of British vegetation, doesn't include these plantations at all. That is because, like arable fields or agriculturally improved pastures, they are essentially cropland. Whether in the private or state forestry sector, the trees are, in the main, grown on a short, clear fell rotation as a utility for profit. Unless this ethos changes, the vast majority of conifer plantations will never develop into real forests with a rich flora and fauna. Proper woodlands are, of course, much more than a stand of trees. They contain complex three-dimensional, interdependent webs of fungi, flowering plants, invertebrates and vertebrates that took millennia to establish and evolve; in sharp contrast to fifty-year-old stands of alien trees planted on open grasslands. Ironically, the new plantations were established on land previously occupied by the original wildwood before it was cleared for agriculture centuries before. The hand-made, made-to-measure countryside of pre-war Britain has mostly slipped away from us by now and these forests are part of the industrialised landscape that has succeeded it. However, as I saw from the results of O. G.'s work, at certain stages they are far from useless for wildlife.

The establishment of commercial conifer plantations has been part of policies by successive governments to encourage domestic timber production. My first encounter with the effects of this was in the early 1970s, when I was warden of an woodland nature reserve rich in the kind of plants and insects that characterise our most ancient woodlands. Adjacent to it was a thicket-stage conifer plantation with some skeletal oaks sticking out of it. This had been part of the original wood – sharing in its nightingales, purple emperor and black hairstreak butterflies – until the Forestry Commission bought it, ring-barked the oaks to kill them and for good measure aerial sprayed the whole wood with herbicide. Who sprays nightingales with herbicide? After that, they planted it with conifers.

I also carry scars from the early 1980s, when specific tax breaks had resulted, for a time, in forestry being an attractive short-term investment for the wealthy. Extensive new plantations were established in some prime wildlife habitats, notably in the Flow Country in Caithness and Sutherland, and closer to home in Llanbrynmair in north Powys, where some of the best blanket bog in Wales went under Sitkas for the benefit of a celebrity's tax bill. The history of conifer plantations is sufficiently recent that I cannot help but mourn what they swallowed up. In 1966, the well-known nature writer William Condry wrote the following about a farm near here called Maes Meillion:

> On these slopes you can find meadows and sheep pastures nearly as fragrant and colourful as meadows in the limestone Alps. In the wetter places there are marsh orchids. On the drier fields there is a scattering of frog orchids and also – but it is very rare and hard to find – the small white orchid, which characteristically shares these calcareous pastures with the frog orchid…. But many people would say that the glory of these slopes is the upright vetch (Vicia orobus) that makes splendid patches of purple-pink in some of the fields.[47]

The same place today is wall-to-wall Sitka spruce. On a recent visit with a group of botanists, we found only the common acid-loving species you would find on any local roadside or bit of boggy ground, and nothing at all under the trees.

Early one peerless morning in late April, I decide to spend some time in one of the plantations adjacent to Craig-y-tân to experience what they are really like. It's the sort of morning I have been waiting for all through a long, cold winter. The interior of the plantation looks like a Bridget Riley op-art painting in brown (an unlikely thought). The trees are forty-foot-tall western hemlocks, which stretch away in a series of vertical stripes in subtly differing shades: nightmarishly this place is the same wherever you view it from. The sun is still low so some lateral light is penetrating the gloom around the edges, but on an overcast day it would be difficult to see well enough to write my notes. I don't suppose this plantation has been touched since it was planted fifty years ago; the trees are now thinning themselves. Some have rotted where they stand; others dropped criss-cross on the floor like pick-up-sticks. The ground, a cushion of conifer needles, is also brown, except for a scatter of green foliage torn from the canopy by the wind. Absolutely nothing grows here.

Over the sound of the river at the bottom of the slope, I can hear a chaffinch, mistle thrush and robin singing; there is also a snatch of wren song by the river, probably outside the plantation. Overhead, a small flock of siskins twitter and buzz through the canopy. There are likely to be other birds: jay, song thrush, coal tit, goldcrest and so on, but, apart from the siskins, they are the kind of bird you would find in any decent urban park. Also, without exception they are in the sunlit canopy; eighty per cent of the plantation is silent and lifeless. I haven't seen a single insect, although sunlight gleaming on the looping threads of spider webs indicates faint signs of invertebrate life.

After about an hour I can't bear it any longer. Part of the reason it is unbearable is because I know from an aerial photograph taken in 1948 what was here before these trees were planted, and is still here today on either side, brutally bisected by the plantation. Rocky grassland, wet and boggy in places, scattered with hawthorn and crab apple trees runs down to the riverbank: a vibrant place with bluebells, heath spotted-orchids and sundews, redstarts, cuckoos, tree pipits and buzzing with insect life in the summer. And it used to be like that right here where I sit. The clues abound: dusty muffled, boulders poking through the forest floor, a spectral section of dry-stone wall leading nowhere. These are parodies of the rocks and walls outside, dressed to kill in lichens and mosses, nest sites for wagtails and wheatears, and this winter an all-white stoat slipping in and out of the crevices. By comparison this place is a graveyard.

To be fair I know that at the thicket stage, for ten years or so, plantations can come alive, as they did behind our house, in a tangle of young trees, brambles and rushes, but that doesn't last for long. Unless we can come up with a radically different way of managing our conifer forests, these sometimes vibrant but mostly moribund ecosystems are doomed to a perpetual 'Groundhog Day' existence of never maturing. It is common enough in Europe to see conifer forest management that includes thinning, selected felling and spontaneous regeneration, all of which contribute to the development of rich and mature forests. Recently there have been signs of a more enlightened approach from Natural Resources Wales (NRW): their new planting schemes are more varied and can include broadleaves, although it will be some time before we see the benefits of these; they are also experimenting with 'continuous cover forestry' in a few places, which crucially avoids large scale clear-felling. In September 2022, NRW opened a public consultation on its revised management plan for Llanuwchllyn Forest, a group of forestry blocks which includes those around Craig-y-tân.[48] The revision has many nature-friendly proposals: maintaining upland heath and blanket bog that falls within the forest boundary; softening the forest edge in a variety of ways; allowing more deadwood to remain for the benefit of wildlife; increasing riparian woodland and diversifying the tree species planted (including broadleaves); long-term reduction in clear-fell systems in favour of continuous-forestry cover. It is very encouraging to see proposals like these being enshrined in forest plans. In many ways, the revolution required in forestry mirrors that in agriculture: an industry that has been focussed on productivity and profitability needing to evolve into one that also willingly delivers non-profitable, and in many ways less tangible aspects, that are essential for the public good. Beyond that, my fervent hope is that a working culture will evolve so that foresters can be proud of the wildlife in their forests, as well as the commercial timber they produce. There are already some rich and interesting state-owned forests, including a couple not far from here: big trees, mixtures with broadleaves, open rivers and streams. In places there are crossbills, nightjars, goshawks and even pine martins but, sadly, where I have been sitting is still the rule rather than the exception. There is a long way to go.

Having fled the hemlocks, I decide to take the steep path up through the higher part of the plantation to the mountain above; for half a mile or so it is still wall-to-wall conifers – Sitkas this time. The experience is much the same, only even darker, and twiggier to get through, so I stick to the path. Stepping through the gate at the top onto the open hill, I sit on a rock with the plantation at my back and take stock. It seems reasonable to assume what is around me now is more or less what the Sitkas replaced when they were planted, and the 1948 photograph bears this out in general terms. I am immediately struck by how much more attractive it is to me and, I imagine, any other sane person. There are slopes of heather-clad scree, rough grassland dominated by mat-grass and heath rush, textured mounds of moss and drifts of bleached rushes in the runnels. Several meadow pipits are calling and a skylark is pouring out joy as it towers up in song. A wheatear flits across my line of sight from one jumble of boulders to another; wolf spiders run across the moss and a bumblebee blunders by. This place feels alive and it is self-evidently richer for wildlife (let alone the human spirit) than the ranks of Sitkas at my back. Crucially, this landscape is fully dressed in native vegetation. A few Sitka seedlings have established themselves amongst it, suggesting the land is only lightly grazed and hinting at a disastrous outcome if the sheep were withdrawn altogether. If this mountain were heavily grazed, as it probably was thirty years ago, it would be less rich in wildlife and not so easy on the eye; lightly grazed mountain land like this has become much commoner in this district over the last twenty years. I'm doing my best to be objective when comparing the conifer plantations with this hillside, but it is no use; I'm with Marged's father. This entire story has been driven by government policy in one direction or the other, with almost no heed for nature.

Fifty years on and the conifers are here to stay. They meet many of the government's countryside policy criteria for timber production, carbon storage, flood prevention, amenity use and rural employment – although the latter is easily overstated. The value of carbon storage in commercial timber is very dependent on the end-use: sawn wood for construction, fencing and the like, continues to store carbon for as long as it is in use, but that is not true of trees that go for wood fuel or pulp, which sadly account for most of the timber produced by Welsh commercial forests.[49] The publicly owned forests allow open access on foot and are much loved by the public, as was demonstrated when David Cameron's government proposed selling them off and was forced to backtrack in the face of a storm of protest.[50] Many of the publicly and some of the privately owned plantations do offer recreational facilities, a number of which are very sophisticated; local to here NRW's Coed y Brenin has some impressive mountain biking trails that have an international reputation.

Much of the early reaction against plantation forestry was on landscape grounds; many people, including the poet Wordsworth, did not like the 'serried ranks' of dark trees in angular plantations, seeing them as marring favourite landscapes in the Lake District and Eryri (Snowdonia), amongst others. For many years, there was very little protest about the effects of afforestation on wildlife. Then in the 1980s, private investors, lured by an enticing combination of a lucrative tax break and planting grants, began putting money into buying land and planting it with conifers. After about ten years, the trees and land were usually sold on and the investors made a handsome profit – largely subsidised by the public purse. Looking for new land to plant, investment companies and individuals began buying up and planting large areas in Caithness and Sutherland on the previously pristine blanket bogs that became known as the Flow Country. This primeval ecosystem was sufficiently important for its landform, vegetation and birdlife to have *global* significance. This did not deter the investors. A huge amount of damage was done to this very special place until, in 1988, Chancellor Nigel Lawson cancelled the tax break, thus signalling the beginning of the end of further planting in the Flows and bringing to an end what Derek Ratcliffe, Chief Scientist for the Nature Conservancy Council, called 'the most massive single loss of important wildlife habitat in Britain since the Second World War'.[51] Thirty-five years later, I still feel angry about this.

Given that these conifer forests are now a permanent and very extensive feature of our landscape, it seems important to consider what they do offer wildlife. Following the Flow Country scandal, the Forestry Commission (now NRW in Wales) began to direct its policies and management to take more account of the landscape impact of their forests and the ancient and native woodland and wildlife found within them. An example of this, local to Craig-y-tân, is about twenty-five years ago, the then Forestry Commission decided to allow half a dozen small plantations that had recently been felled to naturally regenerate. These were blocks that were badly placed in the landscape or perhaps awkward to harvest, so once the timber had been felled and cleared they (admirably) resisted the urge to replant and simply let nature take its course. The result is woodland dominated by birch, rowan and sallow with a scatter of other native broadleaved species and some self-sown conifers. Oaks have also colonised thanks to acorns brought in by jays and squirrels, and these will probably be the dominant trees a hundred years from now. These woodlands are growing up naturally on what was agricultural land sixty years ago, so they have started without the fungal, floral, or invertebrate species that characterise mature woodland. The more mobile birds, mammals and insects will probably have arrived quite quickly and will continue to colonise from nearby woodlands, as will wind- and bird-sown plants and fungi. How long it will take for these infants to become rich and mature woodlands is impossible to say: much will depend on the quality of nearby woods as a source of colonising species.

Locally, most Sitka spruce plantations go through a roughly forty -year cycle from planting to clear-fell. As we have seen, the first ten to fifteen years of a plantation's life is usually richest for wildlife because the canopy is still open, and the structure varied. The fifteen-to-forty-year-old period when the trees are at their most dense is the least hospitable for wildlife. The lack of light penetrating to ground level plus the thick slow-to-rot blanket of fallen spruce needles means that even fruiting fungi are uncommon inside dense stands of trees. A limited, though often abundant, community of mostly generalist bird species inhabit the canopy, some of which breed or feed mostly outside the forest. If the plantation is thinned, meaning a proportion of the trees are removed at twenty to thirty years old, then those remaining have a greater share of the available space, light and nutrients and grow on as bigger, more widely spaced trees. If this does happen and the trees are left twenty to thirty years longer before harvesting, then wildlife increases as more light reaches the forest floor and so plants begin to grow and in turn support invertebrate life. Unfortunately, this rarely happens now, outside of the showpiece forests. More commonly, blocks or whole plantations are clear-felled, wiped clean of being any kind of forest in a matter of weeks, and quickly replanted to restart the cycle. Ecologically this is a traumatic, brutal system, which permanently recycles through colonisation and immaturity, stopping well short of the establishment of high forest. In recent years there has been an attempt, in the public sector at least, to break up the larger, even aged forests into internal blocks, which are felled on rotation. This is an improvement for wildlife as a more varied structure within the overall forest gives plants and animals opportunities to move round within the plantations and so avoid being completely wiped out at each clear fell.

There is a major programme of tree planting across the UK at present, fuelled principally by the government's climate change carbon reduction targets. Trees capture carbon from the air and store it, so planting them is a practical and relatively cheap contribution to this urgent existential problem. How much carbon is drawn down by which trees and in what places is still far from clear. Equally unclear is how much carbon is captured and stored by whatever landform the tree planting might displace, although it is generally understood that woodlands are one of the best habitats for capturing carbon. The re-establishment of woodland across Wales is generally enthusiastically endorsed by conservationists, but 'the right tree in the right place' has become the slightly desperate mantra of those who fear a new wave of conifer plantations. In fact, mostly ecologists would prefer to see trees established by natural regeneration – fence out the sheep and see what comes; it will invariably be the right trees in the right place (as long as it is not dominated by self-seeded conifers!). But the urge to plant trees is compelling, so natural regeneration is rarely considered – despite its economic advantages. The RSPB, when considering nature-based contributions to the government's net zero strategy, has suggested the capacity of new conifer forests to contribute to the scale of change needed for net zero is modest, whereas the potential of new broadleaved woodland to contribute to the ecological crisis would be significant.[52]

The truth is that nature-based solutions to the climate crisis are predicated on everyone simultaneously reducing their carbon consumption and so delivering a net reduction in atmospheric carbon.[53] Sadly, some corporations are now seeing tree planting as a way of using carbon credits to offset their existing (over)consumption and then cynically continuing with 'business as usual'. Farmers in upland Wales are once again being offered good prices to sell hill land for tree planting. The prospect of family farms going out of business to offset corporate greed, their only legacy being millions of Sitka spruce trees, is painful.

Until very recently, comparatively few new plantations have been established in Wales over the last thirty years, so the management of existing forest blocks has been the principal consideration for wildlife. In publicly owned forests, felling blocks on rotation and not replanting along watercourses has been a step forward. Also, large established conifer blocks are sometimes more interesting than they seem at first sight: they have roads, paths, streams, unplanted corners, bogs, ponds, even mine workings and the melancholy ruins of chapels, schools and farmhouses. There are large broadleaved trees dotted about, patches of heather and a surprising amount of deadwood. All of these provide opportunities for wildlife ranging from owls to mosses. What is more, plantations are not usually grazed, a pressure that is almost universal elsewhere in the Welsh countryside. Forest managers preoccupied with timber production may not pay much attention to such things, but they provide additional ecological niches which enrich the forest for wildlife. This often means that conifer forests managed in rotational blocks are richer in wildlife than adjacent improved agricultural pastures, so, despite being an immature and forever transitional habitat, many plantations add to the diversity of an impoverished landscape. Having said that an even-aged, thirty-year-old block of Sitka spruce planted right to the fence is one of the dullest, life-denying living systems you can ever experience.

A significant consequence of the establishment of extensive conifer forests in the uplands has been the opportunities it has given to predators, particularly foxes and crows. Both of these can now find shelter and breed in areas where there was previously little suitable cover, which has given them greater access to large swathes of country. Relatively few people kill foxes and crows nowadays compared to the first half of the twentieth century, when geese and poultry, grouse and partridge, as well as lambs, were vigorously protected in rural communities. The shooting, trapping, snaring and poisoning of a wide variety of birds and mammals including foxes and crows was then widespread and socially acceptable.[54] Once most poultry rearing moved indoors, attitudes towards foxes softened, even amongst some sheep farmers where lambing is now carried out inside. From 1961 to 2009, the number of foxes killed annually by gamekeepers increased threefold according to the Game and Wildlife Conservation Trust, although numbers have changed little since then.[55] Similarly with crows, the numbers present from 1970 to 2013 more or less doubled nationally according to the British Trust for Ornithology's Breeding Bird Survey. However, in Wales there was only a one per cent increase from 1995 to 2020, indicating a more or less stable population.[56] The large increases in the number of these predators in the late twentieth century must have been due, at least in part, to the decrease in human persecution. Hill farmers often loathe foxes and crows because they prey on lambs. The degree to which farmers complain about fox predation varies considerably in my experience, which no doubt reflects local circumstances, but also, I suspect, individual levels of prejudice. Surprisingly, I have been unable to find any solid data about fox predation of lambs.

Hywel and Rhys tell me they lose lambs to foxes every year and, because this issue can be controversial, I asked them how they could be sure the losses are due to foxes. They explained that on the dry slopes in front of the house, where they hold the twins early on, they walk every yard of ground so they would find corpses of lambs that had died of natural causes or by accident. The lambs just disappear in the night, taken, they say, by foxes into the conifer plantation, which is just over their boundary fence. It is to be expected that a medium-sized predator like a fox will take young lambs especially if they are weak or unprotected. Whilst they may initially pick off sickly lambs, there seems to be a general agreement amongst farmers that they do take healthy animals and therefore impact on their livelihoods, but again research data does not seem to be available. Foxes will also sometimes kill lambs, poultry or wild birds surplus to their current needs, some of which they will cache, a habit which doesn't enhance their reputation with farmers and others. Humans have, inevitably, been at war with foxes ever since they started keeping domestic animals.

Hywel is a keen supporter of the local hunt. Typically this operates by sweeping an area of countryside to drive any foxes towards the 'guns' who will endeavour to shoot them as they break cover. The 'guns' are usually a mixture of farmers and other local men. On a single day in early March two years ago Hywel had been out with the hunt and they had shot nine foxes – an unusually high number. A few weeks later, after losing lambs at Craig-y-tân, Hywel called in the huntsmen and they shot two more. On opening them up they found Craig-y-tân's wool mark in the stomach contents of one of them. 'We got the right one,' was Hywel's wry comment. They didn't lose any more lambs that season.

Whether fox (or crow) control is effective in reducing predation of lambs on any particular farm at any one time is open to debate, but it seems reasonable to assume that it can be effective depending on how comprehensive and efficient the effort is. It is also true that you can't 'cull/control' animals or birds without it being a grim, sometimes gruesome, business, which is distasteful to many, especially those whose lives are far removed from these circumstances. All you can hope is that the killing is done efficiently and minimises suffering. And once again farmers feel embattled and misunderstood around this issue – judged by 'out of touch townies and do-gooders'. Personally, I have come to accept that it is a grim necessity, but I need to own that I could not kill a fox myself. Some notes I made recently illustrate why: 'I watched a young vixen, a teenager I would say, on the lawn today – just a few yards away, looking straight at me. She was perfect, not a hair out of place – bright, clean, graceful, poised – moving smoothly, completely in tune with her environment. She seemed to belong in a way we never can.' I can't imagine killing such a creature – but then I don't rear sheep for a living.

Nick Fenwick who farms in Mid Wales offered me a helpful perspective on this: 'Farmers would often take the same delight in watching the young vixen as I did, but not have any problem with killing the same animal at other times of year. I don't think there is a contradiction here, it's just how it is.' Nick went on to say that when you live so close to birth, disease and death in animals every day this become unexceptional; all animals die and often a 'natural' death involves more suffering than by the gun.

More difficult for me is that foxes are sometimes 'controlled' by conservationists when they come into conflict with other wildlife. Recent research seems to support the anecdotal evidence that on moorlands where predators (primarily foxes, crows, stoats and weasels) are controlled to encourage the red grouse population for shooting, the full spectrum of wild birds do better than on moors where there is no culling.[57] This might seem an obvious conclusion, but on such an emotive subject, hard evidence is important. Consequently, as this group of birds are generally declining in Britain, conservation organisations are obliged to consider culling foxes and crows in areas they are responsible for. This is a sensitive topic amongst some supporters of these organisations, many of whom find the idea of conservationists selectively killing wildlife repugnant. The truth is that, because we have modified the wild world so drastically, leaving nature 'to look after itself' no longer works very well. This is partly because we have exterminated other predators (principally wolves and lynx) that used to live here, so in order to retain any sort of balance we need to accept the responsibility of being the top predator in these modified ecosystems. This argument runs strongly with regard to burgeoning deer populations in lowland England, which are having a significant and long-term impact in woodlands by increased browsing of saplings and grazing of ground flora. Since humans have stopped killing deer and other creatures on a routine basis, they lack an effective predator to keep populations in check. The inevitable conclusion to this is that people like me, who are too squeamish to do the killing themselves, should accept and support the necessity for others to do it.

Crows, although universally despised amongst the farming community, do not seem to be considered such a big problem as foxes; Hywel is certainly more relaxed about them at Craig-y-tân. He has a 'Larsen' type of crow trap in which he says he catches six or seven a year, 'just to keep on top of them'. I have come across this trap on the *ffridd* where the twin lambs are put in spring. It is a wire mesh covered structure about three feet square and two feet high. In it there is a 'decoy' crow sitting quietly enough in one half, with food and water provided. The other half is also supplied with a little dried dog food below a perch, which will drop under the weight of an incoming bird, releasing two spring-loaded doors, which shut the bird in. During the breeding season territorial crows will try to drive off the caged 'intruder' but end up getting trapped themselves. The new bird is then killed when Hywel visits the trap. If Hywel needs a decoy bird, he contacts any other farmer he knows who traps crows and they save him a live bird.

Far fewer hands are turned against crows nowadays as people rarely engage with the countryside in the way they did seventy years ago. Even in rural Wales people go to the gym, play golf, or join a cycling club for exercise; there aren't many who poke around the hedgerows anymore, with or without a gun. Consequently, carrion crow populations probably increased considerably in the late twentieth century especially as the new plantations gave them extra opportunities for nesting and shelter. Although it is often said that rooks are found in flocks, and carrion crows singly or in pairs, it is not unusual to see thirty or forty crows together on the farm where I live, when the farmer is feeding 'nuts' to his sheep. Carrion crows will pick on a sickly newborn or half-born lamb, and sometimes a ewe that is ill or stuck in labour. They do sometimes peck the eyes out of ailing lambs when they are still alive. One of the difficulties of assessing the frequency of such attacks is knowing whether the lamb was already dead when the crow found it. Whatever the scale of the problem, it can't be critical as so few farmers now take the time to control crows on their land. Perhaps this is because so many lambs are now born indoors and remain there for the period when they would be most vulnerable to attacks from crows.

Although farmers may have a more relaxed attitude to crows these days, conservationists are less sanguine. A carrion crow is not equipped to take a healthy lamb, let alone an adult sheep, but it is well built to take the eggs or young of ground nesting birds such a lapwing, curlew or hen harrier. The research is now pretty unequivocal that predator control improves breeding success in moorland birds. Gamekeepers on grouse moors will aim to eliminate all crows from their beat as their remit is clear: maximise grouse numbers by all legal means. Whilst it is perfectly legal to kill carrion crows (within certain constraints), it is obviously a difficult choice for conservationists to persecute one bird in defence of another. Personally I enjoy seeing crows in the country-side, I like their dry throaty calls and admire their resilient enterprise. When I worked on the Berwyn we had an estate worker who was expert at gamekeeping work so I never had to face the dilemma of doing the killing myself. It seems ironic that carrion crows can now be as much of a problem for those conserving nature as they are for shooting interests and farmers.

Chapter 6

Peat

At the heart of Craig-y-tân's mountain land is an enormous basin of blanket bog about two miles long and a mile wide, which accumulates near its southern end in an area of quaking ground and scattered pools known as Waun y Griafolen (the bog of the rowan tree). This is the source of the Afon Mawddach that, in its infant form, uncoils from these inaccessible pools and spills over a hard, rocky sill on the western boundary, plunging into Cwm yr Allt-lwyd below, to begin its journey to the sea. This place, cupped in a ring of protective hills, feels as wild and remote as any place I know in Wales. And it is hard to get to – which makes it even more alluring.

I'm keen to get another look at Waun y Griafolen, particularly the area of eroding peat on the western side, which is such a long slog from Craig-y-tân. So, on a fine summer's day with my wife Elen and son Gethin I decide to try a route from the west, which will cut down on the long walk in. It says a lot about this part of Wales that, although the place where we propose to start walking is only five miles from our house as the crow flies, it takes us over an hour to drive there along winding single-track roads and, despite it being a sunny Sunday, we only pass a single car along the way. The nearest settlement to where we intend to park is Abergeirw, which remarkably was only connected to mains electricity about ten years ago. Once the tarmac runs out, we bump along a potholed track until eventually coming to a halt beside a deserted farmhouse: corrugated iron over the windows, swallows flying in and out of its flaking roof. A caravan, green with mould, half buried amongst ragged conifers, only added to the air of godforsaken dereliction that can be so pervasive around profitless hill farming.

A farm bridge over the Mawddach points to a promising looking track winding up the escarpment ahead of us; Waun y Griafolen can't be more than a steep mile from here.

All around in this valley are centuries of worked and built stone: field and boundary walls, sheep pens, barns, pigsties, houses – the product of hard, patient labour and great skill that are slowly falling down, collapsing back into the earth out of which they were hewn. Right by the track is a maze-like complex of sheep pens, now reduced to stone skeletons laid-out under shrouds of moss; they feel 'right' in this landscape and seem to add to its beauty, yet the ghosts of half-forgotten families, even whole communities, stalk these places. No wonder Welsh folk music is so melancholy. Part of that story rings the horizon like shark's teeth: conifer forests, that deadening industry which in the twentieth century swallowed up so much wildlife on open hill land, smothering it with alien trees.

After half an hour of stiff walking we top the escarpment at just over 400 metres and can see through to Waun y Griafolen. Over the last few hundred-thousand years, the river has cut a notch in the ring of protective hills that offers us an open doorway. Ahead we can see the area of eroding peat hags that I am particularly keen to revisit – having been there only once before, three years ago. And they are extraordinary. Ragged mounds of brown peat about ten feet high with teetering topknots of heather and moss are scattered over about two and a half acres. They look like features from the Arizona desert made from chocolate. Between them the rush-covered ground is flat and hard, apparently worn down to the slatey shale that underlies the peat. We are looking at about three metres' depth of exposed peat, which, as it accumulated at about one millimetre a year, is three thousand years' worth of vegetation history stacked up in front of us. The peat is variously spongy, hard or fissured; some slopes have formed into beautiful wave-like patterns when semi-liquid in the rain, reminding me of terraced Asian rice paddies.

Peat really is extraordinary stuff. The gentler slopes and basins of much of upland western Britain are clothed in a layer of it, sometimes, as here, several metres thick. Peat is made up of partially decomposed plant remains, particularly bog-mosses which thrive in waterlogged conditions and are resistant to decay. In places like this, the wet, acidic and nutrient-poor substrates are starved of oxygen, which means that the microbial life forms that break down plant material cannot live in any numbers. Consequently decomposition is inhibited, leaving deepening layers of partially rotted leaves and stems which, when wet, are the colour and consistency of Christmas pudding. As long as rainfall outstrips evaporation and the transpiration from living plants, the peat will continue to grow, giving rise to a landscape draped in it. This is 'blanket bog' a distinctive landscape that rolls gently away in soft greens and brown, sodden underfoot, treeless and mercilessly exposed to wind and rain. Such places are not to everybody's taste, but for me the space and solitude are deeply nourishing.

Blanket bogs are a rare landform globally – Britain and Ireland have twenty per cent of the world's total – and are surprisingly valuable to human society: an example of how our welfare is inextricably and elegantly bound into the health of the natural world.

Firstly, they are an important source of drinking water, with many of our great cities being supplied by the rainfall from boggy moorlands such as these. The taps are kept running in Liverpool, Manchester and Birmingham thanks in large part to rainwater caught and stored in the hills of Wales. This ability to store water in the spongy ground is also vital for flood prevention: an intact bog is eighty-five to ninety-eight per cent water; in effect a huge water-absorbing sponge which allows little lateral movement, so when the rain pours down it is held and then released slowly, rather than careering downhill and engulfing homesteads and villages below.

Blanket bogs also hold huge stores of carbon bound up in the peat, the protection of which is crucial in the fight against climate change. If the skin of vegetation that covers the peat is broken by heavy trampling from people or animals, vehicle damage, fire or atmospheric pollution, then the peat is exposed and begins to dry out, oxidising in the moist air and releasing large amounts of carbon (in the form of carbon dioxide) that had been locked up in the ancient plant remains. The basin in front of me is about four kilometres long by a kilometre wide and if, on average, the peat is two metres thick, then it contains eight million cubic metres of peat. That is a lot of stored carbon in this one small corner of the British uplands – and it is vital for us all that it stays there. Currently around twenty million tonnes of carbon dioxide are released into the air from damaged peat in Britain each year, which is about four per cent of our total greenhouse gas emissions.[58] Ensuring that farmers, foresters and others keep the skin on the soft underbelly of this landscape and prevent it being exposed to the corrosive elements is essential. I don't know what got these peat hags started in this little used corner, a severe fire perhaps, but they will go on eroding and oxidising until there is no peat left. It would be possible to stabilise and reprofile them so that a skin of vegetation could regrow. I don't know if anyone will get to this out of the way place, but I am thankful it is a relatively small and contained problem compared to some of the widespread damage in other areas. During the last ten years or so, as the enormity of the climate crisis has become better appreciated, the value of peatlands as carbon stores has become better acknowledged. A major programme is now underway in Wales and elsewhere to repair and reprofile damaged peat to prevent further erosion and oxidation.

When thinking about peat in this way, as a precious resource to be conserved, it is worth remembering that Marged and E. D. would have seen it primarily as a fuel. Even when I first came to this district, in the early 1980s, there was still somebody selling peat to burn at home on the fire. And scandalously, despite thirty years of lobbying by conservationists, peat is still being cut in the UK and sold in garden centres for potting up tomatoes or petunias. The government is (yet again) proposing a ban on selling peat to amateur gardeners, this time by 2024 – fourteen years after it first announced an intention to ban peat sales for horticulture. It remains 'in consultation' about sales to the trade.

These wild peatlands are probably too inaccessible to have been cut for fuel; I have seen no sign of the tell-tale rectangular depressions. But lower down, in a peaty basin about 200 feet above the house, is the place where Craig-y-tân cut peat for fuel. The cuttings are clearly visible and, ironically, have given rise to wetter conditions in which characteristic bog life is thriving.

Peat harvesting took place in May, once the sheep were back on the mountain and cultivated land had been attended to. Marged and E. D.'s accounts of peat cutting are very similar, both describing labour-intensive work, done by hand – so different from the one-man-and-a-machine-operation, typical in farming today. Special tools were used: a *haearn marcio* (marking iron), a *haearn donni* (cutting tool shaped like a half-moon) and a thin, sharp peat spade. Six divots of peat were lifted from a trench known as a *ceulan* which was six divots wide – the length depended on the quality of the peat. If they had three days of dry weather, the peat was ready to lift and be placed in stacks of three divots, and then, after a further three rain-free days, in stacks of six divots. The men did the cutting and the women and children the carrying and stacking. The last step was to put all the peat divots together in large stacks along the edge of each *ceulan* and, according to E. D., make a peat wall around them to prevent damage from the cattle. Marged said they thatched the stacks with rushes until they were properly dried out, then they were ready to be loaded onto to a sledge which a horse pulled down to the house. All of this was hard, painstaking and very weather-dependent work on which they relied for winter warmth. Of course, this work and the subsequent burning of the peat (as with oil, gas or wood) released carbon into the air, but nothing was known of the long-term consequences back then.

Littered across the eroded ground and protruding from the bottom of hags are bits of wood, some soggy, others bleached as bone, ranging in size from twigs to hulks of timber. These are the preserved remains of the forest that covered this ground 3,000 to 4,000 years ago before the climate shifted into a warmer and wetter phase and blanket peat began to form, gradually burying the remnant trees and so 'fossilising' them forever. Holding a knotted and still fibrous piece of birch, complete with shining bark, in my hands, it is thrilling to realise it is three thousand or more years old: a surviving splinter of the wildwood that occupied the landscape right where I am standing.

Gethin is prowling around the peat hags peering at the ground and I know what he is looking for. When we were here three years ago, he found two fragments of worked flint, which he sent to George Smith, the county archaeologist, who followed up with a further visit and found several more. Smith's subsequent report said five of the flints, including the two that Gethin had found, were 'small blades, probably punch struck, suggesting a late Mesolithic date'. He went on to say that 'very few inland lithic scatters had been found in north-west Wales making this find of particular interest'. He thought it likely that the 'scatter' was the remains of a small temporary summer campsite or hunting site situated on an exposed riverbank in an area that was otherwise forested and was subsequently buried by peat growth. The principal period for this early peat formation was during the Atlantic period, 3,000 to 5,000 years ago, when the climate became warmer and wetter – more oceanic. It is likely that the spread of peat was the main cause of forest decline in areas such as this, but recent research suggests that the small human population at this time may also have had a considerable impact on forest clearance.[59] Philip Marsden, in his book *Rising Ground*, talks about similar Mesolithic flint scatters left on Bodmin Moor in Cornwall by people following the seasonal shifts in their quarry – deer. There are few deer in this part of Wales now, but they were probably commoner then. The woody fragments protruding from the eroding peat, together with Gethin's sharp-eyed finds, give us an extraordinary glimpse of a scene 3,000 to 4,000 years ago, where a group of hunter-gatherer people, probably on a deer hunt, camped right here on the bank of the river in a forested landscape that must have looked entirely different from the windswept moorland all around us.

We walk along the side of the hills that rim the western edge of the bog to get a better overview. To the north-east the Arenig, and its daughter peak Moel Llyfnant, dominate the skyline and to the south, closer to hand, Dduallt rears up out of the bog, nearly sheer for 800 feet. From here I can see that there is a gently humped watershed at the foot of Dduallt, so water drains from it towards us into the Mawddach catchment, and away from us into the fingered streams that begin the Dyfrdwy (Dee) on its journey down to Llyn Tegid (Bala Lake), on to Chester and out to sea across the great intertidal flats of Deeside. Turning to look out across the great expanse of Waun y Griafolen, I can see from this vantage point dozens of pale green parallel lines all across it, and every ten yards or so these are cut with short transverse lines. These are the drainage ditches, which were dammed repeatedly with vegetation and peat using an excavator to try and heal this bog. They look like a pattern of scars – mutilations that have been stitched and are gradually fading. Gethin tells me that one time there were four wide track Hymacs working here simultaneously: it took some serious mechanical clout to close all those ditches, which were dug (with much smaller machines) in the late 1960s, once again incentivised by government grants. Prior to that, there would have been far fewer ditches, that had been dug by hand, and it would have been part of the shepherd's job to keep those open when he was living up here in the summer months. The great web of ditches excavated in the 1960s gradually drained the life-giving water from the bog and sent it careering, peat-stained, into the valley below.

Thirty-five years ago, when I first worked in this landscape, conservationists had barely begun to realise that our blanket bogs had been drying out for decades due to drainage. Then governments were encouraging farmers to drain the land in the belief that it would help boost sheep productivity. Throughout Wales, peatlands have been criss-crossed with hundreds of miles of ditches cut by farmers, hoping to improve the grazing by drying the land. This may have been going on for as long as a thousand years as the early monks are likely to have begun draining boggy land on their granges in the uplands.[60] This, coupled with burning and intensive grazing, has resulted in huge areas of peatland drying out and in places the peat has become exposed and eroded.

Now our understanding and priorities have moved on and our concerns are for ecosystems and the 'services' they provide as well as farming. But from here, looking across the vastness of the mountain land it is difficult to get a sense of this being 'a farm': the farmstead is two pathless miles away across the bog, then over the ridge and down into the valley of the Lliw. It is hard not to be impressed that Hywel and his forebears have lived and worked in this intractable place for generations; shaping the wildness and being shaped by it, in ways that cannot be unbound each from the other.

In 2022, Gethin took me to see some of the most recent peat restoration on the RSPB's Llyn Efyrnwy (Lake Vyrnwy) reserve where he works, only about ten miles cross-country from Craig-y-tân. We hiked up onto a ridge from where heather-clad moorland rolled away for miles in every direction. It was a sunny day in early March but there were no intim-ations of spring: austere, empty and soundless except for a skylark tuning up. In front of us was a mechanical excavator, one of a dozen currently working up here. These machines have specially widened low-pressure tracks for support and to avoid damaging the spongy ground. Beneath our feet the peat was between one and two metres deep. Dotted across this landscape were dozens of glittering pools skimmed with ice. I had never seen scattered pools on blanket bog in Wales; they reminded me of the patterned bogs in the Flow Country in northern Scotland, but these have recently been constructed.

The aim of this work is to cover any exposed peat with vegetation and raise the water table across the whole system. This will reduce carbon emissions from the drying peat and increase carbon capture by the bog-mosses on the re-wetted ground and those colonising the new pools. This will also reduce the risk of flooding in the valleys by increasing absorbency, which slows down the rate at which the water runs off the moors. Biodiversity should also benefit, but the outcomes of this are harder to predict: the pools of open water will provide a habitat for invertebrates, and these will be food for birds such as curlew, golden plover and (on the wish list) dunlin. The re-wetting should also encourage bog plants at the expense of heather – but in reality nobody knows what the outcomes will be.

This is a complex operation: first the area is filmed using drones, then mapped on a computer when gullies, exposed peat and steep undulations are marked for repair; these are then passed to the machine drivers. Their job is to reprofile the steep sides of gullies and then stretch a mat of vegetation back over the wounded peat like a skin surgeon. In the same operation, they dam the gullies along their length in a series of shallow steps, using compacted peat excavated from what becomes the pool. On pristine blanket bog, which no longer exists in Wales, the surface would be gently undulating and scattered with pools, without the gullies and hags that have resulted from centuries of erosion and drainage. These dams may have to be repeated several times in the coming decades to raise the water table in stages; a limitation here is that pools should not be more than 50 centimetres deep to prevent sheep from drowning. Funded by the sale of carbon credits offered through the Peatland Code (an example of natural capital financing), this is expensive work, stretching across whole landscapes. It is also somewhat experimental without guaranteed outcomes, and it is salutary to hear from Gethin that many of the peatland dams made from heather bales during the LIFE Project scheme, of which Craig-y-tân's peatland was a part, are now starting to rot at the bottom and water is leaking through. Some of that work will have to be redone using improved damming methods.

There is a scarce butterfly, the large heath, which is found exclusively in peatland habitats, both upland and lowland. Principally a northern species, it is at the edge of its range in Wales and found in only a few upland bogs, including Waun y Griafolen. I had never seen a large heath, so on a sunny July day Elen and I set out on a quest to find one. This time we decided to go in from the east, which starts along a rough path above the farm of one of our neighbours, who kindly let us park in their yard – which saved us a mile or so.

Our first stretch of walking is through a steep-sided valley stacked on one side with terraced crags from which a kestrel yickers anxiously. The river gurgling through the valley is stained brown with particulate peat washed down from the bog and the surrounding sombre rocks and tumbling screes are lit up with magenta patches of bell heather. A stonechat, headwaiter smart, breaks the silence with its pebble-clacking call from the top of a swaying bracken frond. The land seems barely grazed with only a handful of sheep to be seen, all of which are funnelling up ahead of us through waist-high rushes. In recent years, it appears that many farmers are barely using their mountain land which, considering they get an area-based subsidy, could be courting a financial backlash. But this may be because many are in Glastir agreements which have reduced sheep numbers and exclude grazing altogether for six months through the winter.

We follow vague sheep tracks, which often peter out and then reappear amongst the bracken and rushes as we push on up the valley. Two or three ancient-looking cairns indicate that people used to walk this way more often; they are so slumped and lichen-encrusted that I doubt they were made by modern walkers. Some tumbled sheep pens and a ruined building evoke a familiar sense of ghosts in these landscapes; this valley was once much busier with shepherds, game-keepers, shooting parties and others making regular use of what now feels empty and forgotten.

After plodding on for an hour or two, the valley begins to open out; the sides are lower and less inclined. On our left the other side of the stream is fenced out and the gently sloping hillside is sprinkled with hundreds of young trees: birch, willow, rowan and Sitka spruce saplings that have sprung up spontaneously amongst the heather. This is a vivid reminder that the ecological imperative in most of our countryside is to move towards woodland, if conditions allow. Just over the fence, a haze of golden flowers provides further proof that the hillside is free from grazing; sheep would quickly nibble off these succulent bog asphodels. Their specific scientific name is 'ossifragum', which means 'bone breaker'. It used to be believed that eating this plant made the bones of sheep brittle, but in truth its presence tells you more about the acidic, calcium-poor nature of places like this, which are the real cause of the sheep's problems.

This area of land, owned by NRW, is a conservation success story. In the 1990s, it was part of an early project financed by the EU LIFE fund to restore upland bogs in this part of Wales. The conifers that had been planted here on deep peat were cleared and the drainage ditches blocked to restore the open moorland that was present here prior to planting. It was ill advised to plant trees here in the first place as they would not have grown at all well in these conditions; I doubt anybody could ever have made a profit from them.

To our right, the ridge gradually tapers down to flatness and we are able to turn north onto the main body of the bog. It is hard going stepping over the cottongrass tumps into the soggy sphagnum-moss-filled gaps between, and Elen is soon muttering about 'naturalists going off-piste'. The full swathe of this huge space is spread out in front us now, its northern edge about two miles away. It is rimmed round with rolling grass and heather slopes and at the southwest edge these rear up into the fearsome escarpment of Dduallt which looms over the landscape. The surface of the bog is a gently undulating mosaic of soft brown and green pricked out with the white flags of cottongrass, between which are channels of brilliant green bog-moss. I am struck by the space and quiet; it is like some vast roofless cathedral in which I feel insignificant, dwarfed by land and sky.

The heather here is small and feeble looking, thinning out to a mere scattering, as the bog gets wetter. This is an encouraging sign from a conservation viewpoint as much of the blanket bog in Wales and England has become too dry after decades of draining and burning, a consequence of which is heather thriving on the dried-out peat, at the expense of plants that prefer to have their feet wet. Pools have dried up, bog-mosses disappeared, peat has stopped growing and the specialist wildlife has faded away. By now nobody really knows what pristine Welsh blanket bog should look like. Thankfully it is no longer permissible to burn on deep peat and where drains have been blocked the water table is rising, which in turn may mean the sheep graze it less. Consequently, the vegetation of this place is changing, with likely increases in the wet-loving plants and those that are intolerant of burning, and a corresponding decrease in those that prefer drier conditions. This will also have consequences for the communities of invertebrates and birds that live here, but it will probably be decades before we fully understand the effects of these changes.

Crouching down in this wide-open space under an arching sky, I feel like Gulliver in Lilliput peering into the complexity of a miniature world. There is an unexpected intimacy in the hummocks and lawns of crimson, gold and brilliant green bog-mosses between the clumps of cottongrass and the flesh-pink bells of cross-leaved heath. Red stars of insectivorous sundews glisten with lethal stickiness and wolf spiders sprint across their killing fields. About 400 yards away to our left, I can glimpse the pools known as Llyn Grych-y-waun that are at the centre of the vortex of water that drains into and out of this place. Three years ago, I waded about in that perilous bog with some companions, look-ing for two rare sedges that reputedly grew there: bog sedge and tall bog sedge (*Carex limosa* and *Carex magellanica*). These delicate and barely distinguishable grass-like plants are found in highly acidic bog systems, growing at the edge of pools and in very wet hollows. We held our nerve as the ground quaked and, after much diligent searching, were delighted to find good populations of them both.

By now I am satisfied that we have reached the area that I had been told was best for large heaths so, after an uncomfortable sandwich break perched on wobbling cottongrass tumps with our feet in the bog, we begin to search for them. The conditions are perfect: strong sunshine and only a light breeze – which are not easy to come by up here. Large heaths only emerge for about three weeks in July at this altitude and they are reluctant to fly unless it is sunny, and with very little wind. At rest they are near impossible to find, their dull orange and browns providing perfect camouflage amongst the cottongrass; combine this with the remoteness of their upland habitat and it is not surprising their populations are difficult to monitor. Quartering the ground and scanning the area in front of me intently, I am no longer able to watch my feet and curse as my boot drops into a watery bog hole.

Apparently these butterflies like to keep low, and crouching down I can see that their world has more of cover and structure than you might expect. The hummocks and hollows, runnels and mounds look like an aerial view of this landscape from a low-flying jet. Some of the mounds are worryingly dry with crisp tufts of lichen and patches of bare crumbly peat, but between these are areas fringed with cotton-grass and gleaming with water. A dragonfly with a powder-blue abdomen darts from pool to pool along these miniature highways. The fluttering of an occasional pale, papery moth has me twitching but otherwise, after a couple of hours of careful searching, we have had no sightings of large heaths. Some red grouse droppings on a hummock cheer me but otherwise I can feel a familiar sense of pessimism setting in; an everything-is-going-downhill feeling, which is so familiar to modern-day conservationists. I find myself wishing I had written this book twenty years ago when wildlife populations were more buoyant. I'm standing in magnificent scenery in what looks like high-quality habitat and yet by the end of the day we had only seen two or three skylarks, numerous meadow pipits, three stonechats, two wheatears, a kestrel and an occasional crow. Of course, it is mid-July which is late in the bird season and these things are always a matter of chance to some degree, but it does seem ominously quiet.

It later transpires that hardly any large heaths were seen in upland Wales this year – I heard of only two sightings. Was it just a poor year, or is there a bigger story lurking behind the usual concerns about habitat condition and weather? There has been speculation that these populations, being at the south end of their range, might be under threat from climate change. Because the large heath is confined to peatbogs, it can be seen as something of a coalmine canary for these special habitats. Potential threats such as fire, drainage, heavy grazing or climate change will degrade the very places these butterflies depend upon, so fluctuations in their numbers over the medium and long-term should alert us to the relative health of our peatlands – if we can muster the capacity to monitor them.[61]

Hywel's sheep, unsurprisingly, are mostly confined to the better-drained, grassier slopes that ring the bog. I wonder how much they graze the bogland itself and whether it needs much grazing to support its characteristic wildlife. Hywel tells me his sheep do graze the lower, wetter ground and I have sometimes seen them there, but not in any great number. The lower stock numbers specified in Hywel's agri-environment agreement will have reduced competition for food, so the sheep are now less likely to graze in the soggy areas. The bog is apparently grazed sufficiently to prevent tree seedlings getting a hold on the drier parts; although I have seen several Sitka spruce saplings growing on deep peat today, tortured out of shape by weather and nibbling sheep, but still growing. Although they may never grow into large trees in such a wet and windswept place, they are remarkably tenacious and any number of them would start to dry out the ground, making it more suitable for others to follow. Because Sitka spruce were introduced from north-west America and not planted extensively until the mid-twentieth century, we do not yet know what their tolerances are over the long term. It may be that in the absence of grazing they could gradually populate blanket bog like this, so afforesting land that was naturally open ground. Replacing specialist peatbog wildlife with the very limited range of plants and animals found in Sitka spruce forests would be a very poor deal for biodiversity.

There are still many uncertainties about the long-term ecological impacts of reduced grazing, or the ban on burning, and raising water tables in habitats like this. We think these are the right things to be doing now but experience suggests that conservation practices will have to evolve; there are so many variables in ecological management that it is unusual to get it right first time. Being transparent about our uncertainty and explaining the complexity may help reduce the scepticism amongst farmers. Agricultural development no doubt proceeded by local trial and error, but the application of blanket prescriptions based on current assumptions always runs the risk of lasting damage, if this later turns out to be wrong.

Chapter 7

Moorland
Birds

Thirty-odd years ago, when Elen and I were short of funds, we toyed with the idea of doing bed and breakfast at our house. Mercifully that never materialised, but at the time I dreamed of attracting birdwatchers to stay by advertising that within a three-mile radius of the house you could find hen harrier, merlin, peregrine, short-eared owl, red and black grouse and probably golden plover. I would never have done it for fear of disturbing the birds, but as an ornithological brag it wasn't bad.

Thirty years later and upland birds are generally in decline, but the moorland habitat is still there so I am curious to know how the birds are faring locally. Getting an idea of population sizes and trends is not easy because published information usually only gets down to regional level (in this case North Wales), but I can draw on local knowledge – and my own experience.

On an overcast, chilly day in late April Gethin and I decide to walk up onto the moorland that includes Craig-y-tân's mountain land and see what birds we can find. The cloud is high, and an occasional gleam of sunshine illuminates the enormous view over Llyn Tegid, that opens up behind us as we climb. Above the last farm the *ffridd* is strewn with boulders, billows of dead bracken and ancient ash and rowan trees – variously broken, hollowed or cankered – stand propped amongst them. Tree pipits sob as they parachute down – this is just their sort of country. A pair of pied flycatchers, no doubt eyeing up nest holes in the elderly trees, are anxious for us to pass, fussing from branch to fence and back again. Cresting the slope we drop down, cross a small river and turn into a steep-sided upland valley. Apart from the thin calls of meadow pipits taking to the air, and an occasional lusty wren, it is strikingly silent. Nobody much comes this way.

Above us are some dark fissured crags where a pair of peregrines nested for many years, but not anymore. When I first came to this district, peregrines were still recovering from their disastrous population crash in the 1960s caused by pesticide poisoning. After some years, pretty well every suitable crag had a pair of peregrines once again and we were able to relax, but recently they have started to disappear again. This nest site has been taken over by kestrels, one of which flies off, 'yikkering' loudly at us as we pass. Kestrels too are declining so it is good to see this bird, but what makes this place, rather than another place, good for them I will never entirely understand; as Mary Midgley wrote, 'The world in which the kestrel moves, the world that it sees is, and always will be entirely beyond us.'[62] But I still mourn the loss of peregrines, one of our avian aristocrats.

Ironically, the overall UK population of peregrines is increasing and may now be larger than it has ever been.[63] This is mainly because they are doing so well in urban areas, having adapted to nesting on tall buildings, from where they are growing fat on feral pigeons. But in the uplands, they have been declining.[64] Rather surprisingly, one of their main sources of food in the hills is racing pigeons, but these have become scarcer as pigeon fanciers got wise to the peregrines and changed their race routes.[65] It seems it is now easier for peregrines to make a living in Wrecsam than Eryri, but, despite this, the overall population in Wales is in worrying decline.[66]

We follow the faint path up the valley. After about a mile, Gethin suddenly stiffens, exclaiming 'harrier'. He had heard a characteristic 'yip yip' call and sure enough up to our left is a male hen harrier drifting away across the heather and over a conifer plantation, before being lost from view. 'Probably a food pass,' Gethin says laconically. Unlike me, he has less reason to get excited; at this season, surveying moorland birds is right at the centre of his work for the RSPB. In fact, he is so focussed that I begin to feel laboured and slow – there was a time when I taught him this stuff.

There is no doubt that hen harriers are the pin-up birds for moorland conservation, particularly the males. Apart from anything else they are beautiful: soft, pale grey plumage – almost white in some lights, with ink-black wing tips and large yellow eyes. Their long slim wings and a tail that flexes and fans are superbly adapted to tilt and slide across the heather, pouncing at the slightest movement from a vole or panicky pipit. I once held one and remember how its beautiful yellow eyes looked back at me with the blank indifference of planetary moons – the gaze of untroubled evolution. Endlessly patient, they drift like pale ghosts across this dark landscape, conspicuous and yet often unseen in places where people rarely go.

Gethin sets up the telescope and settles into his own patient vigil. He is completely tuned in, scanning the hillside for the smallest movement and eventually it pays off: he sees the male settle on a rock about half a mile away and nearby he finds the female, her streaked brown plumage finely camouflaged against the heather. She seems to be eating something, probably from the food pass. When the female is incubating eggs, the male will fly in with food and use that 'yip yip' to call her off the nest. The food pass is often spectacular with the female turning upside down in mid-air to catch the prey in her talons as he drops it.

Gethin was concerned that these birds were rather close to a forestry plantation, which could give cover to foxes and crows, both of which will take harrier eggs and chicks. The mixture of pleasure and anxiety we experienced was very familiar: there are now only about thirty-five pairs of hen harriers in Wales, down by about forty per cent since 2010,[67] but their population levels do tend to fluctuate, so there is always hope of an upturn.

Until recently, we assumed hen harriers in Wales were free of the illegal persecution associated with grouse shooting that had so disgracefully suppressed their populations in England, almost to the point of extinction. This arises because, although hen harriers mostly eat voles and pipits, they also eat grouse chicks. As hen harriers are fully protected by law this persecution is a scandal, which is far from being resolved – although a significant improvement in the fledging rate on English moors in 2022 was encouraging. Fortunately, incidents of persecution have been rare in Wales over the last thirty years, but this was blemished recently when young harriers fitted with tracking devices mysteriously disappeared over a grouse moor about twenty miles from Craig-y-tân. Gethin had watched over one of these birds from egg to fledgling, so he was understandably angry and upset. There is little *direct* evidence that grouse-shooting people are responsible for these disappearances, but there is a long and repeated pattern: hen harriers disappear far more often over grouse moors than anywhere else.

Considering this, Gethin and I are pleased to have found a pair of harriers on our doorstep, so we set off up the valley in good spirits – at least one of the birds on my bed and breakfast brag is still with us.

Climbing up and over the ridge to our north we look down on the wide expanse on Waun y Griafolen and Craig-y-tân's mountain. The rolling treeless expanse in front of us is in effect a huge basin draining down into pools out of which the Mawddach arises. The slopes around us are now dominated by cottongrass and a scattering of heather with the soft underlying peat deepening as the ground levels out towards the bottom of the slope. We set up the telescope on its tripod and settle down on the side of the ridge to see what we can find.

One bird we would both love to see is a merlin. This dashing little falcon can be elusive; the best chance is often when one hurtles noisily into the air in pursuit of a crow or buzzard. I have never seen a merlin here, but I am always hoping. Two ornithologists who conducted moorland bird surveys for the Nature Conservancy Council and RSPB in the 1980s and 1990s tell me they saw merlins here at that time. Back then it was generally assumed that they were present on most heathery moorland locally, but nobody assumes that anymore. Numbers have declined significantly in the last thirty years across Wales and it is estimated that less than fifty pairs remain. Successful breeding pairs are likely to be far fewer than that.[68]

Conservation managers are often preoccupied with habitat condition, but in the case of the merlin this seems unlikely to be the significant factor. As merlins are northern birds and ours are on the southern limit of their European range, they could be withdrawing northwards due to the influence of climate change.[69] Many upland birds are declining in the southern part of their ranges, and modelling has suggested that the climate in Wales may become unsuitable for them at some point during this century.[70] It is a depressing thought that birds like curlew or black grouse may become extinct in Wales as a result of the climate damage already 'in the pipeline'. Whilst climate change is a powerful driver, there is likely to be a combination of other factors, that vary from species to species, also contributing to declines. For merlins it may be an unholy mix of increased predator pressure, reduced prey availability linked to habitat condition and contaminants affecting breeding condition as well as climate change; but for now we lack enough hard information to unpick causality.

Another bird that Gethin and I discuss while sitting amongst the heather and cottongrass tumps is the short-eared owl. This mysterious owl, which in our area is confined to remote upland bogs and heather moors, is not often seen. It has a reputation for being diurnal, but this may be something of an illusion. Recent work in Scotland using satellite tags found that the birds were largely nocturnal. [71] As the researchers said, 'If they can get away with being nocturnal, they will,' but the demands of dependent young combined with varying levels of vole availability and short summer nights means they are forced to hunt in daylight some of the time, and that is when we see them. There is still much to learn about short-eared owls, but we do know that their numbers are tied to the cyclical peaks and troughs of short-tailed vole populations, which are their principal food source. Their floppy yet buoyant, almost moth-like, flight and dappled cream and brown plumage make them a striking sight drifting over a remote treeless heather moor – such a strange place to see an owl. In 2018, there were estimated to be around twenty pairs in Wales, but less than half that a year later.[72] Short-eared owl numbers were probably higher in the 1970s and 1980s, when they could take advantage of the high vole numbers in the long grass of newly planted conifer plantations from which sheep were excluded, but there has been little new planting in the last thirty years. Further afield short-eared owls have declined significantly in Mid Wales and across southern Britain,[73] and this is another bird that the climate in Wales will probably become unsuitable for in years to come.[74] Perhaps they are still here on these moors from time to time depending on the vole numbers. Hywel told me he saw a group of five owls in the late summer heather on his mountain a couple of years ago – they can only have been a family party of 'shorties'.

A bird that is on the increase is the goshawk – they are not often seen, but they are here. This impressive raptor can, along with the fox, claim to be the apex predator in our countryside these days. Other than humans, it has nothing to fear and it is a formidable hunter. Goshawks were driven to extinction in Britain by the late nineteenth century; the present population originates from escaped falconers' birds or those deliberately released. From these, a rapidly expanding population has become established: by 2018 it was estimated there were about 310 pairs in Wales, and that may be an underestimate due to the remoteness of many forestry plantations.[75] Goshawks prefer large undisturbed conifer forests where they will hunt along the moorland edges as well as inside the forest blocks. Although their diet in Welsh forests has been recorded as principally pigeons, crows, thrushes, grey squirrels and rabbits, they do occasionally take other species such as black grouse, kestrels and young merlins.[76] Even if their level of predation is not significant it seems likely that they could make a breeding territory untenable for merlins by the 'terror' effect of their presence.

It is early May and I have decided to have another look at the birds on Craig-y-tân's mountain, this time approaching from the northern end, taking the rough path up from behind the farmstead. I get going early; such is the clarity of the morning light it seems as if I could reach out and touch the opposite side of the valley. Above the farm, ewes with single lambs at foot dot the hillside; tree pipits and redstarts sing from the crooked thorn trees. Higher up I can hear a cuckoo, its call echoing off the crags, which gives it a rasping quality like a dog barking. Another replies further along the valley at the top edge of the woodland. Hywel tells me he has heard up to three calling at the same time this year. These parasitic birds will mostly lay their eggs in meadow pipits' nests on the mountain land; they are a familiar sound locally and we almost take them for granted. However, according to recent research, there has been a seventy per cent decline in the UK cuckoo population, mostly in the lowlands where the moth caterpillars on which they feed have declined dramatically, probably due to the effects of intensive farming. The caterpillar's decline has been less marked in the uplands, at least so far, particularly in the strongholds of the north and west, but who knows if that will last. [77]

By the time I reach the top of the slope and step onto the rolling heather it is only half past eight in the morning, but I am already hot and sweating. The path is slippery and I pass a dark pool Hywel has fenced out to prevent the lambs from drowning; the sheep's sharp feet have churned the peat into a chocolate brown sludge. After a short distance I make my way up onto a rocky promontory and spread out in front of me is the Waun y Griafolen basin, which stretches about two miles left to right and a mile across. Putting my rucksack on the ground, I settle down against it: my intention is to spend most of the day looking and listening to get a better idea of what birds are here.

What strikes me straight away is the silence, only the lightest breeze and no other sound. I'm looking over thousands of acres of heather moorland and nothing moves except the ewes and their lambs, following their well-worn paths to the grassier places.

There are still red grouse on Craig-y-tân's mountain, but they appear to be scarce: Hywel says he sees one or two now and again, but there must be a fraction of the numbers there were when the Glanllyn estate was in its prime. To know how many there really are I would have needed to come up here just before dawn in April, which is when the territorial males call against one another. But getting here in the dark would be difficult, the way up is over steep and often very wet ground without a defined path; so far the doing of it has been beyond me.

A decline in heather management is not the only factor that has been working against red grouse in Wales: widespread upland afforestation in the 1970s and 1980s and, up until the 1990s, overgrazing by sheep both reduced and degraded the available heather-covered moorland. Consequently, the red grouse population is much reduced away from the few moors still managed for shooting. It is often claimed that the red grouse is the most thoroughly researched bird in the world, so we do know how to maintain populations, but without the economic incentive of commercial shooting to manage the heather and kill the foxes and crows this is unlikely to happen here. These soggy hills clothed in blanket bog are not optimum habitat for red grouse, which thrive on drier, less acidic heather moors. As things stand, it seems unlikely that commercial grouse shooting has much of a future in Wales, in which case red grouse populations are unlikely to increase and could eventually disappear altogether due to climate change.[78]

Black grouse are large handsome birds, which are particularly known for their unusual 'lekking' behaviour. The lek is a traditional grassy patch on the moorland edge where the males, known as blackcocks, gather on early spring mornings to strut, spar and cackle, their red wattles inflated and tail raised to show off their snow white underwear. This is watched by the discerning greyhens, which will mate with the males that impress them most.

Black grouse have a rather chequered history in Wales, compounded by attempts to introduce, or reintroduce, birds by people interested in shooting them. One thing seems to be clear: they increased significantly in the twentieth century with the coming of the new conifer plantations;[79] they are a bird of transitional habitats on the moorland edge where trees, heather and bilberry mingle. When the new plantations were established and the sheep fenced out, a mixture of young trees and resurgent heather and bilberry provided abundant black grouse habitat – for a while. These strong-flying birds tended to crop up wherever new plantations were being established within their range in Mid and North Wales. But of course, these conditions were ephemeral: the trees grew up and closed together, shading out the heather and bilberry, eventually leaving a hard edge along the fence between the plantation and the moorland. In the late 1980s, the government removed the tax incentives for establishing new plantations, much to the relief of conservationists, but without new plantations to replace those now maturing, the black grouse population began to decline again. In the 1980s, there was a small population here on the plantation edges to the north and south of where I am sitting. About fifteen years ago the edge to the south was remodelled specifically to provide habitat suitable for black grouse, with scattered trees amongst the heather and bilberry. Despite this numbers continued to dwindle; the last time they were recorded here was in 2014. This is the trend across most of the North Wales moors and by 2018 more than eighty per cent of the Welsh population were confined to Ruabon Mountain and the Clwydian Hills;[80] both of which are to the north and east of us. It is difficult to account for this decline: is it habitat condition, predation, an underlying shift northward due to climate change or a mixture of all three?

Two black grouse studies illustrate the difficulties faced in providing the right conditions for species of conservation concern. One suggested that *both* low and high intensity grazing were required, the former to encourage certain moth caterpillars and the latter some sawfly larvae, both of which black grouse need to feed their young.[81] The other said that young (five-year-old) native woodland near to lek sites was beneficial,[82] but of course it would not remain young for very long. Sometimes nature conservation management seems like the art of the impossible. This complexity can make the 'no predetermined outcome' of rewilding seem a very tempting proposition.

In the 1990s, there was an experimental five-year programme to control foxes and crows on the nearby Berwyn Mountains to see what effect this had on bird populations. The results were disappointing: there was no overall beneficial effect to bird numbers except for black grouse, which did show an increase.[83] Perhaps that was coincidental with some other favourable change, as it seems unlikely that the reduction in predators would not have also benefitted other ground nesting birds, such as red grouse. What strikes me is that, despite multiple conservation designations, frequent land management strategies, and a great deal of knowledge about these two species of grouse, we are still here wringing our hands and speculating as they decline.

I move my vantage point several times during the day, shifting to get a different angle as, inevitably, there is some 'dead ground' you cannot see from any given place. My final vantage point gave me the best view across Waun y Griafolen looking out towards the pools at the source of the Mawddach. This is the wettest part and it got me thinking about a bird that likes such places and used to be here – the curlew.

It is still quite a shock to say 'used to be here'. Curlews are an entirely familiar bird of moorland and wet pasture to me; a bird that farmers recognise easily and care about. When I worked on the Berwyn in the 1980s, curlew were as much part of the landscape as heather and sheep: a large-scale bird survey between 1983 and 1985 found approximately 240 pairs spread right across those hills.[84] Today they have almost completely disappeared. In 2018, the RSPB had only one pair on the thousands of acres of moorland on its Llyn Efyrnwy reserve on the Berwyn.

Similarly, when I first came to live in Llanuwchllyn they were widespread in the area, even breeding in the damp fields below our house. Each spring I used to listen for their evocative bubbling call, but gradually these faded away and for the last twenty years they have not been back at all. And they have gone from Craig-y-tân's mountain as well. When I was talking to Hywel and Rhys about this earlier in the year, Rhys asked what a curlew looked like: he is in his late twenties and has spent all his life on hill farms, yet the curlew is an unfamiliar bird to him. As Britain holds a quarter of the world population of Eurasian curlews, a seventy-five per cent drop in our population between 1990 and 2020 is of global significance.[85] Wales saw a sixty-nine per cent loss from 1995 to 2018, and almost certainly the situation is worse than that now. We face the real possibility that this once common bird could become extinct in Wales within the next ten to fifteen years.[86]

A consequence of all this has been a flurry of research into curlew ecology, to try and understand such an abrupt and catastrophic decline. So far in the uplands some of the usual suspects have been identified.

The amount of afforestation adjacent to moorland blocks is negatively associated with curlew populations, most probably because they harbour foxes and crows.[87] In some areas, the very large numbers of pheasants released into the countryside for shooting may be maintaining artificially high fox populations which turn to wild bird eggs and chicks when the pheasants are no longer available after the shooting season. Some people are in no doubt that predation is a critical factor: Ian Newton, in his authoritative book *Farming and Birds*, states baldly that 'some species, notably waders, may now be unable to persist in many upland areas unless foxes and crows are controlled'.[88]

Other suggestions have been that warmer and drier weather in the breeding season due to climate change may be reducing the number of soil invertebrates that curlew chicks rely on. This is likely to have been exacerbated by historic drainage drying out the ground. Gamekeepers on north Berwyn are saying that the flush of wavy hair-grass that characteristically occurs following moor burning is much greater than it used to be twenty years ago.[89] This grass is an indicator of increased atmospheric nitrogen, which could be affecting vegetation in ways not so far understood. Also, the reduction in sheep grazing and lack of burning over the last twenty-five years means heather is often taller now and less suitable for curlews.

We woke up to the decline of the curlew rather late – perhaps too late. They are long-lived birds and so it was quite a while before we noticed that too few young were being reared to replace the adults that eventually died. Once again, this highlights how complex the ecology of a single species can be and how difficult it is to understand what causes populations of wild animals and plants to decline – even for a conspicuous bird like the curlew. The time, money and expertise required to find out is daunting, even for a single species. Perhaps it is a statement of the obvious that all of the factors being considered as contributory to the curlew's decline are anthropogenic, even if indirectly. We are responsible, so we must fix it: the background music of our age.

Looking out over the wet bog, another bird that comes to mind is the golden plover. This species was once relatively numerous and widespread in Wales in suitable habitats, but by the late 1970s was reduced to 250–300 pairs.[90] By 2007, it was estimated numbers were down to just thirty-six pairs.[91]

Various reasons have been suggested for their decline, many similar to those put forward for curlew: changes in vegetation and availability of habitats, drying out of moorland due to historic drainage and/ or climate change may reduce the availability of crane fly larvae – an important food source. An increase in crow predation due to the decline in moorland gamekeeping could also have impacted.

Thirty years ago, golden plovers probably bred here around the pools and peat hags of Waun y Griafolen; up to three pairs were reported there in the mid-1970s.[92] Golden plovers in Wales now tend to be found only in the wettest blanket bog areas and on exposed ridges, which have shorter vegetation. As with many populations which are under pressure, they have retreated to the very best habitat – deserting more marginal places.

As the day ends, I count the number of birds I have seen or heard during seven hours of careful watching and listening: twenty meadow pipits, two skylarks, two wheatears, one stonechat, and flying over – one raven, buzzard and red kite. For such apparently prime habitat on a beautiful day in May, with no human disturbance, that seems like a pretty dismal haul. I also recorded six different lots of fox droppings, which may be part of the story.

An additional concern is that this depressing litany is about birds: a popular, conspicuous, and well-researched group of animals. We know a lot about birds, but still clearly not enough. This said, many of the birds discussed above are doing better further north in Britain – where there is generally more predator control and heather management on moorland than in Wales.

Welsh populations tend to be on the southern edge of their ranges so perhaps they are retreating north in the face of climate change. From the range of possible causes outlined above we have no sure idea which are the most critical and it is likely that some, or all of them, are acting in combination. Bigger populations of these birds were consequences of land management practices that have changed or disappeared altogether. Now conservation managers are having to pick up the baton, without the economic incentives that drove the other systems, to see if they can make improved numbers of curlews or black grouse a consequence of their actions. They are cutting vegetation, re-wetting blanket bogs, controlling predators and adjusting grazing patterns to see what works. It is a painstaking process to shape the land in ways that suits the many, and not just sheep and grouse. Such work is in its infancy compared to agriculture or even grouse shooting and has a long way to go. As Rachel Taylor, an ecologist working on curlews in Wales, wrote in 2022: 'The drivers of their decline are as simple – and as complex – as the way humans use and manage landscapes.'[93]

The fluctuations in moorland bird populations over the last 200 years have mostly been driven by human activity. Waders may have thrived in the late nineteenth and early twentieth centuries, when predator control by gamekeepers and other country people was at its height. On the other hand, raptors, seen as competitive predators by farmers and shooters, were suppressed. After the Second World War the number of gamekeepers declined, farming became highly mechanised and fewer people kept domestic poultry, and so the raptors and persecuted mammals began to thrive again and in turn preyed on the waders. Then the extensive upland conifer plantations arrived in the second half of the twentieth century, swallowing up hundreds of thousands of acres of hill land, the growing trees providing temporary habitat for some birds but also refuge for predatory foxes and crows. In the 1980s and early 1990s, incentivised by government and the European Union, sheep numbers were probably at their highest level ever on the Welsh hills. This suppressed the vegetation, particularly heather, which may have made it better for some birds like golden plover and worse for others such as red grouse. The change in government subsidies means the number of sheep in the hills is now much lower and most farmers have stopped burning heather (see Chapter 11); both had further consequences for moorland birds. In this way we keep on shaping our wild land and the wildlife reacts accordingly. However, these twists and turns are now against an insidious backdrop of climate change and aerial pollution, which may well tip some bird populations beyond their capacity to recover.

If we take birds to be the 'canary in the coal mine', then what does this story imply about populations of moths, sundews or bog-mosses and the like, about which we know so much less? For example, a recent study found that there has been a startling fifty-five per cent decline in the number of species of bees and hoverflies in the British uplands since 1980.[94] Is the whole moorland ecosystem being quietly hollowed out, leaving this magnificent landscape windswept and empty?

As I trudge back down the escarpment at the end of the day, I come across the first grouse I have ever seen on Craig-y-tân. The quills have been cleanly sheared, most probably by the teeth of a fox, and its wing and feathers are scattered amongst last year's withered bracken.

Chapter 8

The River

The river Lliw is a constant companion at Craig-y-tân. It defines the eastern boundary of the farm for about a mile, gurgling or thundering along in symphony with yesterday's weather. These steep mountain rivers are highly responsive to the rainfall in their boggy catchments, bursting their banks for a day only to quieten with surprising suddenness the following morning. With underlying rock that is often hard and impermeable, little water is absorbed along the way which, coupled to high rainfall and steep gradients, means upland rivers can seem capricious, running from ferocious to gentle and back again with little warning. The Lliw is only about six miles long from its source to the point where it disgorges into Llyn Tegid (Bala Lake), so much of it is associated with Craig-y-tân. To celebrate and better understand this beautiful river and the valley it has been forming for thousands of years, I decide to walk down it from the source to the farm.

On a fine morning in May, Gethin gives me a lift up the gated road along the opposite side of the valley to Craig-y-tân and then along a rutted farm track, dropping me off high up the river. At this point the stony riverbed is no more than a metre wide with the rock forming a series of shallow steps over which the water cascades in a glittering staircase. A grey wagtail, disturbed by my arrival, bounces away downstream, flashing its chrome-yellow underwear. Above here the river branches out into a network of small streams, any one of which could be called its source.

At this height the river is only a shallow nick cut into miles of rough and rolling pasture, brushed with the bleached tops of rushes and mapped-out by weathered walls. Sheep are scattered across the landscape and in one place there are cattle, an uncommon sight in the uplands these days – their absence is significant for conservation. Cattle are less commonly kept nowadays partly because they are more labour intensive than sheep – too valuable to be left unattended for long periods. With an aging, often single-handed and even part-time workforce, grazing cattle in remote upland pastures is not often viable. But cattle crop vegetation differently from sheep: they are less choosy and will eat coarser material. This has proved critical in boggy areas of the Welsh uplands that have high rainfall but only shallow peat because this is the habitat for purple moor-grass (commonly known by its scientific name, *Molinia*) which has become increasingly dominant over large areas. This tall, tussock forming grass crowds out less robust plants, and is unsuitable for moorland birds such as golden plover to nest in. The now largely absent cattle loved to eat it and so kept it in check, but it is shunned by sheep. Add a helping of fertiliser from atmospheric nitrogen and Molinia is doing well at the expense of less competitive species.

A similar story has unfolded on better drained areas, including those surrounding me, where the decline in cattle and inexorable rise in sheep numbers during the second half of the twentieth century has led to a species-poor grassland flora dominated by the less palatable mat-grass.

A cocksure wheatear flirts his tail from the top of a wall as I pass. Trees and bushes are non-existent here, save one: an ancient looking hawthorn permanently bent by the wind, which is still flowering defiantly. Feeling my age, I note the metaphor, tip my hat to the tree and walk on. I have mixed feelings about this landscape: on the one hand there is the grinding attrition of the vegetation from centuries of stock grazing, which is personified by the single derelict hawthorn, and on the other hand the sheer magnificence and freedom of just being here, in this exhilarating sense of space. Despite it being a fine spring day, if I meet anybody else all day it will be a surprise.[95]

Half a mile downstream I come to an abandoned, but tidy, stone house in the middle of nowhere. Barring two sturdy sycamores, so often the signature trees of hill farms, there is no longer anything to anchor it to place. The roof is still good and trustingly the front door key is hanging up on the outside. In the downstairs room is a scatter of wooden shearing stools, a cracked mug on the cast iron range and some rusting tinned food in a cupboard. Upstairs in one of the bedrooms several desiccated swallows lie on the dusty floor – they must have got trapped inside, somehow. This house is a vivid reminder of how many more people lived and worked in the hills 150 years ago. Within sight of here, Gethin's friend Owen has just moved into what must surely be, at a shade below 1,500 feet, one of the highest inhabited houses in Wales. A young man on his own with no main services needs a certain kind of grit, especially in winter, but I suppose he was born to it, as his family farms much of the surrounding land.

Below Blaen Lliw, the river widens out a bit and, because it has been dry and water levels are low, a layer of blotchy pink stone the colour of drowned flesh has been exposed below the usual moss-darkened boulders.

It must be very different when the river is in flood compared to this easily fordable gurgle; in places there seems to be more gravel shelves and boulders than running water. Here and there are green skeins of slimy, filamentous algae swaying in the current, a sure sign of nutrient enrichment from land and sky that is concentrated by the low water level. Swallows and sand martins are working back and forth along the river, which suggests it is a source of emergent insects for them to feed on. A common sandpiper flicks away downstream on stiff wings, piping loudly. I'm pleased to find they are still on the river because, although the diversity of wild plants and animals is naturally low on acidic and torrential rivers like this one, they do have some characteristic wildlife – such as common sandpipers.

The water in the headwater streams of the Dee, of which this is one, has been found to have little pollution compared with the lower reaches,[96] and the water quality in the Lliw has improved from 'moderate' to 'good' between 2015-21,[97] which is not something you can say about many British rivers. However, as the algal growth suggests, there is some pollution, probably from a solution of sheep and cattle dung running into the river, plus the background nitrogen coming down with the rain, which will 'enrich' any water flowing into the river; but overall this is probably insignificant except in times of low water like this. The lack of sediments where pollutants can accumulate, plus the flushing-out effect in times of spate, also minimises this problem. Fortunately applications of artificial fertilisers to the pastures in these upper catchments is uncommon.

This far up the Lliw there are no invasive alien plants such as Japanese knotweed or Himalayan balsam. The latter has been a problem in recent years closer to Llyn Tegid on various rivers, including this one, but the National Park staff, working with volunteers, have done an impressive job in controlling it by hand. The kind of conspicuous and attractive plants associated with rivers, such as water lilies or purple loosestrife, need quieter and less acidic conditions than these, with bottom sediments and soft, marshy banksides.

In these scoured and rocky conditions it is the mosses, liverworts and lichens clinging to the boulders that provide the floral richness. The Lliw is also probably clear of alien aquatic invertebrates such as the signal crayfish or Chinese mitten crab, which are increasingly frequent in the low reaches of the Dee. The characteristic birds of a mountain river like this are dipper, grey wagtail and common sandpiper, all three of which have declined markedly in Britain since the 1970s. Thankfully the most recent information for North Wales seems to raise little concern for them at present.[98] Kingfishers are sometimes present lower down the Lliw and may occasionally breed in the soft earthy banks nearer to Llyn Tegid, but I have never seen one this high up.

Further on, one or two rowans begin to appear on the riverbanks and in the top of one, about fifteen feet up, is a tidily refurbished crow's nest. I contemplate climbing up to see if it contains eggs or young, but think better of it. There is something reassuringly domestic about this homely nest in such a bare, windswept landscape, although it also seems an unnervingly exposed place to incubate eggs and feed chicks. Overhead a red kite wheels above the river, crossing the valley with barely a wing beat. We met Owen's father, Stephen, on the way up and he told us it had been around for several weeks, probably feeding on the afterbirths from lambing – so providing a useful service. When I first arrived in the district, every red kite's nest in Wales was monitored and there was considerable secrecy concerning their whereabouts. The British population of this species had been reduced to near extinction in the nineteenth and twentieth century with only a dozen or so pairs clinging on in the hills of Mid Wales at the lowest point. Since then, thanks to dedicated conservation work by many committed people, the Welsh population has gradually increased until it is now commonplace to see these magnificent birds drifting overhead in most parts of Wales. Kites cannot really be considered upland specialists; they are more generalists, effortlessly covering great distances in search of food. Although they do eat small mammals and birds, they are not expert hunters and are mostly looking for sheep carrion when cruising over the moors.

The valley is more rugged than rolling now, heather and bilberry mix with the cottongrass. There is a good covering of heather on the steeper slopes, an indication of reduced grazing pressure from sheep; a scatter of fifty or so young rowans growing amongst the rocks reinforce the point. Sheep numbers in the upland have been reduced since an historic high in the 1980s and now, on some less accessible slopes and rocky places, the beginnings of new woodlands are springing up. I listen in vain for a ring ouzel. If populations were strong there would surely be a pair in one of these heathery gullies. Every now and then a green-veined white butterfly passes me, always going upstream into the wind, their erratic yet purposeful flight is surprisingly effective. I can only think this must be a local migration: flying up over the watershed in the hope of sunshine and 'cabbages' further west. Probably valleys such as these are important local routes for some flying insects and birds.

Where the valley widens out there is a sizeable bog and it is hard going across the lumpy cottongrass – which is just beginning to wave its white flags. The wind sighs through a rumpled line of waist-high tussock sedges growing in the wettest part. Apparently the tussocks of these enormous plants used to be trimmed into hassocks for kneeling on in chapel years ago. A grasshopper warbler is reeling off its drunken song somewhere out in the rushes and nearer at hand a reed bunting is picking out a much more hesitant tune. Two ravens flying tight together towards the ridge, deep in croaking conversation, are disinterested in me. I fill with gratitude for the solitude of this wild place.

The weird thing about waterfalls is that you can't hear them from upstream until you are almost upon them. This is the case with the Afon Lliw as it plunges over a shelf of hard rock just above Buarth Meini; seventy feet of crashing, glittering water that orchestrates every other sound. Set amongst rocky hillsides studded with birch and rowan trees, it is wonderful sight. In much of Britain it would probably have a car park and picnic site; up here there isn't even a path.

The birches are the first I have seen since starting out this morning and they provide a song post for a willow warbler – neatly pointing up the link between habitat and species. Clambering across the water-scoured rocks at the top of the falls, I find bluebells in deep cracks and some violets the texture of plush velvet. There is even a straggling thyme plant clinging on precariously. I can't imagine how these plants survive when the river is in spate. Getting down the side of the falls is a struggle as the steep rock-strewn ground is knee-high with heather and clumps of purple moor-grass. I experience a twinge of fear: this is leg-breaking terrain and there is no phone signal up here.

Below the falls the air is thicker; a sheltered and intimate place compared to the wide-open uplands above, where I had felt like an ant creeping across the landscape. This bit of land beside the river is fenced out, perhaps to protect the sheep from the danger of the falls, and it has become lush. There are hawthorns and hazels and even a young sycamore; marsh marigolds and wood anemones are flowering beneath the trees and a lizard slips away from my boot. A singing blackbird conjures the warmth and security of village lowlands. The absence of nibbling sheep in this sheltered place has released the land, allowing it to move towards its wooded climax.

A hundred yards further downriver, I stumble upon a ruined farmstead huddled beneath a rocky bluff and screened by ash trees. It is of Lilliput proportions – the house no bigger than a modern lounge. Although the roof has long gone, ferns and moss soften any sense of absence. The window sockets, chimney and a slate threshold are still intact but a massive fireplace lintel is only just above the collapsed rock and moss by now. Out front are a barn, sheep pens and several small meadows mapped out by crumbling stone walls, some of which are muffled with cushions of silver-grey moss a foot deep, like an insulation against history. The whole forgotten place is slowly sinking back into the earth from which it arose. Yet 150 years ago there would have been a family here with, no doubt, multiple children crammed into this modest house. Whenever possible life must have been lived out of doors. Oats would have been grown, bread baked, cows milked and buttermilk made.

E. D. wrote of living in a house like this when he was a boy: the *hen dŷ Tynfron* – the old Tyn Fron house – which was only half a mile downstream from here on the opposite bank. The family moved into a new house built close by around 1890 (see Chapter 1), when E. D.

was about ten years old. The old farmhouse, 'an undecorated cottage by a stream', had a granary next to the house and a cowshed beyond that and lastly the *penty* (lean-to), all arranged along its length and divided by thin walls. The floors were earth and the roof thatched with rushes, which leaked when it rained. There were (and still are) plenty of rushes on the rough grazing towards the river, which in autumn they cut and made into bundles to store for patching the roof in the winter. Inside, the house was divided into a kitchen and living room with a ladder up to a *croglofft* (a loft space for sleeping) where all eleven of them slept. The kitchen had an earth floor with a stone hearth, but the living room probably had slates on the floor. The external chimney was made of wood and E. D. was amazed that it never burned down. They drew their water from a spring, which arose straight out of the rock – he never remembers it freezing or failing. This description of houses with rush roofs and earth floors is a very literal connection to centuries of European peasant farming, a culture that has now almost vanished, but from which Hywel is only two generations away.

Families in these houses would have laughed and quarrelled, hoped and feared just like the rest of us. Most of all they would have worked, the endless physical work that is the lot of subsistence farmers the world over. A sense of community and interdependence amongst the handful of farms scattered through the valley, coupled to strong traditions and a sense of humour, would have helped temper the hard labour. Expectations must have been very different then, as most people rarely left the valley and the edge of their familiar world was probably within a ten-mile radius of here. With just a little more phone signal I could find out what is happening in Beijing right now. Sitting here on a mossy boulder in this slow-moving place, that seems totally absurd.

I clamber over a fence and step onto Craig-y-tân land; the mile or so of riverbank ahead of me is very familiar and there are few places I would rather be. Rough pasture dotted with cranky old hawthorns and crab apple trees, the deep pink buds of the latter just beginning to open. Tree pipits love to perch in these trees and sure enough one flits away in front of me with a wheezing call. The river is much broader and noisier here. There are bits of grass and twigs caught in the bankside willows a full four feet above today's water level, reminding me how violent this river can be; something the inhabiting wildlife has to be able to withstand. The banks are now tree lined – ash, rowan and willow mostly – which is encouraging as this provides better habitat for birds and bats and the invertebrates they feed on. I come across a large and previously unnoticed oak amongst them, which is plastered with lichens. The water, black from a distance, is crystal clear close up, with no brown staining from suspended particles of peat. A dipper arrows downstream like a wind-up toy, fat belly grazing the water as its sharp cries puncture the quiet. A six-inch fish, probably a brown trout, darts upstream. The river smells like a river should – perhaps it's the previously submerged vegetation exposed and mouldering in the low water levels – but it seems fresher than that. The sound of the water is absorbing, like watching a fire, and it loosens a knot in my chest that I didn't know was there.

The Dee and its catchment (of which the Lliw is a part), is one of the best rivers in Wales for brown trout, sea trout and Atlantic salmon.[99] Although there were serious declines in numbers during the twentieth century, there is some cause for optimism now, mainly due to determined conservation efforts by the angling community, who now put back nearly all the fish they catch, and the LIFE Dee River habitat restoration project managed by NRW and funded by the EU. Trout and salmon require gravelly riverbeds to spawn in, of the kind that occur on the Lliw, especially lower down. The falls at Buarth Meini are presumably an obstacle they cannot overcome when swimming upstream to spawn in the spring; however I am told that there is a population of brown trout that live permanently above the falls. Otherwise the only fish likely to be found in the highest parts of the Lliw are minnows and sticklebacks. These rivers are no longer artificially stocked with brown trout as they were ten years ago; the policy now is to encourage wild populations. A catastrophic flash flood down this river in 2001 scoured the riverbed so severely that it probably eliminated most of the trout population; stocks are likely to have been slowly rebuilding since then, although to what level I don't think anybody knows.

Strolling along the bank through the short grass I am reminded that this riverside is heavily modified by sheep. The area below the falls was a glimpse of the potential this land has for increased biodiversity once released from the incessant grazing; but, as described in Chapter 4, this rough pasture is still far richer in plants and animals than an improved agricultural field, so perhaps it is a good enough compromise between farming and conservation.

Just beyond the footbridge over the river I stop to look at some water crowfoot flowers in a quiet eddy and startle a pair of goosanders into flight. They wheel around over my head and fly off southwards calling softly. These elegant saw-billed ducks have increased significantly on Welsh rivers over the last thirty years and breeding is now quite widespread. Fishermen dislike them because they are fish feeders and are seen as competing for trout or salmon, but there is unlikely to be conflict on this quiet stretch of river, which is rarely fished these days – although at least one person I have spoken to locally is indignant about the quantity of fish he says these birds are eating. I would be pleased if they bred here, but I wonder if there are many trees big enough at Craig-y-tân to have the kind of holes they require for nesting.

A little further on I come to a place that reminds me of a pleasing moment last June, when I had come across Hywel by the barn. We hadn't seen each other for a while and, after a bit of catching up, he asked, 'Have you seen my globeflower?' and, pulling out his phone, showed me a photograph of one he had found by the river.

The globeflower, related to buttercups, is found in damp pastures and stream sides in mountain districts; it has beautiful pale-yellow flowers whose petals curve over into an elegant globe shape. They are scarce now and getting increasingly hard to find. The general view was that they had gone from the Lliw, the last few having been destroyed in 2001's violent flash flood. But Hywel had found this one a couple of weeks before, right here at Craig-y-tân. He thought it may have finished flowering by now but was keen to show it to me just the same. We walked down to the river and in a rocky scoop in the bank, somewhat sheltered from the current, there was the single plant. With its flower over and seed head developing it was difficult to spot. Hywel had put some rocks and a log on the bank to prevent the sheep from reaching it and nibbling it off. He thought the plant looked vulnerable to getting washed away in a flood and raised the possibility of transplanting it or growing more from seed. We agreed that this would only be practical if a place could be found where the sheep couldn't reach it, such as inside his fenced woodlands. It was rewarding to be with a farmer who took so much pride in a single flower that he had found on his land.

Half a mile further on, as I was watching a common sandpiper bobbing anxiously on a rock in the river, a loud yammering above the conifer plantation on the opposite bank startled me. A big peregrine, probably a female, was rising up steeply and then stooping down at speed, calling loudly all the while. It seemed to be aiming at a small crag almost buried in the conifers. It repeated this manoeuvre several times before flying off strongly towards the mountain. It was a thrilling sight, especially as peregrines are scarcer here now than they were ten years ago; I didn't know what to make of its behaviour. It was as if it was trying to repel a predator or intruder from its nest site, but that seemed unlikely on such a small crag deep in a spruce plantation. I made a mental note to try and get to the crag and have a look outside of the breeding season.

Just where the river leaves Craig-y-tân, it starts to cascade down through a gorge littered with boulders, ranging in size from a suitcase to a small car. When the levels are high, water smacks against the stones, sending up a mist of spray that settles on your clothes and hair. Lining the banks are oaks, ash and hazel, and behind them walls of conifers form a canyon of trees. These conditions combine to produce high humidity and relative shelter in this short stretch of river, which for many mosses, liverworts and lichens is very good news. The boulders are plastered with a green, brown and grey patchwork, which in close-up resembles the canopy of some exotic rainforest. Veteran bankside oaks are decorated with filigreed lichens, like long-service medals. High up on one ash tree is a patch of tree lungwort: a scarce and extraordinary looking lichen – veined, membranous and parchment thin – said to resemble the lining of lungs. This place could give you the impression that it has been unchanged for an eternity if you overlooked the conifers.

On 3 July 2001, 3.5 inches of rain fell in three hours in this river catchment, and that wasn't all of it; a wall of water gathered in the upper Lliw and hurtled down the valley, gaining force as it went. It was laden with boulders, timber and gravel that sliced and blasted the riverbed and banksides – killing and maiming trees. The ash tree with the lungwort has a six-foot-high scar to prove it. Lower down, this cataract swept caravans from a field and smashed them against the bridge at Llanuwchllyn. It was a 'once in a hundred years' weather event and by the time it was over the gorge had been stripped of vegetation and completely reconfigured.

In the summer of 2015, a concrete weir was built across the Lliw just above the gorge. An intake pipe in the water, just upstream of the weir, has been routed underground down the hill, parallel to the gorge. Through this the river water flows with accumulating force to a pumping station at the bottom, driving turbines, which generate electricity to be delivered to the national grid. The water is then returned to the river lower down. Small hydroelectric schemes like this, with financial incentives from the government, are springing up on steep mountain rivers across North Wales. Renewable energy may yet save us, and our wildlife, from the worst consequences of climate change and this scheme is a small contribution to that.

At first sight, this would seem to be a conservation success story: only local disruption to the river around the weir and renewable energy generated for years to come. But there is a snag. Growing in the gorge are a number of 'oceanic' mosses and liverworts, so called because they are restricted to Atlantic coastal areas in Europe, especially in the mild damp conditions of western Britain and Ireland. Their limited distribution and often exacting habitat requirements means they are of particular conservation importance. Mostly these are small, and some are tiny, growing on rocks, trees and occasionally soil. They are fussy about where they will live, having particular requirements around such things as humidity, water levels, shelter and aspect. There is still much we don't know about the needs of these plants.

Identifying bryophytes is a specialist business – even to many naturalists they seem obscure. I wanted to understand more about those in the gorge so I asked my friend and expert naturalist Andrew Graham, who had looked closely at the bryophytes in this gorge twenty years previously, if he would show me some. Scrambling over the slippery river boulders, we found an intricate and fascinating matrix of tufts, lobes and filaments, many of which I found hard to distinguish from their neighbours. Andrew showed me one special liverwort growing on the stems of a moss that, even through a hand lens, looked like nothing more than a blob of creamed spinach. By the end of the afternoon, it became clear to Andrew that these plants were much diminished compared to when he had looked at them twenty years before. We concluded that, as with the fish, the flood of 2001 must have blasted them away.

The snag with the hydroelectric scheme is that, except in times of drought, up to forty per cent of the river's flow can be diverted down the intake pipe, and so missing out the gorge. The concern for conservationists is that reduced water will mean less spray and humidity, which might threaten the survival of some of the special mosses and liverworts. The great flood of 2001, a seemingly natural event, probably did enormous damage to these specialised plants, but at least re-colonisation from those that survived is still possible, even if it takes one hundred years. Permanently reducing the water flow might be more damaging in the long run. Then so might felling the conifer crop that forms the sheltering canyon – but they can't have been there for longer than fifty years. There are many imponderables.

The complexity of this one local conservation problem brings home to me just how difficult it is to anticipate the effects of our actions. Getting it right for species such as otters or kingfishers is comparatively easy. They are large, appealing and we know a great deal about them. It is a different story with these obscure and little-understood plants. Which has the greater benefit: generating some renewable energy to reduce greenhouse gas emissions, or saying no to the hydroelectric scheme and so ensuring that it does no harm to the plants in the gorge? It seems to me we have an obligation to minimise harm to all living things, but in practice that can be very difficult, not least because the interdependent nature of living systems means that any conservation action unavoidably impacts other plants and animals and people, sometimes in ways we can't predict. As Robert Ingersoll said, 'There are in nature neither rewards nor punishments – there are consequences.'[100]

Chapter 9

Shaping the
Wild Woods

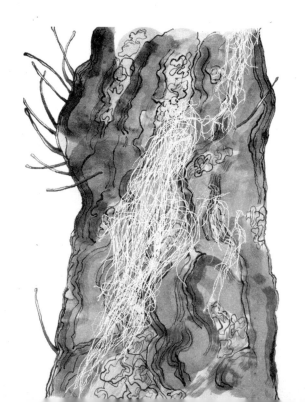

While researching and writing this book, it's become clear to me that in Britain nature doesn't just happen – it needs help. Farmed landscapes rich in wildlife were a slowly evolving by-product of human activity over many centuries, but in the last one hundred years most of these have been so seriously damaged that we are left with countryside that is largely devoid of wildlife – for example, forty-one per cent of species have declined in abundance, among these farmland birds, which have reduced by fifty-four per cent.[101] The only route back to wildlife-rich farmland is to manage the land in ways that are sympathetic to the needs of wild plants and animals. Hill farmers are entirely familiar with adjusting conditions to rear more and better livestock: factors such as pasture condition, drainage, fencing, stocking rates and winter-feeding are second nature to them. The same kind of attention to conditions is often needed for wildlife to thrive on their farms, although due to the complexity of natural ecosystems this is rarely simple. This is nowhere truer than in woodlands.

Perhaps it wasn't such a good idea to come back to the woods in late July – the bracken is head high and as tough as tangled leather. To make matters worse, I can't see where to put my feet amongst the chaos of boulders. But once under the canopy of the trees, the bracken becomes scattered and I can get around more easily. Hywel tells me bracken has been getting thicker in the woods since the grazing was reduced, but here in the heavy shade it is sparse and puny compared to the thugs on the woodland edge.

I am at the north end of the Craig-y-tân woodlands, in a part known as Coed Dolfudr, after the old farm that lies in ruins in the pasture below. I am back at the place where I found the Wilson's filmy-ferns in the spring and I feel a charge of excitement rediscovering them on the north side of several large boulders. They look parched and shrivelled in these dry conditions: perhaps they are tougher than they look, but the hot, dry conditions we have been experiencing in recent summers will not suit them. Filmy-ferns, like many other plants of these western woods, like cool summers and warm winters with plenty of sum-mer rainfall. The actual and predicted effects of climate change are ominous for these tiny plants.

Filmy-ferns are so small it is best to look at them through a magnifying lens, which takes you down into the kind of miniature and intimate world children so easily inhabit. Found only in small clusters on damp, shaded rocks and tree trunks, these tiny ferns could easily be mistaken for a moss, their delicate translucent fronds cupped one over the other like the hands of a saint. The two species of filmy-ferns found in Britain are both confined to undisturbed and humid situations, mostly in ancient woodlands in the north and west. The delicate appearance and specialised requirements of these miniature ferns seems to epitomise the enchantment of these upland woods.

Close by the filmy-ferns is a grove of aspens. I knew they were here because you can see them from the other side of the valley in the late autumn, when they stand out like yellow flames in the soft browns around them. Inside the wood you can also pick them out because their fallen leaves, slow to decompose, sit in grey skeletal mats beneath the trees. On the tree their leaves constantly tremble in the wind, making a distinctive rustling sound that you could recognise with your eyes closed: because of this aspens are sometimes known locally in Welsh as *tafodau hen wragedd* (old women's tongues).

Aspens are a rather localised wild poplar, which spread principally by suckers, so they are often found, as here, in clonal clumps. I am pleased to find dozens of suckers ranging in size from 15 to 60 centimetres under the parent trees; these are highly palatable to sheep, so the growth of suckers confirms that removing the grazing pressure is helping tree regeneration in these woods. The caterpillar of a tiny moth (*Ectoedemia argyropeza*) found only on aspens bores its way between the surfaces of the leaves leaving a distinctive trail. I have found it here, miraculously sustaining a population in this house-sized clump of trees.

This end of the wood is particularly steep, and it is hard going on a humid afternoon. In places the terrain is more like a mountainside than a wood but it is prettily clothed in grasses, quilts of moss and sheaves of ferns. It is necessary to test every step with my stick for fear of dropping a foot, or whole leg, into a mossed-over crack between the rocks. Craggy birch trees and scattered rowans dominate the low canopy with well-grown hazel stools in between; a few sallows are scattered in the damper parts. The woodland floor is covered by grasses and moss stitched together with marsh bedstraw and the dried remains of bluebell flowers. Sheets of bog-mosses are everywhere, not just in boggy pockets but slung across the surface of otherwise bare rock. Clumps of ferns sprout from every crevice, including delicate beech ferns along a streamside. In the low light the yellow flowers of common cow-wheat, clinging to fissures on a rock, look like lit candles on a Christmas tree.

This place has been hushed by its solitude; there is no movement except the fluttering of pale moths amongst the tree trunks. Not even the faint animal paths found nearer the farm mark the ground in here. Hywel tells me the sheep never come here as Glastir does not permit grazing in this northern-most section of the wood, not even in winter. It is very quiet; bird song is mostly over now and some, like the cuckoo, will have already left. Resting on a boulder I soak it all in, knowing I cannot be objective about such a place. The tilt of the light, smell of scuffed moss, the papery moths, all set in deep stillness, along with a host of memories and associations, add up to so much more than a list of species or descriptions of ecological processes. Such harmonious complexity has an absolute quality, a truth that is undeniable. Briefly I am present only to the perfection of the moment, feeling an absolution from the guilt and anxiety that is the white noise of twenty-first century conservation.

Looking around, it is the mosses and lichens, the so-called 'lower plants', that strike me. I grew up mostly in the lowlands of England and it wasn't until a visit in my early twenties to Wistman's Wood, a famous 'wildwood' relict on Dartmoor, that I first felt the enchantment of the woods of the western uplands. And these woods are very special: classified as Coastal Temperate Rainforest, a globally rare habitat, which has more in common with forests in parts of southern Chile, New Zealand and north-west America than those in eastern Britain.[102] They thrive mostly because it rains so much: there are more than 200 wet days a year and in excess of 2,000 millimetres of rain in places like Craig-y-tân. High humidity and only narrowly fluctuating temperatures also play an important part. Although flowering plants are relatively sparse, these 'Atlantic' woodlands contain as wide a variety of bryophytes and lichens as almost anywhere else on Earth.[103] In the clean air and undisturbed conditions are found an assemblage of bryophytes, lichens and ferns that are globally rare – Wilson's filmy-fern is one of them.

To my eye, Craig-y-tân's woodlands look in good condition for these special plants and lichens, especially here in Coed Dolfudr, but like all living systems they are dynamic and moving, even if on a different timescale from us. Fencing out the woods to allow only limited, or in this case no, winter grazing will have been a stimulus for accelerated movement in this ecosystem. We do not yet know if that is in a direction favourable or detrimental to these Atlantic bryophytes and lichens. And it seems unlikely that Glastir, and whatever comes after it, will have the manpower or expertise to find out.

Back in the 1960s, when conservationists first began to think about the ecological health of upland woods in Wales, what seemed to be needed most was more young trees. Many of the woods were dominated by even-aged trees, which had regrown from stumps after widespread clear-felling 200 years before.[104] The subsequent intensive sheep grazing that became almost ubiquitous in Wales meant that very few saplings were growing up to replace them: an inevitable death sentence for any woodland. For the same reason there was often no shrub layer and the ground flora rarely got to flower or set seed. The imperative seemed to be fencing sheep out of the woodlands to give new trees a chance to grow. Although it was already recognised that some of these woodlands were special for the Atlantic bryophytes and lichens, it was assumed that these would continue to thrive without grazing. One of the best examples of Atlantic woodland in Wales is the complex at Ganllwyd, about eight miles west of Craig-y-tân, and it is instructive to consider what has happened there.

Various areas of the Ganllwyd woods were fenced off from the 1960s onwards to promote tree regeneration, and then more or less left to their own devices. What eventually resulted was an invasion of exotic rhododendrons and vigorous regrowth of young trees and brambles which combined to shut out the light from the lichens and smother the bryophytes on the lower tree trunks, rocks and fallen timber. Once conservationists woke up to the scale of the problem they had precipitated, it took years of hard and expensive work by organisations such as the National Trust, and others, to get rid of the rhododendrons and thin out the thicket of brambles and trees. To ensure this did not happen all over again, some form of grazing was clearly needed to keep the regrowth in check. Recently, a small number of Highland cattle have been introduced into the woods and are now contentedly munching away at the brambles and saplings; the hope is this will keep the woods open enough for the lichens and bryophytes to recover. Whether the cattle will leave enough saplings to grow into replacement trees remains to be seen.

If these bryophytes and lichens are unable to thrive today in a wood left entirely to nature, it seems reasonable to wonder how they ever prospered in the original wildwood. Until three or four thousand years ago when humans began to have an impact, the wildwood, whatever it looked like, was very extensive and within it a scattering of veteran trees would have lived for 500 years or more, before gradually decaying and eventually falling apart. Alongside these, middle-aged and older trees would have ensured a varied and reoccurring habitat for bryophytes and lichens. Over millennia the interplay between climate and the effects of large herbivores and their predators would have influenced their abundance, but there was plenty of room for fluctuation then, without risk of extinction. What we have now are small fenced-in habitat relics and, with the wild herbivores gone, the woods often become a dense tangle which is unsuitable for lichens and mosses. And if local conditions become unfavourable, there is now nowhere else to go, especially if you have the limited mobility of a moss or lichen.

The challenge now is how to keep conditions continuously favourable for the bryophytes and lichens in relatively small and isolated woodlands, whilst ensuring the long-term continuity of trees. Recently conservation managers have been experimenting with 'pulse grazing' – which involves reintroducing grazing every eight to ten years for a limited period to push back some of the undergrowth. In between times, young trees could get established and become the replacement trees for the future. Whether this will work in the long-term is largely untested.

Such proposals are difficult enough to deliver on nature reserves, let alone farms. If woodlands are left ungrazed, thickets of brambles will eventually develop, which are impenetrable to woolly-coated sheep; hardy cattle or goats are then required to browse back the brambles, and thin the thickets of young trees. It would require a lot of flexibility on the part of farmers, and the schemes paying them, to deliver grazing every eight years or so. Perhaps part of the answer is to plant trees in the canopy gaps and, until they are established, protect them from grazing sheep. That way light woodland grazing with sheep in the winter, as at Craig-y-tân, could continue.

Sometimes the understanding required for managing wildlife can be very subtle. For example, concerns that regrowth in ungrazed woodlands will shade out bryophytes may be a problem that is particular to Wales.[105] There has been heavy grazing here for five to six hundred years resulting in a very short ground flora which has allowed specialist bryophytes to colonise lower parts of the trees and rocks, where the microclimate is at its most humid and equable. In an ungrazed wood, the taller plants and shrubs would shade out the special mosses and liverworts, and unfortunately conditions higher in the trees don't provide the climatic conditions they require. Apparently in western Scotland, where it is even wetter than here, the bryophytes can grow higher up the trees and so are less likely to be threatened by shading from a taller ground layer. If this is right, it implies that grazing in the Craig-y-tân woodlands needs to be quite tight to benefit these plants.

As lichens are so important in these woodlands I was interested to understand more about them, so I contacted Dave Lamacraft, who is the expert for Plantlife, the wild plant conservation charity, and he generously agreed to visit the Craig-y-tân woodlands with me.

He arrives carrying the usual naturalist's kit, including a shoulder bag stuffed with intriguing lichenology gear, and we walk up to the north end of the woods, which I thought looked promising for lichens.

After an hour or so two things about lichens stand out for me: many of them are very small and all of them, until recently, were only referred to by Latin names. At least now there are some with English names, which can help get a handle on things, especially if you are a beginner, as I am.

It turns out that lichenology is a bit like alchemy, and it is best taken slowly. Watching how Dave goes about identifying them is fascinating: most must be examined through a hand lens, which you hold to your eye and then lower to the plant, which means you spend hours with your nose up against a branch or boulder. Close up, these lichens come in many forms: flaky, cupped, crenulated, fissured and strap-like; some were encrusted, others slapped on like face cream or pats of cold porridge. Some of those we found were easy to identify such as the fishbone beard lichen (*Usnea filipendula*), which hangs down like a hank of grey hair; or the barnacle lichen (*Thelotrema lepadinum*) whose fruiting bodies do look remarkably like barnacles. But many others were difficult, which is where the alchemy comes in. Dave variously shines an ultraviolet light as some species show up a different colour or dabs them with bleach for the same reason. He even chews fragments saying, 'If this tastes really horrible, I will know which one it is!' More often he cuts off a tiny piece, carefully folds it in paper, and stows it in a collecting tin for later identification under the microscope.

The group of lichens known as 'Atlantic' species, characteristic of these high-rainfall west coast woodlands, are, due to the scarcity of their habitat, some of our most treasured species and we have a particular duty to care for them. To my delight, by the end of the day, Dave has found a good selection of them at Craig-y-tân. He also finds several others that are indicators of a long continuity of woodland cover, supporting the idea that this is an ancient wood, perhaps a direct descendent of the original post-glacial 'wildwood'.

He was particularly impressed by the abundance and luxuriance of the lichen community found in Coed Dolfudr, which is the least disturbed part of the Craig-y-tân woodlands. The frequency of *Usnea* species on the hawthorns and rowans adjacent to the wood also suggests to him that levels of acidic atmospheric deposition are low, which is encouraging. As we walk back to the car across the *ffridd*, Dave stops to examine the old hawthorns and birch trees scattered across the pastures. He is looking for nitrophilous (nitrogen loving) species of lichen and, despite this valley having some of the cleanest air in England and Wales, he finds some: only scraps, but there they are, in line with the wind and rain sweeping in from the west bringing nitrogen dioxide in solution. One of these, *Xanthoria parietina*, a conspicuous chrome-yellow crusty species, is often common along main roads and at motorway service stations because it thrives on the nitrogen from exhaust fumes. It seems odd that we should get even a small amount of this pollution here, when there are so few settlements and little industry to the west – where the prevailing winds blow from – but it seems that exhaust fumes from cars and trucks and even offshore shipping are enough to push atmospheric nitrogen over a critical threshold anywhere in these high-rainfall areas.

Once Dave has identified all his specimens from Craig-y-tân woodland, he sends me a report in which he concludes that it is one of the best examples he has seen of the 'Atlantic woodland acid bark community of lichens, which points to it being old, at least in terms of woodland cover'. On the formal scoring index, the wood comes out as a 'nationally important' site for lichens. Further confirmation of its importance later came from a visit to Coed Dolfudr in 2019 by the British Bryological Society who found 'some very nice species of humid Atlantic woodland' on the trees, boulders, rotten wood and seepage points under boulders. Amongst the 143 species they recorded in and around the wood were an impressive twelve species of bog-mosses (sphagnum).[106] Besides being exciting confirmation of my hunch about these woods, both specialist visits are salutary examples of how little we know and are able to cater for the specific needs of species. 'Lower plants' are a cited feature of the Special Area for Conservation (SAC) designation at Craig-y-tân, but whether NRW has the expertise or capacity to monitor their condition at present seems very doubtful. Meanwhile Hywel manages the land, but he clearly can't be expected to know what these specialist organisms need.

Dave Lamacraft's visit points up another difficulty: surveying of this kind needs time, expertise and often money. Craig-y-tân is not a nature reserve, it is a farm, albeit part of an SSSI (Site of Special Scientific Interest) and rich in wildlife habitats, so perhaps it is unrealistic to expect detailed information on which to base decisions about land management. It would be equally demanding to find out about the

myriad beetles, flies, moths or fungi, some of which might be as important as the lichens or the birds. Woodlands are the most challenging
habitat of all for assessing conservation value due to the immense
number of species that can inhabit spaces from the tops of the trees
down to the leaf litter and soil. Some generalisations can be made as to
the value of rotting wood, high humidity and lack of disturbance being
important for a rich variety of beetles, flies and molluscs, but in truth
woodlands such as these are often as unexplored for invertebrates as
a remote tropical forest. Every wood is also different according to its
geology, aspect, altitude, past and current land use, which can make
the formulaic prescriptions favoured by agri-environment schemes so
frustrating for conservationists and farmers alike.

It is mid-October and I am scrambling about in the woods above the
house at Craig-y-tân. There is no mistaking the season: a softening
underlies everything and only the first thin seeps from redwings in the
treetops smack of urgency. It is also the beginning of the quietest time
on the farm; the mountain has just been cleared of sheep and they have
been trucked out to their winter pastures. At least the dogs are quieter
now I am out of sight; I made the mistake of entering the wood in view
of their kennels and they set up a terrible racket, which echoed back
off the hillside until I was out of view. A couple of sheep amble away
through the trees. There is a large gap in the canopy where I am standing but no tree seedlings amongst the grass and sparse bracken – which
is a puzzle. There were quite a few small birches protected by the thick
bracken on the woodland edge where I came in. Perhaps the sheep, even
at this light density, nipping off any accessible seedlings, rather than a
lack of gaps in the canopy, prevent new trees getting established.

As I edge my way across the steep ground along the boundary fence
at the top of the wood, I come across a big rowan that has recently
blown over in a gale, its vertical root plate still pitted with soil and
rocks. Stretched across it, as tight as a piano wire, is a bisecting fence
that has been wrenched above the ground by the fallen tree. I scramble

over it and find myself stepping into the future. This small section of wood, perhaps three acres, has been fenced off separately and so sheep have been completely excluded – until now, as they are beginning to get in where the rowan has lifted the fence. Unless Hywel reinstates it, any further tree regeneration will be inhibited.[107]

But for now, the successional story that I have been speculating on for months is spread out in front of me. In great contrast to the rest of the woodland at Craig-y-tân, in the next half an hour I find two young oaks, a holly sapling, a twenty-foot-high western hemlock that has seeded in from the nearby forestry plantation, and two areas thick with brambles, some of which are head high and bearing fruit. There are also thickets of young birch and rowan along with new growth of blackthorn and sallow. If Craig-y-tân's woods were left entirely ungrazed, this is what they would look like in twenty years' time – almost impenetrable.

Some of the tall birch saplings are growing in the shade of a nearly closed canopy, giving more support to the idea that it is grazing, rather than lack of light, that is inhibiting new trees getting established. I find myself bristling about the hemlock, an exotic conifer, needing to be cut out before it gets old enough to start seeding. The implications of all this growth for the rest of the woodlands depends on what kind of wood you want. Maybe the present light winter grazing is doing enough to hold back the brambles and conifers, but that also means no oaks, holly or replacement birches and rowans. It also implies reintroducing grazing in Coed Dolfudr before too much longer – it would be tragic to see that submerged in a tangle of brambles. It might seem odd to conclude that reintroducing human 'interference' would be beneficial to the wildlife of these woods, but historical stock grazing has created conditions that suit a rich assemblage of lichens and bryophytes that would be hard to let go.

To avert the worst consequences of climate change, we need to draw down much of the carbon we have already pumped into the atmosphere. Various technological fixes – most notably carbon capture – have been proposed for this, but these are likely to be expensive and mostly still unproven at scale. A cheaper, more immediate and, to many people, more appealing option is trees: they absorb and store carbon dioxide from the air and release oxygen as a by-product – which in turn allows us to breathe.

New woodlands will certainly be established in Wales in the coming decades to help meet the UK government's target of 'Net Zero' greenhouse gas emissions by 2050, but what kind of woods, where and how extensive they should be is a complex question. The Centre for Alternative Technology in Machynlleth, in its well-regarded *Zero Carbon Britain* report, suggests Wales needs about an extra 260,000 hectares of woodland to meet its share of the UK total. The UK Climate Change Committee has recently suggested a smaller figure for Wales – an additional 152,000 hectares of forest, of which sixty per cent should be broadleaves and forty per cent productive conifer plantations.[108] The Welsh government has also recently proposed a new National Forest for Wales, which the First Minister described as 'an ecological network running the length and breadth of Wales', although the details of this are still rather hazy.[109] But, as discussed in Chapter 5, which trees should be planted and in what places is a vexed question.

Farmers in upland Wales are once again being offered good prices to sell hill land for tree planting, but there has already been some public push back against such proposals: a London-based firm that bought four farms in Wales in 2021 was forced to change its plans to plant these with commercial forestry plantations in the face of a petition signed by 17,000 people.[110] Conservation bodies, such as Trees for Life, are also beginning to use carbon credits to help finance tree planting and rewilding projects; I can only hope they are screening people who are buying carbon credits to ensure they are simultaneously reducing their carbon output, and that the planting is not just part of a 'greenwashing' exercise. If we don't all reduce our carbon consumption, no amount of tree planting will meet this crisis.

Having said that, there is clearly an admirable public urge to 'do something', and planting trees resonates with people: it seems like a 'good thing'. The Woodland Trust are currently looking at where all these new trees might be planted or allowed to regenerate in Wales. It is likely that they will recommend that the bulk of the broadleaves are situated in or on the sides of valleys, in which case most of the 60,000 hectares of conifers are likely to be in the uplands. As we have already seen in Chapter 5, commercial conifer plantations are not good news for biodiversity; what wildlife needs are native broadleaved woodlands that are left standing – they will also draw down carbon indefinitely. It is true that the UK uses considerably more timber than it grows. Even in Wales we use about twice as much as we produce annually, but the need to sequester carbon is now so urgent that reducing timber imports must surely be secondary.

If more trees are going to be planted in the uplands, it will invariably be on native, semi-natural vegetation – most sheepwalks are not agriculturally improved. It now seems to be accepted that tree planting should not take place on deep peat (although countless acres went that way in the past), as the ploughing and drainage required for the trees to prosper exposes raw peat, which then oxidises, releasing quantities of stored carbon into the atmosphere. Deep peat should be left alone.

There are still extensive peaty podzols and other soils in upland Wales and these are likely to be targeted for tree planting, especially plantation conifer crops. The loss of native vegetation and associated invertebrates, plus the increased pressure on ground-nesting birds from predators using new plantations, would almost certainly result in a net loss for wildlife. On the other hand, allowing broadleaved woodlands to establish naturally and stand indefinitely could lead to a net gain for wildlife, especially in the long term.

The prospect of extensive new conifer plantations in the Welsh uplands is profoundly depressing. It is true that young, fast-growing conifers are good at capturing carbon from the atmosphere but, as discussed in Chapter 5, the carbon is released again if the wood is burnt or used for short term products such as paper, wood pellets or short-lived fencing. Of the UK's 2018 timber harvest, only twenty-three per cent was used for construction, which locks up the carbon for decades. It is argued that, as long as the other seventy-seven per cent of trees are replaced each time they are harvested, they are in effect carbon neutral. Twenty-three per cent of trees giving a net gain will not be enough to meet the climate emergency.[111] On the other hand, a self-regenerating broadleaved forest would draw down and store carbon, potentially for centuries, as well as providing a better range of ecological and social benefits – and it would cost very little to set up and maintain.

Where and how the land can be made available for all this tree planting in upland Wales seems quite another matter; all the land is owned by somebody and most of it is farmed. If large areas were to be covered in conventionally planted trees, then they would effectively be lost to farming for ever; in which case a lot of farmers would go out of business, albeit with fat cheques in their pockets. The Woodland Trust, in an unpublished report from June 2020, suggested that a proportion of the new tree cover in Wales could be in areas of agro-forestry, where light sheep grazing co-exists with growing trees. This seems an imaginative proposal which, if it proved practical, could offer a solution to increased tree cover and continuity of farming.

How does all this apply right here at Craig-y-tân? All of the habitats on the farm are variously good at carbon capture and the deep peat on the mountain is a major carbon store, and therefore unsuitable for tree planting. Trees could be allowed to regenerate naturally on the mountain land and/or the slopes adjacent to the existing woodland, but Hywel would have to be persuaded to reduce his grazing levels even further, or more likely, stop altogether for a significant number of years. Judging from nearby examples, a mixture of rowan, Sitka spruce, sallow and birch would gradually become established on the drier ground. It might be possible to reintroduce sheep once the trees had become established but that could take twenty years on the exposed and climatically challenging mountain, during which time Craig-y-tân would become unworkable as a farming unit. Assuming the establishing woodlands were left unmanaged (certainly the cheapest option), then perhaps over several hundreds of years they could become biologically diverse, even as rich and interesting as the wild woods that currently drape the slopes at Craig-y-tân.

Chapter 10

Shearing

Managing sheep on a hill farm requires a great deal of knowledge and skill, most of which is passed on in a line of almost unconscious tutelage. On farms like Craig-y-tân, this is as much an expression of identity, culture and language, as it is of farming. Enabling this local, family-based culture to thrive in the context of a highly regulated and subsidised farming industry is difficult. Now society is beginning to demand an even wider variety of 'products' from the farmed landscape, creating yet another level of challenge to the Welsh hill farming culture. Craig-y-tân is no exception to this.

It is early July and time for the sheep to be 'gathered' from the mountain and brought down to the farm for shearing. Hywel has suggested I walk up to Craig Dolfudr, a vantage point high above the farm, from where I would be able to get a clear view of what is going on. When I set out, it is cool and damp with a blustery wind; the smell of bracken, bleating sheep and an occasional burst of song from a wren accompany me as I plod up the steep hillside. I am a bit unsure of the route, so I look out for the footmarks of Hywel and his companions who will have walked up ahead of me an hour or two earlier. It has rained a lot in the last two weeks and the ground sucks at my boots along the sheep paths that snake through the bracken and hummocks of cottongrass. Every step up the escarpment disturbs numerous small dark craneflies; there must be hundreds of thousands across these hillsides today: surely an abundant food supply for meadow pipits and other birds, but I don't see or hear many as I trudge along. The escarpment is relatively sheltered, but, as soon as I crest the ridge, a harsh wind is straight into my face; I am glad to be wearing plenty of layers.

This is hard country to farm, yet it never ceases to amaze me how tenaciously people cling to their land. I have known young men who are desperate to break into farming despite the hard work and lack of profitability, and others who have a day job but rent or buy a couple of fields and work long hours, just to have one foot on the land. Despite the high market value of agricultural land, selling up rarely seems to be an option, unless infirmity or calamity makes it unavoidable. If that tenacity ever breaks, the character of rural Wales will change forever.

Scanning the huge expanse of moorland and bog spread out in front of me, I can't see any sheep or people, even through binoculars, but after a few minutes I realise most of the sheep are a mile or so away, on the drier grassland that rims the moorland. The wind is spitting rain into my face but I keep watching, and slowly the scattered sheep begin to coalesce into lines which thread this way. Then I see a figure on the distant horizon who is also heading in this direction. The cloud is lifting and visibility improves; a pale patch of sunlight sweeps towards me across the heather like a searchlight and is gone in seconds.

You might think that humankind has had no influence on this vastness – it looks impervious – but just behind me I can see a single yellow flower of goldenrod clinging to an inaccessible crag: a tiny clue to what might have been in the absence of sheep nibbling for centuries. As Roger Deakin so aptly put it, they 'keep the contours clear, sharp and well defined … constantly at work on every detail'.

The light settles back into a soft damp blanket over the muted greens and browns. I watch as a large swift-shaped bird becomes a hobby and turns at speed out over the bog – no doubt hunting dragonflies. It is already half a mile away. So much space makes me feel insignificant and powerless.

From here it seems like a conjuring trick: sheep out of nothing, trickling together like lines of milk down the side of a huge bowl. But after about an hour they have all disappeared into dead ground between two ridges and do not reappear. It dawns on me that they might be keeping to the ground in between and will come round behind me. I dash back to the edge of the escarpment and there they are: the trickle is now a stream flowing round the end of the ridge heading towards an open gate.

I see a man, who is whistling to his dogs, moving slowly down the rocky hillside; and then another one on the path below. Hywel phones me to check where I am – mobile phones are surely the most startling innovation in this ancient process. The long line of ewes and lambs is snaking across the hillside towards the gate. Amid a constant chorus of bleating and men whistling, they funnel through like sand in an egg timer and out onto the lower mountain, where they will be held until shearing. We meet up by the gate as the last of the sheep are pushed through: Hywel, Rhys and Jac – Hywel's brother – plus eight dogs. Setting off down the slope I had climbed earlier, we slowly follow the sheep. Hywel and I walk together and the other two ahead. 'If you take them gently they don't lose their lambs and have to go looking for them, so it's quicker that way,' Hywel explains.

There is a cacophony of bleating as ewes and lambs call to each other; this is how they stay in contact, despite the hubbub. The ewes with their lambs will remain here, on the shorter grass, until they are dry; their fleeces are heavy by now, after a year's growth of wool. Tomorrow Hywel and Rhys will take them down to the farm in batches: there are 350 to shear from today's gather.

'We have walked some miles today,' Hywel says with a quiet smile. Unusually for this day and age, he doesn't use a quad bike on the mountain: the terrain is difficult and he prefers to be on foot. Neither does he use the bike round the farm very much, although he admits 'it is handy for feeding hay in the winter'. It seems to me that Hywel really is a shepherd, in the fullest sense of that word, like his uncle and grandfather before him, and so for him walking is the proper way to do the job.

As we follow the sheep down, our conversation inevitably moves to what the post-Brexit proposals for farming might be.[112] Hywel is concerned – he knows he can't keep going at Craig-y-tân without subsidies. He says everybody is worried, but all they can do for now is speculate amid the uncertainty.

The mountain is gathered four times a year: in spring for ear tagging and dosing, at this time in July for shearing, in August for weaning and separating the lambs for sale, and finally in October to clear the mountain for winter. The sheep are more or less walking themselves down now – they know the way. The dogs are sloping along, sometimes snapping and snarling or mounting each other, like a pack of wild dogs. The men, wearing full waterproofs, are unhurried, strolling – making the long walk look easy. Steeped in the ways of sheep and hill farming, they move easily in their natural environment.

Hywel explains that at the top of the gather earlier this morning they had fanned out, walking about 200 yards apart with the dogs in between, gradually working their way down driving the sheep ahead of them. It was hard going amongst the tussocky mixture of cottongrass and heather. The dogs prevent the sheep from doubling back, 'although one or two usually get away'. The whole process is like a river catchment starting with the trickles and ending with the torrent that is in front of us now. Once again, it is the continuity that strikes me: Hywel's grandfather, and probably his grandfather before him, would have walked with the ancestors of these sheep down these same paths through the bracken. The only thing that's really different now is the mobile phones.

Although the sense of community is still very strong here, farming neighbours pooling labour to help one another out is now mostly a thing of the past. Despite this, the farming community is still particularly important to Welsh language and culture because it provides continuity from generation to generation, each informing the next about that particular land, to which they are deeply attached in every sense. They represent a tradition where people belong to places rather than places belonging to people; identity is tied to place.

Language shapes our view of the world and Welsh, having evolved primarily as a rural language, is rich in vocabulary and expression about the land and our relationship with it. I can sense that there is a cultural way of understanding that outsiders like me can barely grasp. I often feel its presence separating me from Hywel (let alone Marged) despite our best endeavours. Besides being a wonderful manifestation of human culture, the richness and complexity of the language provides a window into the past that is beyond price. Anyone with an urge to repopulate the hills with wildlife by depopulating them of people should pause and know that there is more at stake than agri-culture and biodiversity. Language and its cultural expression represent a way of looking at the world, which is an expression of being human, and deserves to stand shoulder to shoulder with biological diversity. We must not lose sight of the fact that we belong here – even if we behave badly.

And yet this whole way of life remains invisible to many outsiders. It can seem as if the Welsh-speaking culture lives in a parallel universe to the English-speaking world. In many parts of Wales, farmers, and others who are concerned with the land, strongly prefer to speak about it in Welsh and they don't speak 'out' very much – consequently,

English tends to command the wider discourse. When a new idea comes up, Welsh-speaking farmers tend to talk about it amongst themselves in what can seem like hermetically sealed spaces, whilst the English speakers from outside that community are often louder about generalised concepts and lines on maps. Fortunately, there are a few who can do both, but we need more of them. This schism means that farmers here frequently feel misunderstood by the wider world. They are parochial, a term often intended as pejorative, but in its original sense it means localness, something the movers and shakers could often benefit from knowing more about.

Despite this localness of culture, Hywel can by no means do what he likes on his farm. And it is important to try and understand the tangle of regulations which ensnare him, and modern farming in general. Craig-y-tân sits within the Eryri (Snowdonia) National Park but this has little impact on Hywel's farming system. It is more likely to be a constraint for erecting or changing structures such as a hydro scheme, wind turbine or a house extension.

Most of Craig-y-tân is part of a very large Site of Special Scientific Interest (SSSI) designated primarily for the upland blanket bog and heather moorland that clothes the surrounding hills. Superimposed on top of the SSSI are both a Special Area of Conservation (SAC) and a Special Protection Area (SPA), both of which are EU wildlife conservation designations representing the best of Europe's wildlife areas; SACs are primarily for vegetation and SPAs for birds. These designations remain in place post Brexit and most conservationists fervently hope that will not change. From this tangle of acronyms it becomes obvious that Craig-y-tân is part of something pretty special for wildlife conservation. Hywel is not keen on the SSSI, but apart from some minor horse-trading over boundaries around the farmstead, he has to put up with it. What is more, it comes with a list of 'notifiable operations', e.g. grazing levels and seasons, burning heather or opening ditches for all of which he must obtain 'consent' (or not). It sounds draconian but these designations are to ensure that farming operations don't damage our best wildlife sites – not all farmers are as positive or understanding about nature as Hywel.

A more recent development is agri-environment schemes, which are administered by the UK's devolved governments. The most recent scheme in Wales is called Glastir, a voluntary scheme for farmers designed to incentivise environmentally sensitive management of their land. These schemes were financed from the EU's Common Agricultural Policy (CAP) and the UK government has pledged to continue these payments in the short term, until the new, post-Brexit schemes are finalised. These replacement arrangements are awaited with some anxiety amongst farmers, especially those in the uplands – and with good reason. On average hill farmers in Wales make a £3,800 annual loss on their farming business:[113] currently, hill farming is fundamentally unprofitable. After the Second World War, the Hill Livestock Compensation Allowance (HLCA) was introduced in recognition of the hardship of farming in the uplands and as an incentive to keep people working in the hills. Eventually this hardship support for upland agriculture was subsumed into the Basic Payments Scheme within the CAP, and farmers receive annual payments for every hectare they farm. In return, they have to demonstrate good husbandry and farm 'sustainably', but it is generally agreed this so-called 'cross compliance' delivers very little, other than a tangle of regulation and paperwork for the farmer. Beyond this, there are more proactive schemes like Glastir that provide payments for additional environmental work, such as adjusting grazing or fencing out woodlands. All of these must be agreed in advance and are binding over a renewable five-year management period. Hywel opted to enter one of these schemes twenty years ago and, in effect, he is bound into a five-year rolling management plan that he must abide by. Currently there is a strong culture of fines (by withholding payment including arrears) for any discrepancies including paperwork errors. Common gripes amongst local farmers are that Glastir is bureaucratic and lacks sufficient flexibility, expertise or manpower to enable the scheme to deliver well for all concerned. On the other hand, its funds are a financial lifeline for many, and even lucrative for some.

At Craig-y-tân it is Glastir (with the SSSI regulations lurking behind it) that is responsible for the fencing out of the woodlands, changed grazing patterns and restricting the flock size to about half what it was in Hywel's uncle's time. It also forbids further drainage of the marshy pastureland and specifies winter-feeding sites for sheep. Similarly on the mountain they prescribe the conditions for heather management such as burning or cutting. In exchange for abiding by these restrictions Glastir makes compensatory payments to Hywel for 'income foregone/costs incurred', which are sufficient, along with the Basic Payments Scheme, for him to stay in business and have Rhys work on the farm part of the year. Without these payments there is no possibility that Craig-y-tân could continue as a farm; in return Hywel must sculpt his farming system to fit the restrictions.

A real-life example illustrates the complexity of such arrangements: Glastir specifies that no sheep can remain on the mountain at Craig-y-tân between mid-October and the beginning of April. Given that the mountain land is such a large part of his farm, Hywel doesn't have grazing for all these animals elsewhere, so he sends most of them away, including the pregnant ewes, to winter on lowland farms, where inevitably they feed on more nutritious pastures. A consequence of this extra nutrition is significantly more ewes giving birth to twins. But there isn't enough grazing for all these extra lambs at Craig-y-tân, so Hywel is now obliged to rent additional land locally in order to be able to rear them all.

This brought home to me how different each farm is, and why, if wildlife is to benefit and farming remain viable, agreements need to be flexible enough to take account of very local circumstances. Agri-environment schemes provide a framework for caring for the land in a more environmentally sensitive way, but they also add to the multitude of agricultural, animal welfare and trade constraints that our highly regulated and globalised world places on farmers, as it does on many of us. The image of the rugged, independent hill farmer being master of his own destiny is very far from the truth. Whether schemes like Glastir are delivering for the environment is debatable. At the entry level, the benefits accrued to wildlife have, so far, been disappointing across wider wildlife populations, although there have sometimes been local benefits, but these tend to be concentrated in arable areas, e.g. increases in tree sparrow or corn bunting populations.[114] Recent research into the effectiveness of agri-environment schemes in Wales rather reinforces the view that they have been minimally effective at 'maintaining and enhancing species abundance', with few differences found between sample areas inside or outside schemes. Some positive differences were observed, but again mainly in species using arable farms in the areas surveyed – for example, there were local benefits to arable plants, yellowhammers and hares. There was little in these results relevant to hill farms.[115] However research always lags behind practice and work on the ground is being refined all the time, so it may be too soon to draw definitive conclusions.

There is a higher level (Glastir Advanced – in Wales) to these schemes where management requirements are specifically targeted to the particular wildlife features on the farm, and this level may be proving more effective as management can be more focussed. Craig-y-tân is in one of these, and I can see positive effects: restricting drainage of boggy pastures for the benefit of characteristic wet ground plants and invertebrates; significantly reduced grazing pressure on the heather moorland; restricting winter-feeding sites for sheep. The fencing out of the woodlands with light winter-only grazing might be just the right prescription to sustain the lichen and bryophyte interest.[116] Unusually nearly all of Craig-y-tân is classified as 'habitat land' by Glastir, which means there is very little Hywel can do to it except graze it within the prescribed limits for each habitat type. There are further restrictions too: for example, tree cutting (including dead trees), opening ditches and use of fertilisers are not permitted. Hywel is paid per hectare to comply with these arrangements and has adapted his farming system to accommodate them. But some concerns remain: if, for example, the woodland grazing turns out to be too light and brambles begin to invade who will notice, and if they did is the scheme flexible enough to change the grazing prescription? Officers from Glastir rarely visit to check this kind of thing and often lack the expertise to make a sound assessment anyway.

These agri-environment schemes are now being phased out as the new post-Brexit schemes for farming are being firmed up (see Chapter 3). These are likely to be based more around 'public goods for public money' and 'payment by results'. In other words, they may not continue to subsidise food production but would pay for such things as improved biodiversity and carbon storage. Current thinking is they will also introduce a baseline payment for 'universal actions' to provide income that is not discriminatory wherever you farm.[117] Measuring 'results' for biodiversity (as we saw in Chapter 2) is difficult, if not impossible, over a five-year management period; it requires too much time and expertise, and there are many variables involved in delivering wildlife targets. Habitat condition, which is a widely used measure for SSSIs, might be a way forward as a basis for payment, but it can miss a great deal, e.g. a fine heather moorland can be almost devoid of specialist birds (for reasons that are still poorly understood – see Chapter 7) or plant populations may be declining due to atmospheric nitrogen deposition, which clearly is outside the farmer's control. Eventually I would like to see these new schemes result in farmers seeing themselves as land managers, rather than just food producers, and be paid accordingly for the non-commercial aspects of their work. Hywel or Rhys could assess the situation with brambles and invasive conifers in their woods and undertake or supervise the work to control them if this was structured into their scheme. At present they might be wary of such a role, but with training and encouragement it could gradually become a part of work at Craig-y-tân that they take pride in.

The following day I was back to see the shearing, which takes place in the farm's modern utilitarian barn. The lambs, noisy and fidgeting, are penned outside whilst their mothers are held inside packed together in batches, panting slightly, but quiet. Hywel and Rhys are both shearing although Hywel is a little wry about how many Rhys can get through compared to him these days. 'He's the chief shearer now,' he says with a smile. The ewes are touchingly passive as the men grip them upright and belly out, first between their legs and then down on one knee, as the electric clippers slide between pink skin and the dense matt of the fleece until the skinny sheep, looking like a supermarket chicken, is released leaving its former self spread on the floor like a trophy rug. The back of the fleece is a dense spongy net and the long fibres of wool are loaded in lanolin, which makes it highly waterproof.

The wool from these tough mountain sheep is not high grade commercially; it will go for carpet making and, as Rhys says wryly, the price will depend on the Chinese, who buy the bulk of the wool these days. It is a vivid example of globalisation that the wool from the backs of these rugged mountain sheep will end up in a carpet made in China.

The shearing is done to a pattern, a New Zealand style that arrived here in the 1970s. Firstly the head is clamped between the shearer's knees with the underside outwards so the dirty wool around the belly and tail can be clipped and discarded; then the clippers glide along the legs, up each flank, over and down the back from the head in a beautiful fluid rhythm. It takes about three minutes per sheep, and repeat, and repeat. Father and son are working quickly but steadily; this is intense work and concentration is needed. Once sheared most sheep sprint out, kicking and leaping for freedom: although a few are momentarily dazed, walking uncertainly towards the door.

Rhys explains that these Welsh sheep are lighter to drag out than the down-country breeds but they do kick, the others being 'too fat to kick'. He says the art is to grip the sheep with your legs and feet leaving your left hand free to keep the skin tight – a bit like a man shaving his face. You then clip with your right hand, coordinating legs, hands and eye in one flowing process – almost like undressing the ewe. 'It takes a while to get the hang of it and then it's alright,' he says in his understated way.

Rhys' girlfriend, Glesni, is wrapping the wool. She is not from a farming family but 'knows a bit', she says, pulling a 'not much' face and laughing. Hywel is in fine form, twinkly eyed and laughing, teasing me, Glesni and Nesta, his wife, who comes in and out.

Once all the ewes are shorn they will be reunited with the lambs and then turned back onto the mountain. They mostly go willingly as they prefer to be up there at this season, but Hywel says he might have to 'put a dog behind the stragglers in about a week'.

Cooperating and getting along with your neighbours was, and still is, important in hill farming, but it was especially so when some tasks could only be accomplished when labour was pooled. The biggest communal event on the farm each year was shearing. Many older farmers are still nostalgic for the times when they exchanged labour with their neighbours, particularly at shearing time. Mechanisation and economics now mean that farming has become largely solitary work, even in a district like this that places such a high value on community.

Marged spoke about shearing with great enthusiasm, and it was clearly as much an expression of community (and food) to her as it was a job of work. She recalled how the first Friday in July used to be shearing day at Craig-y-tân, although wet weather would sometimes hold them up; the sheep's fleeces needed to be dry for shearing. Once a neighbour complained that he had been 'waiting so long with Seimon Jones for dry weather that he had learned all the words on the HP sauce bottle'. About eighteen neighbours came to help with the shearing, and there was an understanding about responding in kind when the turn of the other farms came round. Each shearer had his own bench and set of hand shears. Marged was nostalgic about hand shearing: 'I would prefer to hear the clicking of the shears and the shout for another sheep any day, than the constant sound of those noisy machines, like wasps in your ear.' As well as the shearers, there were those that caught up the sheep in the pens and others that wrapped and bagged the wool. A big peat (and later coal) fire was lit to heat pitch for marking each sheep with the brand of the farm after it had been shorn. It was the children's job to pick up the scraps of wool that had fallen. 'Pick up each little bit and it will pick you up later' was what they were told, which Marged said never made sense to her as a child.

Special food was prepared for shearing day: a big oven full of white bread, and another with *bara brith* (traditional fruit loaf), a yellow rice-pudding and an apple and rhubarb tart. A joint of home-cured ham was boiled. Marged spoke (nearly) as fondly of the joking, teasing and general good neighbourliness on shearing day as she did of the food. And she said there was great satisfaction in seeing 'the one white flock' returning to the mountain at the end of the day.

It is late August and Hywel and Rhys are sorting the sheep in the ancient stone pens in front of the house. These pens must be hundreds of years old so have seen this operation countless times before. The task today is to separate out the ram lambs to be sold for slaughter;

the older ewes to be sold as breeding animals to lower farms; and the smaller ewe lambs to be kept down on the better pasture around the house to put on weight. The younger ewes and 'good' lambs go back onto the mountain until October. In addition, all the lambs need to be dosed with minerals and medication. Sheep are flowing in endlessly changing patterns, propelled by dogs but controlled by men, who are the still centre of the operation, issuing soft and sometimes harsh commands to the darting dogs. Rhys is typically laconic but sometimes lights up with a shy smile. His job looks impossible to me: a single file of sheep is running at him between the walls and he is working a smaller metal clapper gate opening to one side or the other. He selects instantly by eye whether a sheep needs to be separated to the left or right. It happens very fast and needs great concentration; he tells me he has always to look three sheep ahead.

There is a passing shower and we pull on waterproofs; the sky is inky dark, bringing the rowan trees laden with berries into heightened relief. Late swallows are swooping around us, no doubt picking off the insects stirred up by the milling sheep. The stone walls of these pens have been patched and mended repeatedly over the years, and additional fencing and corrugated iron with numerous makeshift gates turns them into an intricate system to hold and channel sheep.

Once they have been sorted it is time to dose the lambs: two men in a six-by-four-foot pen crammed with lambs – some of which are now almost fully grown. Hywel and Rhys are constantly handling them: grabbing, lifting, pushing – cooperating with practised ease, only speaking occasionally and even then, quietly. The air is full of animal noise and stink; after a couple of hours I am mesmerised – the world reduced only to sheep.

They are injecting mineral pellets into the throats of each animal and squirting an insecticide along their backs to treat for ticks and blow-flies. In the middle of this mayhem, Hywel somehow spots a sheep with the earmark of their neighbours at Buarth Meini and he hoicks it out to be delivered later. Each farm has its distinctive earmarks that are cut into the lamb's ears at the first gathering in June. Hywel finds one of theirs that they had missed and shows me how it is done. Using special miniature shears, he cuts the Craig-y-tân mark into each ear: a notch in the tip of the right ear and an L-shaped cut on the bottom edge of the left ear. There is a little blood which Hywel wipes from his hand on the sheep's fleece, but the animal doesn't flinch. These marks were established many years ago to provide a way of identifying which farm a sheep belonged to, which was especially important when the mountain land was unfenced and sheep more likely to stray into another flock's *cynefin* (territory/heft). Nowadays the mandatory plastic ear tags are colour coded by year, which is a great help to aging them at a glance. Nonetheless, I am impressed by how much else these men know about a sheep – sex, condition, health, potential – just from a quick look. They answer questions with good-natured tolerance of my ignorance about what must seem obvious to them.

Many aspects of caring for sheep are relatively unchanged at Craig-y-tân: repairing walls and fences, branding and cutting ear marks, lambing, gathering and shearing. One thing that has changed is washing the sheep, or rather their fleeces. At one time, wool was worth more if it was clean and much of the lanolin washed out of it; farmers would submerge the sheep into a deepened place in a stream or river, the *golchfa* (washing place), sometimes with crooks or long poles, until the wool was clean. This had to be done about a fortnight before shearing and in good weather so the fleeces would dry out. This process is different from dipping sheep in an insecticide solution to rid them of parasites, which came later and has now thankfully been abandoned, as many of those solutions were highly toxic compounds, which were lethal to invertebrates and fish if they got into rivers. They could also cause serious and long-lasting illness to farmers. These have now been superseded by the less harmful and more targeted 'pour-ons'.

By late October there is an underlying quieting, a pulling-in that could not be mistaken for any other season: leaves are dropping and sap subsiding. I feel it in myself – this stilling. At Craig-y-tân the rams are sitting chewing peacefully in a steep pasture by the house, but it won't be long before their indolent year changes abruptly; they will be put to the ewes for tupping (mating) next month. Unexpectedly to me, they must be taken out to the farms where the breeding ewes are over-wintering and left there for six weeks to ensure all of them are mated. Under Hywel's Glastir agreement, all sheep must be cleared from the mountain by 21 October and there is insufficient grazing for them all elsewhere on the farm, so most of the ewes must leave immediately. Taking the rams to the ewes in early November ensures the lambs are born soon after the ewes return home, at the end of March.

Today about half of the six hundred sheep that winter away are being moved out and when I arrive most of those are already crammed into the big stone pen; they spook a bit when I look over the wall. This lot will go north-west to a farm on the Llyn peninsula, the others to Henllan north of here in Denbighshire; both farms are significantly lower than Craig-y-tân and have better pasture. Two big trucks have arrived and one is backing up very precisely into the entrance to the pen; the ramp is lowered, hurdles tied into place with baler twine and the sheep are walked slowly forward, their hooves rattling on the metal ramp. There is a bit of whistling and arm waving from Rhys and the two drivers but mostly it is quiet, familiar and quick. A sheep coughs like an old man as the truck pulls away. These sheep will spend the winter on farms where the pastures are empty, as the cattle are housed indoors until the spring. In addition to the extra income, the cattle farmers like to have sheep over the winter because they graze differently from cattle and clean the pasture.

Hywel tells me ruefully that away-wintering is expensive, £18–20 per head,[118] and his sheep are small so there are more to the acre, which is a better deal for the host farmers. Now they are gone, leaving without fuss, and the farm will be quieter until the end of March when they return pregnant, and the annual cycle begins all over again.

Chapter 11

Heather

Heather is almost synonymous with moorland in Britain, covering huge areas of wild hill land across the west and north. But these landscapes are far from natural; they are artifacts principally of farming and recreational grouse shooting whose land management over hundreds of years has profoundly influenced both their appearance and their wildlife.

It is 12 August and I am head-down into the rain, plodding up the escarpment from Craig-y-tân; the ground is saturated, so my boots are in water most of the way up. Somebody, Hywel probably, has hung a ram's horn on the top strand of the fence by the mountain gate; it puts me in mind of hunting trophies and idly I wonder why we do that – hang up trophies. Perhaps it is an appropriate question to be asking on the 'Glorious Twelfth', the first day of the grouse-shooting season.

These slopes are quite different from the gently rolling peatlands above; here steep, rocky outcrops are interspersed with wet flushes, streams and extensive stands of bracken – which is largely absent on the deeper peat higher up. There is still a good scattering of flowers: tormentil, devil's-bit scabious, cross-leaved heath and one of those yellow dandelions that are so difficult to identify. After about an hour of steady climbing, I reach the break of slope and an enormous bowl of rolling moorland opens up in front of me. On the opposite side, a mile or so away, is the hazy purple outline of Dduallt and through the binoculars I can just make out the peat hags we visited earlier in the year. From here it seems as if you could walk forever out across this great waste. And it is true: if you set off west you would stay on rough wild country practically all the way to the sea.

Part of the reason I have come here today is to take a closer look at the heather on Hywel's mountain. Scanning with binoculars I can see there are no sheep in the heather; most of them are, as usual, scattered across the grassy slopes on the opposite side of the bog. And why would they try and plough through this dense, not very nutritious tangle of heather, especially as they have their lambs with them. It is in winter when grass is in short supply that sheep would be forced to graze the heather, but Hywel's Glastir agreement specifies that the mountain land is closed to stock between October and early May, so sheep probably have little impact on the heather under this regime.

In which case, now that the ditches have been blocked and the water table is (we hope) rising, most of the influences on the vegetation are no longer from current human land use. These moors have, however, been profoundly shaped by human activity, so it would be foolish to call them natural, but perhaps the cycle of growth, decay and regeneration is less distorted now than at any time in the recent past. Given that much of our heather has been continuously grazed, drained and burnt for centuries, how does it fare if you do nothing to it? Later that day I found something that provided a clue: an old heather clump that had collapsed outwards like a star, and, in the decaying centre, the one small place where there was enough light and exposed soil to germinate, was a heather seedling. This is the textbook way in which heather replaces itself, if left to mature and die naturally.

Repeated thousands of times across a moor at any one time, this would perpetuate heather cover, and with a more varied microstructure than the even-aged carpet that results from a combination of burning and sheep grazing, as is the case here. Nearby I also found the other way it does it: elderly collapsed heather stems root into the moss carpet at the point where they touch the ground. In this way, when the old connecting stem dies and rots away, a new independent plant will remain. These are slow processes but without interference they would continuously renew the heather cover. But without any grazing, trees would colonise, at least on the shallower, drier peat, and woodland could eventually become established, shading out the heather in the process. The present level and seasonality of grazing is probably just about right to maintain open heather moorland here, but the heather is stuck in an even-aged blanket resulting from the burning and grazing patterns of the past.

The rain has eased, and patches of sunlight are sweeping across the whole expanse, lighting up the flowering heather with a soft magenta. There is some at my feet and close up it looks much too pretty for a place as austere as this. What quickly strikes me is the lack of 'heath' rather than heathery blanket bog. The distinction between the two can seem arcane, cloaked in botanical obscurity, but it is important nonetheless. The difference is dependent on the presence (or absence) and abundance of characteristic plant species such as heather, bilberry, cottongrass and various bog-mosses.

Roughly speaking, blanket bog occurs on peat deeper than 50 centimetres and has plenty of cottongrass and bog-mosses and not much heather, whereas upland heath is found on shallower peat with often dominant heather and bilberry and not much cottongrass. Although there are gradations from one to the other, the broad distinction is helpful when considering how best to manage for the benefit of wildlife.

Vegetation on upland heath is tolerant of burning traditionally carried out for the benefit of grazing sheep and grouse shooting, whereas some blanket bog plants, as well as peat, are easily damaged by fire. In practice, farmers and gamekeepers in this part of Wales have made little distinction between the two over the years and burnt any heathery landscape, which has not served blanket bog well. Heather will regrow quickly after burning on drier ground, if the grazing is light. Periodic burning of heath keeps the heather low and therefore accessible to sheep; the regrowth also has a higher proportion of young and palatable shoots compared to the woody branches of mature heather plants which, additionally, are difficult for sheep to push through. Burning also allows palatable grasses and other vegetation, which is shaded out by mature heather, to thrive whilst the heather is regrowing. By contrast, heather on blanket bog is less vigorous and grows more slowly due to the wet conditions; it often seems to stay in the same low and straggly state for years on end.

The great swathes of heather-covered blanket bog in front of me will have been burnt for generations: by Hywel's uncle, his grandfather and no doubt long before him. They would have burnt patches on rotation each year so that those most recently burnt were left to regrow and the oldest were next in line. Up until the middle of the twentieth century this would have been done in cooperation with the Glanllyn estate, which owned the land – Hywel's family being tenant farmers at that time. The estate's principal interest was shooting red grouse, an entirely wild bird which feeds largely on heather, particularly the young palatable shoots of regrowing plants. Their other important requirement is taller vegetation to nest in and hide from predators.

Patch burning provides them with both, side by side, repeated over a large area. Simply put, more sheep and grouse can be sustained per hectare on rotationally burnt heather moorland.

Back then the blanket bog was drier due to the well-maintained network of drainage ditches, so the heather was probably taller and more vigorous – better suited to burning. There are no significant areas of heather on Craig-y-tân's mountain land that could be classed as heath, and therefore considered suitable for burning according to recent thinking. Additionally, the concerns about climate change now mean that any burning of vegetation in the countryside is frowned upon due to the amount of carbon fires release into the atmosphere.

Due to the long history of burning and drainage, this blanket bog is not in good condition – as in so many other moorland areas in Wales. This dried-out state has allowed heather to become more wide-spread and vigorous even on deep (but drier) peat, which of course encouraged further burning, and so the pattern of subtle degradation continued. High quality blanket bog like that in the Flow Country in northern Scotland has small pools and 'lawns' of bog-mosses that we rarely see in Wales; the vegetation there is low and somewhat sparse with only a scattering of straggly heather. It is richer in plants, insects and birds than most of what lies in front of me. Due to differences in climate and latitude, pristine Welsh blanket bog would probably be somewhat different to the Flow Country, but it would not look like this. It took me a long time to fully appreciate that magnificent scenery such as this is not necessarily in good shape for wildlife.

This history of land use means there are no extensive areas of un-modified blanket bog in Wales remaining for comparison, and conse-quently conservationists don't know quite what to aspire to. Here, the centre of the bog around Llyn Grych-y-waun is the wettest area and therefore the least favoured by grazing sheep. It has probably rarely been burnt and there are certainly a greater variety of plants and insects. The grazing/burning/drainage regimes were, by and large, beneficial for grazing sheep and shooting grouse, but now that carbon storage, flood prevention and biodiversity are important considerations, land management is having to be adjusted. Hywel would like to burn the heather on his mountain because it would provide better grazing and easier access for his sheep, but as the land is currently being managed for the benefit of wildlife, as well as farming, the management is a compromise, which is reflected in the payments he receives from Glastir. Incentives designed to promote carbon storage and flood protection are not yet available to farmers, but we hope they are coming.

The conservation of heather moorland in Wales has sometimes been contentious. When I arrived on the Berwyn Mountains in 1983, things were very tense. The then Nature Conservancy Council was attempting to notify a very large moorland SSSI at a time when farmers were being encouraged by another branch of government to convert rough grazing to reseeded pasture, as well as receiving payments per head for keeping sheep, which inevitably encouraged high stocking densities. At the same time foresters, through tax breaks for the wealthy, were buying up similar land to plant conifers. It was a perfect storm, which led to a long, and sometimes bitter battle on the Berwyn, and to a lesser extent on other moorland areas in Wales. Fortunately, much has changed over the last forty years.

Back then the imperative for conservation was not to lose large chunks of heather moorland habitat and to prevent what remained from being grazed to death. We spent years pursuing designations to protect sites (SSSI, SAC, SPA, NNR[119]) and negotiating management agreements with farmers, principally to reduce the size of their flocks in exchange for financial payments. The good news is that, by and large, it worked. The designations stopped the outright damage, and the management agreements (and agri-environment schemes that followed) reduced the grazing pressure. Much of the heathland and blanket bog vegetation across the North Wales moors has recovered from grazing damage. From the perspective of the early 1980s that is a huge achievement.[120]

Conservationists are still unsure of the best way to graze blanket bog and other upland vegetation for the benefit of wildlife, especially when it needs to be coupled to farming that is both practical and profitable. Large swathes of upland vegetation in Wales have become dominated by purple moor-grass (*Molinia*) on wetter deeper peat, and by mat-grass on drier, less peaty areas – both of these to the detriment of their wildlife interest. Generally, these grasslands have been derived from heathland and bogs over time through livestock grazing and sometimes the influence of burning and drainage. This process accelerated in the latter part of the twentieth century due to high densities of sheep and the decline of cattle grazing in the uplands – *Molinia* and mat-grass are both palatable to cattle, but not sheep. Although it would be interesting to know what part the fertilising effect of aerial nitrogen deposition is playing in all of this.

The great benefit of cattle from a conservation perspective is that they eat *Molinia* and mat-grass, but reintroducing cattle in the uplands is a big step in farming terms, as per head they are much more valuable than sheep and require more frequent attention. They also need winter housing and feeding; although a few breeds such as Galloways and Highlands could be wintered on the hills, but they would still need supplementary feeding.

Mountain ponies can also be useful in this context: they are winter hardy, lighter on their feet, and don't need close supervision. However, they are not keen on eating *Molinia*. Although sheep numbers have decreased on mountain land since the days of headage payments, they are still significantly higher in some places than they were in the early twentieth century. Sheep nip rather than tear the vegetation and are more selective grazers, so they tend to eat the delicate plants, and leave the coarser species, which consequently become more dominant. Over time this leads to structurally simplified, species-poor vegetation and a corresponding loss of diversity and abundance of invertebrates and small mammals. Heavy grazing also causes soil compaction which, coupled to the shorter vegetation, encourages fast rainwater run-off and increases flood risk in the valleys.

Coupled to which type of animals is how many to have in any given area (stocking density). As if this wasn't complicated enough, there is the added problem of getting the stock to graze where you want them to. Naturally any animal will gravitate to the sweetest grazing, the most sheltered areas, or congregate in places where they receive supplementary feeding – consequently they inevitably over-graze some area and neglect others.

Reintroducing traditional shepherding could help with this, but it is a time-consuming and expensive option. Another possibility is 'virtual fencing', using radio collars combined with audio signals and a mild electric shock when an invisible boundary is crossed. The animals soon learn to recognise a warning sound when the boundary is approached so rarely receive a shock. The RSPB has been experimenting with this method at Haweswater, but it is still too early to know how effective it can be.[121] There is an urgent need to find grazing solutions that will enable wildlife rich moorland vegetation to arise from practical farming.

Change has been happening in other ways as well. Farmers are getting older: their average age in Wales is now sixty-one, and many of those are part-time – farmers juggling more than one job are even more likely to opt for a system that requires minimum labour. The reduced flock sizes in recent years, compared to thirty years ago, means there is less competitive pressure for sheep to graze the steeper and higher moorland vegetation; consequently, some of this is being colonised by trees. This is exacerbated by farmers keeping fewer hardy Welsh Mountain sheep; the more profitable crossbreeds that have replaced them are even less keen on rough grazing. The upshot of all of this is that many farmers now make little use of their mountain grazing for much of the year. NRW has begun to specify minimum numbers of sheep in their management agreements, which is an extraordinary turnaround since the 1980s. Amongst conservationists there is now much talk of farmers 'under-grazing' and 'de-stocking'. Back then some of our stock reduction requirements may have seemed too stringent, but, in the face of the chronic grazing damage to heather, drastic action was required. The practical information on which we drew to make the calculations was scant; upland conservation management was still in its infancy, and much more has been learned since then. And there is still a lot to learn: after all, hill farmers have been refining and evolving their land management for hundreds of years. Conservation can't claim much more than fifty.

The switch to area-based farm payments, which began in 2005, is probably the most important change in the history of grazing these moors for a very long time. Farmers began to see low stocking rates on their mountain as a viable and voluntary option. Progressive though this was, there some unforeseen consequences. Although grazing damage to heather still occurs locally, usually in places with a grass and heather mix, parts of the Berwyn and Migneint are now so lightly stocked they have developed a closed sward of heather and moss where there are virtually no grasses and (without burning) precious little young palatable heather. This vegetation is virtually un-grazable. Coupled with the shift to less hardy crossbreeds, this means that the remaining hefts, the self-sustaining territory of a sheep flock, which are critical to flock management on open moorland, have broken down irretrievably in some places.

Over the last fifty years or so, much of the mountain land in our area has been fenced according to each farm holding, including here at Craig-y-tân. Prior to that, very large tracts of mountain land were open, yet each flock kept to its own heft, the boundaries of which were defended by castrated rams, known as 'wethers' which passed the knowledge onto the next generation by example. Seventy years ago, in Hywel's grandfather's time, sheep were still shepherded on the mountain: confined to one area or moved to another by a man and his dogs on a regular basis. Farmers, now often single-handed and even part-time, need to reduce their supervision of sheep to a minimum, relying on fencing and allowing the sheep to range as they like.

Moorland gamekeepers used to say that all you needed to manage a moor was 'a box of matches and sheep's teeth': the matches to burn heather, and the sheep's teeth to prevent the vegetation from becoming too 'rank'. By now we have fewer sheep's teeth on Welsh moors and the matches aren't often needed, as burning has mostly been outlawed or abandoned. There are usually only a few days when the weather is suitable for burning during the period when it is permitted (October to March) and there are no longer enough people employed on farms to get the job done safely.

Burning heather is a skilled job in which knowing the lie of the land and understanding the weather, particularly the direction and strength of the wind, is critical. If the wind picks up or changes direction unexpectedly, you can find yourself with a wildfire raging towards a valuable timber plantation, or worse still human habitation. Having enough experienced and competent people to tend a heather burn is essential, consequently very little now gets done.

On this moorland Hywel would now need NRW's consent to burn, which would not be forthcoming as most of it is blanket bog on deep peat. In recent years, burning vegetation has generally become frowned upon in environmental circles as it releases extra carbon into the atmosphere; this is especially sensitive on peatlands because they are huge carbon stores.

In the early 1990s, some moorland managers began experimenting with cutting heather using tractor-powered machinery. This has the big advantage that it can be done in all kinds of weather and uses very little labour; the resulting letterbox-shaped strips became a familiar sight across the hills of North Wales. At Llyn Efyrnwy the RSPB have experimented with linked cutting patterns to enable sheep to distribute themselves across the moorland, so grazing it more evenly. This has attracted interest from other moorland landowners as a possible way forward for reinstating grazing on neglected moors. At Craig-y-tân access to the mountain is so difficult for machinery that Hywel doesn't see heather cutting as a realistic option at present. Cutting, and previously burning, are probably only necessary at all if sheep graze the moorland; ponies or cattle can cope with taller heather.

An unintended consequence of the decline in grazing and burning on some heather moorland has been the colonisation by self-seeding trees, sometimes birch and rowan, but more often Sitka spruce, which is now the principal seed source for trees in upland Wales. This is not just a few trees here and there, but a significant and re-occurring problem on moorlands close to plantations, of which there are many.

In 2009 and 2010, the RSPB removed 11,500 spruce trees on heather moorland on their reserve at Llyn Efyrnwy. This colonisation was due in part to another unholy coincidence: by the time the conifers planted in the 1970s and 1980s were mature enough to produce seeds, grazing levels on adjoining moorland had been reduced and most burning had ceased; consequently, the Sitkas found a good seedbed in the tall, open heather and the resulting seedlings were not nibbled off by sheep.

Birches, rowans and Sitka spruce saplings are now springing up over many areas of upland Wales. Hywel, who is no lover of conifers, pulls up dozens of Sitka spruce seedlings every year on his mountain. Left to their own devices, these colonising trees would eventually develop into woodland: perhaps not a bad thing if reducing atmospheric carbon is your goal, but woodland dominated by Sitka spruce is mostly bad news for biodiversity, and whether this would pull down and store more carbon than the heather moorland is still unclear.

Grouse shooting has been an important part of the land use history of these moors. Local accounts have it that, in the first half of the twentieth century, Craig-y-tân's mountain was part of an important and productive grouse shoot for the Glanllyn estate. Shooting grouse became fashionable for the gentry in late Victorian and Edwardian times and any moorland landowner would have wanted to provide shooting for his guests.

There is an important distinction between 'driven' and 'walk up' grouse shooting. In the former, the birds are flushed by a line of noisy 'beaters', often local people hired by the day. They drive the flying birds over a line of 'guns', as the shooters are called, who are concealed in 'butts', which are excavated holes in the ground or blinds made of earth or stone. To have enough birds to provide a day's shooting of this kind, you must manage the moor intensively to produce an artificially high population of grouse. This means manipulating their habitat into a chequerboard of burning to provide optimum conditions for breeding and survival. Additionally, to produce sufficient grouse, gamekeepers must kill as many potential predators as possible – foxes, crows, stoats, weasels and often, though now illegally, birds of prey such as hen harriers, goshawks, sparrow hawks, peregrines and golden eagles. If all these conditions are met and the weather has been kind, a grouse moor can have a large surplus of birds in the autumn available to be shot. Driven grouse shooting, a pastime peculiar to Britain, can be very lucrative for moorland owners, with customers paying thousands of pounds for a day's shooting.

However there is considerable and increasing friction between driven grouse shooting and various other sections of society, including nature conservation. At the heart of the problem is the need to manage moorland very intensively in order to have the high numbers of grouse available to be shot that a driven shoot requires. Heather is burned frequently so it rarely gets more than about eighteen inches tall before it is burned again, resulting in a monoculture which, whilst optimal for red grouse, supports a low diversity of other wildlife. Whilst burning on deep peat is forbidden in protected areas and discouraged elsewhere, it is still carried out on some grouse moors.

Intensive burning causes a lot of aerial pollution as well as producing a ground layer of ash; the latter can discolour drinking water and is expensive for water companies to filter out. Shorter vegetation and a diminished layer of mosses are less effective at absorbing and then slowly releasing rainwater, which contributes to flooding downstream. Intensive predator control is less acceptable to the general public than it would have been fifty years ago; in fact, it is now repugnant to many. The illegal killing of birds of prey on and around grouse moors is widespread in parts of England and Scotland (although less so in Wales where intensive grouse shooting is very limited) and is a public scandal, about which the shooting community has done very little. It is this above all else that has led to some conservationists attempting to get driven grouse shooting licensed, or even banned.

In contrast, a 'walk up' grouse shoot, which is done by a small group of 'guns' and their dogs walking the moor, is usually less intensively managed in all aspects. It seems to mostly be a sport for the landowner and their guests, rather than a profit-driven business. Although some predator control and heather management is still necessary for walk-up grouse shoots, the lower intensity means that gamekeepers are less likely to feel pushed into killing birds of prey.

Historically both forms of grouse shooting have taken place on moors local to here. The remains of butts can be found on the Berwyn and the Migneint, but I haven't found any at Craig-y-tân, which suggests that it was a walk-up shoot, even in the heyday of the Glanllyn estate. Regardless, back then predator control would have been ruthless and comprehensive, and at that time the killing of birds of prey was perfectly legal. Any bird or mammal that was considered to conflict in some way with human interests would have been persecuted in rural areas; every hand was turned against them, and the slaughter was commonplace.[122] That alone may have been enough to encourage a thriving population of red grouse. The only direct evidence I have found of historic heather burning at Craig-y-tân is an aerial photograph taken by the RAF in May 1948, which shows what appear to be sizeable patches of burnt heather. These are nothing like the intricate patchwork of burns characteristic of intensively managed moors; they were probably as much for the benefit of sheep as grouse. Marged told me that her father was paid to burn the heather on the mountain by the Glanllyn estate although, surprisingly, she said the gamekeepers did not take a direct hand themselves.

One other tangible evidence of grouse shooting on this mountain is visible from where I am sitting looking out over Waun y Griafolen. Just below me, tucked under the lip of the escarpment, are the remains of a simple stone building: a doorway at one end, a window at the other and a single forward-sloping pitch where the roof would have been. As usual there are no slates to be found, there never are – perhaps they were too valuable to leave scattered around a ruin, or maybe the roof was thatched. The stone walls and lintels are flecked with lichens and mosses; a jumble of large stones may have been a wall, but I am not sure. By now it looks more like a natural feature than a building; grown back into the place, it is being assimilated.

There are several similar buildings like this dotted about this landscape; Rhys tells me that they were 'stables' – places where the ponies were taken to on shoot days. I imagine them bringing up the lunch for the guests and taking the 'bag' (the shot birds) back down at the end of the day. The shooting party could have taken shelter in these bothies, no doubt very welcome in some weathers. I wonder if they were originally built for shepherds to live in when they tended the flock in the summer months. These shepherds' summer houses – *hafodydd* – were widely used when the mountain land was unenclosed, and the sheep needed closer attendance than they do today. This system of moving the animals on foot between separate winter and summer pasturage was part of the tradition known as transhumance, which still hangs on in a few parts of Europe. Poking about in the rushes, I cannot find anything that gives me a clue to who used the building, no rusting artefacts or scratched initials. It doesn't belong to us anymore; the mountain is reclaiming its own, with the usual indifference. Although shots would have echoed around these moors on the Glorious Twelfth for many years, there is little to suggest that grouse shooting has left a lasting impact on the ecology of these hills.

No grouse shooting takes place on Craig-y-tân's mountain now; in fact there are precious few grouse here anymore, perhaps because their predators aren't killed and the habitat isn't optimised for them. It is an interesting thought that this wild bird may be close to extinction here and yet it thrived in bloodier times. I would have expected the grouse population to have settled out at a lower level and their predators to thrive, being no longer persecuted: that a natural balance would have been restored but, despite appearances, these are far from natural conditions.

Moorland is anthropogenic in origin; in modern Wales it is an agricultural landscape formed principally by the grazing of sheep and the burning of heather. It may look and feel wild, mainly because it is high and covered in native vegetation, but it is mostly a product of farming. The inescapable conclusion of this is that if we continue to value it, then we need to go on grazing it, otherwise it will become something else. Although heather burning or cutting is necessary for sheep farming and grouse shooting, it is not clear to me that it has many wildlife benefits. Whilst some species of birds such as curlew, golden plover and dunlin can do well on grouse moors this is mostly in their strongholds of northern England and eastern Scotland.[123] This likely due to a number of interdependent factors rather than just habitat management (see Chapter 7). It is also likely that a wide range of other wildlife such as plants, lichens, fungi and invertebrates are suppressed by intensive burning regimes. Moorland conservation managers, like farmers, foresters and gardeners often have a strong urge to 'do something' but I wonder if there is sometimes a case in heather dominated areas that farmers have given up on, for doing nothing – letting the heather grow tall, fall open and die. This would allow new seedlings to arise in its place: a sort of waist-level rewilding, where not much would be required, except to cut out colonising trees. The moths, fungi and even the odd hen harrier might bless us for that.

Chapter 12

Wilding

Rewilding has become a much used (and abused) buzzword in recent years, but it is important to acknowledge it is a serious element of conservation thinking and practice; it can also be controversial in some situations, including in the uplands in places like Craig-y-tân. There are many definitions of rewilding but in essence it is about freeing land from human manipulation and allowing natural ecological processes to take charge, with no outcome in mind. As a term, 'rewilding' has morphed into a catchall for any place where landscape and habitats are moving in a 'wilder' direction, intentionally or otherwise.[124] As Dafydd Morris Jones wrote somewhat caustically, 'it can mean anything from not mowing your lawn to the reintroduction of apex predators'.[125]

As an approach to conservation, rewilding originated in the United States where it was mostly concerned with very large areas of wild land. In Britain, until recently it appeared to be a niche conservation concept, but it has now become well and truly mainstream. Even ten years ago, government finance for rewilding would have been unthinkable, but Brexit and then the 2021 United Nations Climate Change Conference (COP26) and the UK government's commitment to Net Zero changed the political landscape around agricultural and environmental support. Rewilding is now frequently mentioned by government ministers and is an element in the post-Brexit Environmental Land Management Scheme proposed for England, although not, perhaps significantly, in the Sustainable Farming Scheme proposed for Wales. Rewilding, along with large-scale tree planting, is often seen as a (relatively cheap) way to help meet the government's targets for carbon storage, flood prevention and increasing biodiversity.

Despite this, rewilding is a controversial topic and has provoked and polarised opinions, perhaps particularly in Wales. Some farmers here view rewilders as people who think 'to hell with food, rural communities, language and culture', seeing them as having an agenda not unlike the Highland Clearances – the forced eviction of residents of the Scottish Highlands and Islands in the eighteenth and nineteenth centuries, ironically to make way for sheep. However rewilding has undoubtably struck a chord, perhaps particularly with the urban-based public, but also environmentally concerned people living in rural areas. Sometimes, in this often divisive and polarised issue, farmers are viewed as wilful destroyers of nature from whom the countryside needs to be rescued. Rewilding can evoke images of 'nature healing itself' and 'untouched wilderness' which, although appealing, are often at odds with the countryside as a place where humans belong (ecologically), and so naturally live and work. Because rewilding has become a fashionable term it is liable to get attached to almost anything, including species reintroduction programmes. This may account for apprehension amongst farmers who see pine martens or eagles to be the thin edge of the wedge towards a depopulated countryside.

In recent times many more people have become concerned about the finer points of animal welfare, an important strand in the growth of veganism. Rewilding is appealing to this viewpoint as it implies a reduction or abandonment of farming livestock. Some, including George Monbiot, are promoting new technologies of 'cultured' or lab-grown meat, which they foresee could eliminate the need to farm animals for food; by implication that could make large areas of land available for rewilding.[126] It is easy to see why this kind of talk creates tension with the farming community.

In 2013, George Monbiot published *Feral*, a polemic for rewilding which inspired many, infuriated a few and sparked a national debate about the future of our countryside.[127] Personally, *Feral* inspired and provoked me in about equal measure – which would no doubt please Monbiot. At the time he was living not far from here in Machynlleth and parts of his book draw on his views about the Welsh uplands, which has given the rewilding debate a particularly local flavour and helped polarise opinion. His basic premise is that the current species and site-based approach to conservation has failed us, and consequently our countryside is now one of the most wildlife impoverished in Europe. He considers that conservationists are fiddling about in a farmed landscape using agricultural methods and have lost sight of the full wild potential of our countryside. Allowing nature to take its unfettered course would, he argues, result in a landscape that is richer in wildlife and aesthetically more pleasing, as well as better at capturing carbon and preventing flooding. To achieve the full potential of this approach he advocates introducing wild grazing animals and their predators.

As more than eighty per cent of Wales is farmed, rewilding will not become significant here without the cooperation of farmers, which until recently seemed unlikely. But new schemes that allow absentee investors to claim carbon credits on land set aside for tree planting are beginning to persuade some to sell all, or part, of their farms, even though it would take the land out of farming, potentially for ever. But, as we've seen in previous chapters, this has happened before – many farmers sold mountain land for afforestation in the 1970s and 1980s.

As neither Hywel's sheep nor the moorland birds seem to be making much use of his mountain land in its present condition (see Chapter 10), it seems reasonable (if distinctly uncomfortable) for me to consider whether rewilding could be a better use for Craig-y-tân's mountain from an environmental perspective.

The most obvious implication of this is that Hywel would no longer be able to farm there; his farming system depends on the mountain as summer grazing for the ewes and lambs – there simply isn't room for them elsewhere on the farm. And as things stand he has no choice: his Glastir agreement specifies both a maximum and a minimum stocking level of 1.2 and 0.6 sheep per hectare respectively, so he is obliged to go on grazing the mountain – at least for the duration of his agreement. This points up how vital the continuity of government support is for conservation on farmland. If the scheme that replaces Glastir does not provide equivalent funds, Hywel would have to calculate the most viable option for farming Craig-y-tân, which might mean increasing his flock size and going back to using the mountain land more intensively. Conversely, if the new scheme favours rewilding and provides him with sufficient funds to buy or rent summer grazing land elsewhere, he could choose to leave the mountain ungrazed throughout the year – and let it go wild. For most hill farmers there is something deeply antithetical about letting open land grow over with trees; as his grandfather said, 'once the mountain is gone, you will never get it back again'. Given a choice, I am sure Hywel would prefer to go on grazing the mountain and keep the farm intact, not least because if you exclude the mountain, (and, in effect, the woodlands) there wouldn't be much of a farm left. This points up the significant social and cultural implications of rewilding, which in my view should always be integral to the rewilding debate.

It is also important to ask what would actually happen to this land if you gathered the sheep, closed the gate and left it to its own devices. Whether rewilding the mountain would lead to a more desirable outcome for wildlife is an interesting question. As it happens, there is a place no more than a couple of miles away from Craig-y-tân that can provide part of the answer.

If you take the mountain road from Llanuwchllyn to Trawsfynydd and look down into the catchment of the Afon Gain, you will see something remarkable: a wood is growing up. Not just a bit of scrub in the valley bottom but a 400-hectare mixed woodland. It is still at the thicket stage and studded with patches of Sitka spruce, but where else in Wales can you see a freely regenerating woodland of this size at 500 metres?

Known locally as 'the Ranges', the history of this place is fascinating. From 1903 to 1965 a large area of these hills was used by the Ministry of Defence as a firing range. In the mid-1960s, shelling was discontinued and the core area handed over to the Forestry Commission. It was something of a poisoned chalice, since the ground was full of unexploded ordnance. Three brave drivers in armour-plated caterpillar tractors ploughed it ready for planting. Gangs of local men, reputedly on 'danger money' (and apparently with a lucrative sideline in brass scrap from shell casings), then planted it, largely with Sitka spruce. By the turn of the millennium, it was ready for felling and the timber was extracted in 2001 to 2003. This time a man with a metal detector walked ahead of a mechanical harvester, which had a long reach and bulletproof windows. The Forestry Commission now had a 400-hectare clear-felled site littered with unexploded shells – still a hazardous place to work. The decision was taken to leave it to its own devices and allow a natural upland woodland to establish – perhaps the largest in Wales. Here and there, birch branches, laden with seed, were stuck in the ground to encourage regeneration; otherwise nature was just allowed to get on with it.[128]

The view westward from the top of the pass is impressive: the jagged frieze of the Rhinogydd frames a great bowl of land chewed into shape by generations of sheep. In the centre is a big spread of seemingly random clumps of scrubby birch, sallow and Sitka spruce linked with open patches dominated by heather and grass. In stark contrast to the surrounding bald and bitten hills, the vegetation between the young trees is luxuriant. It overflows with bilberry, crowberry, bell heather, tormentil, heath milkwort, various sedges and a profusion of lichens. The bird life is equally rich with short-eared owl, hen harrier, black grouse and cuckoo all regularly recorded in recent years, as well as smaller birds such as whinchat, stonechat and grasshopper warbler. A high vole population, which is characteristic of these early conditions, no doubt draws in the raptors. If you drive through at night, thousands of moths are sometimes visible in the headlights, surely just a hint of the huge supply of invertebrates emerging in this dynamic young woodland. All of this has been achieved by doing absolutely nothing, except maintaining the boundary fence to keep out the sheep.

Of course, this wood is only twenty years old and changing rapidly. We don't know exactly how it will evolve; over time some of those species will be lost and others will arrive. My conservationist's instincts are to cut out the conifers and keep the heathland and boggy areas free of trees, but it would be prohibitively expensive to make the Ranges safe enough to work in, even supposing NRW agreed with me. If spontaneous re-afforestation is widely encouraged in future for the benefit of flood prevention, carbon capture, and biodiversity, then this is just the kind of mixed woodland that is likely to arise in the Welsh uplands. In the 1960s, the Ranges must have been an open sheepwalk covered with a mixture of heather, bilberry, grasses and rushes. Now in places it is thick with self-seeded Sitkas and thickets of birch, sallow and rowan – grown from seed carried in on the wind or dropped by birds.

Hywel pulls and cuts young Sitkas from his mountain every year and I have seen them growing there on deep peat half a mile from the nearest plantation, so they clearly have the potential to get started. Blanket bog in good condition is naturally treeless, but in Wales, where much of the peat has been dried out, that could change if we don't interfere. At Craig-y-tân a higher water table resulting from the ditch blocking will, I hope, prevent tree regeneration in the wetter parts, but on the extensive drier slopes young trees would become established in the long heather (beyond the reach of sheep) if Hywel stopped pulling them out. If the mountain was left ungrazed, we would probably be looking at a young woodland much like the Ranges, fifty years from now.

From a wildlife conservation perspective, would that be more desirable than what is there now? In its present condition, Hywel's mountain land is not very interesting for wildlife – as blanket bogs go, although that could be improved by making the peat as wet as possible and creating uneven-aged heather cover. But if woodland became established there, moorland specialists such as red grouse, hen harrier and a range of invertebrates and plants would gradually be lost. As a comparison, the Ranges at its current stage of development is certainly richer in wildlife inside than outside the boundary fence; a similar outcome would be likely at Craig-y-tân, at least in the medium term. However we are not short of secondary woodland in the UK, but blanket bog is a globally scarce landform and wildlife habitat[129] – so, from a nature conservation perspective, maintaining Craig-y-tân's mountain as blanket bog is always likely to be the priority.

Of course, left to its own devices a young wood will eventually become a mature one, and at a thousand feet or more above sea level, on the deep peat of Craig-y-tân, we don't really know what one of those would look like. It would most likely contain introduced as well as native species in novel combinations rather re-establishing the original native woodland. The chances are that, from the point of view of wildlife diversity, flood prevention and carbon capture and storage, it would eventually be an improvement on the present situation. Whether aesthetically such a landscape would be more pleasing is subjective. A survey in the Lake District showed people a photograph of Borrowdale as it is now and another with woodland digitally added: sixty-nine per cent preferred the more wooded version. On the other hand, the desolate beauty of Waun y Griafolen stirs something in me that I would be very sad to lose. I would also be unhappy with the large numbers of Sitka spruce that would inevitably arise there; this is a tree native of North America which does not 'belong' in our wild places. But as Sitka spruce is probably the most numerous tree in Wales by now, with a super-abundant seed source, it is clearly here to stay – so I'd probably better get over it. This also highlights an important principle of rewilding: it is 'process led' without a desired outcome, so my preference for a Sitka-free landscape would not be relevant. From that perspective, what is happening on the Ranges can only be right. I wonder if that would be acceptable to many people if, for instance, it was rhododendron (an introduced and invasive plant that has covered large areas in the Welsh uplands) that was spreading across the heather. I am not clear if, for those promoting rewilding, 'no desired outcome' includes undesired outcomes. As Tom Williamson wrote, 'The simple act of ceasing to manage land will not lead to the restoration of Britain's "natural" landscape, whatever that was like.'[130]

Rewilding has become a catchall term for a variety of situations. George Monbiot is interested in what our countryside would become if we excluded human activity and domestic stock and then introduced herbivores such as deer and horses and their predators – notably lynx and wolves. As well as radically altering the soils and vegetation, humans have eliminated the predators as well as the original wild cattle, horses, pigs and, in some areas, deer. The current ecosystem is structurally different from that of the prehuman era, even in the wild-looking areas of upland Britain. It is also different because of natural changes in the climate since then: we could never get back to the original state from here. There is, however, a good deal of ecological curiosity about what the 'new natural' would look like. For this reason, some have suggested that 'wilding' is a better term for this process, which is not about getting back to some pre-existing state, but rather letting nature go where it will.[131] Also, there is no time in the past that we can use as a baseline; the ecological profile was always dynamic and moving.

George Monbiot and others have suggested that rewilding experiments should be concentrated in the agriculturally unproductive uplands, which he provocatively terms 'sheepwrecks', in his book *Feral*. He argues that the forest and scrub resulting from rewilding the hills would, given time, become much richer in wildlife and be more attractive to humans. The developments on the Ranges, although still at an early stage, seem to support this. It is also important to acknowledge that the interplay between vegetation, herbivores and predators in his fully developed model of rewilding would eventually result in something richer and more varied than just taking the sheep off and letting it be.

One of the distinctive things about Wales in this context is the relative lack of deer: in much of Scotland and England deer are very significant ecologically. They have been increasing in number in many English counties over the last fifty years or so, presumably because – like so many mammals and birds – they are no longer persecuted to the degree that they once were and, unlike many parts of Europe, the British seem to have lost their taste for hunting for the pot. In addition to the native roe and red deer, a variety of exotic species, particularly muntjac, have become established and started to spread. These increasing populations are having a significant impact, particularly in woodlands where they browse the ground flora, tree seedlings and coppice shoots. Wales is not immune from this expansion: recently both roe deer and muntjac have been colonising from the east; so far their impact has been minimal, but it could be significant in future rewilding schemes.

A natural ecosystem in Britain would have a suite of herbivores that grazed and browsed the vegetation, plus their predators. A wilded landscape without herbivores would be different in form and structure from one with deer, horses, cattle, etc., and one that included predators would be different again. It seems important to acknowledge that the most significant native predator – humans – are still very much at large, so perhaps we have an ecological responsibility to manage these populations. At present, in Britain, there are potentially three significant versions of rewilding: landscapes without herbivores, those with, and those with predators as well. The first is the easiest and cheapest to set in motion, the second more complicated but still potentially practical, and the third largely impractical because we don't have enough space to introduce predators without conflict with human interests.

As discussed in Chapter 9, it is currently fashionable to promote extensive tree planting on less productive land, particularly in the uplands, in the service of carbon capture, flood prevention, clean drinking water and increased biodiversity. Largescale tree planting that is subsequently unmanaged is, in effect, a version of the 'no herbivores' style of rewilding that has been given a kick start. If planted trees are native broadleaves, rather than (even more) conifer crop plantations, then I presume they would eventually become self-sustaining high forest that needs very little intervention. The benefits of this for biodiversity are as yet unproven. Many of Britain's previously managed woodlands are now neglected and have grown into closed canopy forest, losing much of their species diversity in the process.[132] This is because much of our wildlife originates from edge habitats, which are usually lost in homogeneous woodland; an enclosed, unmanaged wood eventually has very little edge habitat. Also planting trees, or allowing natural regeneration, on bare hill land which has not been forested for thousands of years, would mean there are no specialist woodland fungi, flora or fauna readily available to colonise the new treescape. Such a place would not become a fully functioning wild forest for hundreds of years. That 'a wood is more than a collection of trees' could not be truer than a planted sheepwalk. As Tom Williamson has said, 'The easy assumption that rewilding will, of necessity, improve biodiversity in all or most situations needs to be challenged.'[133]

To get an idea what might happen to another upland area with the 'no herbivores' version of wilding, I visit an experiment in the heart of Eryri (Snowdonia) about thirty miles from Craig-y-tân.

It is late June, pushing thirty degrees Celsius and there doesn't appear to be any prospect of shade. Standing at the edge of the lake in Cwm Idwal and looking up at the majestic thousand-foot rock wall that wraps around its upper end feels very exposed, but the geomorphology is impressive. This is what geographers call a hanging valley, a colossal scoop of rock that was gauged out by glaciers millions of years ago leaving a classic cirque cradling a lake. The complex geology was folded under immense pressure into strata that are writ large across the towering headwall. It has to be one of the most spectacular places in Wales.

Cwm Idwal is also a special place in the natural history of Wales as many of its rare mountain plants such as moss campion, various saxifrages and the Lili'r Wyddfa (Snowdon lily) were first documented here by Evan Roberts, a quarryman and self-taught botanist from nearby Capel Curig, who established an international reputation for his knowledge of mountain plants. About forty years ago, I stood with a group of botanists high up on these cliffs in a place known as the Devil's Kitchen or Twll Du. Our guide, the then warden of this National Nature Reserve, was Iorrie Ellis Williams and I remember how he pushed his stick in the ground, spread his arms wide to the stupendous view and declaimed dramatically, 'This is God's own country.' On reflection, I don't think he just meant that it was beautiful and rich in rare arctic-alpine plants, both of which mattered to him; I think he was intuitively referring to how as a place with its rugged mountain landscape, tradition of upland farming and association with Evan Roberts (a man of the people), it represented a quintessentially Welsh perspective on life.

Cwm Idwal has been, like most of upland Wales, significantly influenced by farming; hundreds of years of sheep and cattle grazing have drastically modified the vegetation here. It is also much loved by hill walkers and climbers: many famous names – Chris Bonington and Joe Brown among them – have cut their teeth on the Idwal Slabs. On top of that, tens of thousands of 'ordinary' folk come here every year just to soak up the splendour. That is how it is with wild places like this, everybody thinks it's 'theirs' and inevitably they view it from different perspectives, not all of which are harmonious.

Tugging my hat down against the heat, I take the path that runs above the eastern shore of the lake, which is paved with rocks artfully levered into place by a gang of local men whose speciality is repairing mountain paths. Working with stone is an indigenous skill around here. Without this work, a combination of trampling feet and heavy rain would reduce these paths to eroded gullies. The slopes above and below are cushioned with heather and bilberry, interspersed with tall grasses and patches of heath rush; this might look like any other lightly grazed bit of upland vegetation, but it was what I had come to see. Until recently, these slopes were grazed down to contouring hugging lawns embedded with vestigial, barely surviving, heather and bilberry plants. Then, twenty years ago, the grazing tenant retired and Barbara Jones, the upland ecologist for the Countryside Council for Wales, persuaded her employers to buy the tenancy and let the National Trust, who own Cwm Idwal, take it 'in hand'. Barbara's reasoning was that the arctic-alpine plants that are so special here were not doing well probably because, being at the southern limit of their range, they were beginning to feel the impact of a warming climate. The other major stressor on these plants was grazing from sheep and feral goats. She saw an opportunity to find out if removing grazing pressure would enable the plants to thrive even in the face of climate change. So it was arranged that there would be no further grazing in Cwm Idwal for the foreseeable future and that natural processes would be allowed to take their course. Barbara calls this 'a hundred-year experiment' – which is probably as realistic as it is ambitious. A neighbouring farmer is paid to shepherd out any sheep that trespass via the higher slopes, which are impossible to fence. At present, the rare plants mostly grow in difficult-to-reach ledges and crevices, perhaps as a last refuge from years of grazing. Unfortunately, the 'wild' goats, which are very popular with visitors, are better at clambering to such places; so now, if their numbers build up in the cwm, they are discreetly culled to more acceptable numbers.

By the time I get to the head of the lake, I am frying. The only patch of shade I can find, in the overhang of a huge boulder, is already crammed with five other people, so I have to put up with the heat. Here in places the flowers are conspicuous: thyme, bog asphodel and butterwort are flowering profusely, where previously they would have been grazed off. But what really takes my eye is the burgeoning heather and bilberry, which are beginning to close over these previously grassy slopes. Here and there whippy rowan saplings have taken root; in the absence of sheep and goats, berries dropped by birds now have a chance to germinate.

Having started up along the steep path to the Devil's Kitchen, I take a break to recover my breath. Sitting beside the path, the shouts of encouragement and clink of the gear from a group of climbers on the Slabs seems quietly reassuring in the hot, still air. The whole cwm felt rested, as if convalescing after the hard years of grazing.

I come to see how this experiment is progressing every few years. Apparently, when the scheme was first mooted, there was some concern from the public that 'the place would become a jungle', but changes to the vegetation have been so gradual that hardly anyone has noticed. A harsh climate, high altitude and poor soils mean these upland ecosystems move slowly. Barbara tells me that, mossy saxifrage excepted, there has been little or no visible effect on the arctic-alpine plants after twenty years; their growth is so gradual it might be thirty to fifty years before any change is visible.

The way down from the Devil's Kitchen is more like a staircase for giants than a path, each step needing careful negotiating. Beside the path, mountain sorrel, beech fern and starry saxifrage sweeten the effort. Coming to a spot where a trickle of water flows over a rock, I startle a pair of twite who have come to drink. They fly off uttering hard metallic calls, which echo around the rocks. I am pleased to see them, as this is now the only area in Wales that you can find these upland finches.

Making my way along the west side of the lake I come across a slope that is thigh deep with impenetrable gorse and heather, a vivid illustration of why the local farming community objected to this scheme. They thought it a 'waste of land' and that furthermore it would be impossible to reintroduce sheep 'in due course'. From their point of view, mountain land doesn't look right without sheep or cattle. This was dereliction. Perhaps they also feared this was the thin end of the wedge for farming in Eryri (Snowdonia) – that once this land was let go it would be lost to farming forever.

A cheerful group – Eastern European, I think – are picnicking on the lakeshore and frolicking in the water. A bit further on, posing (no other word will do) on the top of a rock, a young, scantily clad couple are in a passionate embrace. This might be a National Nature Reserve, but clearly not everyone is here to ruminate about vegetation succession and conservation management. It's a beach, a romantic walk, a climber's training ground, abandoned (stolen) farmland, naturalist's treasure house – and no doubt more.

So where is this experiment heading? As far as the arctic-alpine plants are concerned, nobody really knows. For the rest, probably continued slow development to heathland with scattered trees and eventually light woodland – changes that will barely be noticed by most people. From the traditional farming perspective that will look like derelict land, but perhaps that attitude will begin to soften if a new era of 'public goods for public money' in farming support becomes a reality. It seems to me that we need bold experiments like this to help us understand and be flexible in the face of a changing climate and a globalised world. I hope all concerned in Cwm Idwal can hold their nerve, and report back in eighty years' time.

Cwm Idwal and the Ranges are examples of the level of wilding that is easiest to consider in Wales. If a farmer was willing to give up grazing his mountain you could gather the sheep, shut the gate and wait for it to become woodland – although you might have to wait a long time. Whether the presence of exotic conifers and rhododendron in the arising mixture would be acceptable I have heard no opinion, other than my own. If so, then maintaining the boundary fences might be the only significant management input, although deer culling could be a consideration in the future. There is also likely to be pressure from any surrounding sheep farmers to reduce the fox population that would inevitably dwell in such places. Other than that, it could be a cheap option.

The next level up is to introduce grazing animals other than sheep. Although it is still possible to find cattle grazing in the uplands of Wales – there is a fine herd of Welsh Blacks near Cwm Idwal – they are no longer common. Similarly, there are not many areas where semi-domesticated horses can be found, one exception being the ponies on the Carneddau just across the valley from Cwm Idwal. This, plus the general absence of deer, means that proxy native grazers are mostly absent from the Welsh hills. Sheep would be no substitute for our lost indigenous herbivores, not least because they only graze soft herbaceous vegetation and leave the coarse or woody growth.

Away from the uplands, this level of rewilding has notably been done on the Knepp estate in Sussex, in a fascinating experiment that catches the exciting potential of wilding. Most of this 3,500-acre estate was, until twenty years ago, a mixed arable and dairy farm on the Wealden Clay, an hour south of London. However it was only turning a profit two years in ten; that clay, it seems, is difficult to farm as it is a slippery mess in the wet, and bone hard when dry. The owner of Knepp, Charlie Burrell, had always been interested in wildlife so, inspired by a visit to a Dutch rewilding project at Oostvaardersplassen, he and his partner Isabella Tree decided to try something similar back home. They removed all the internal boundaries on the estate, introduced longhorn cattle, Exmoor ponies, fallow and red deer and Tamworth pigs – as proxy species for our original wild herbivores – and let them loose to feed and roam as they pleased across 2,500 acres. The results have been spectacular.

When considering Knepp it is important to remember the debate about the 'original' vegetation of Britain. As mentioned in Chapter 3, I grew up with the notion that pretty well everywhere below 2,000 feet, in the original vegetated landscape of Britain, was high forest – with an overarching canopy of majestic trees. But Frans Vera's theory that the original 'wildwood' was more akin to savannah than high forest is a serious challenge to this picture. Some ecologists do broadly agree with him, suggesting that parts of pre-Neolithic Britain were covered by a mosaic of vegetation types set in open country with scattered old trees, patchy thorn scrub and areas of dense woodland.[134] But others support the idea of a landscape much closer to the closed-canopy woodland model that was commonly accepted prior to Vera's work.[135] Frans Vera is a valued advisor at Knepp, so understanding how such a landscape evolves has become very much part of what the project is about: they call it 'process led conservation'.

When I visited Knepp in 2016, what confronted me amongst the fine old estate oaks is a mess of sprawling hedges thirty feet wide at the base, big blocks of sallow and large open areas dotted with patches of bramble and scrub – some of which shelter young oaks from the browsing animals, just as Frans Vera predicted. This landscape is prompted, manipulated and sculpted by cattle, horses, deer and pigs. Some of it is low grade habitat at present, particularly the overgrown fields covered in ragwort and fleabane; but to everyone's surprise populations of some nationally declining species such as turtle dove, nightingale, cuckoo and purple emperor butterfly are increasing at Knepp. What this landscape has, in effect, is lots of transitional woodland-edge, which would have been plentiful in Vera's vision of a dynamic wildwood; this could account for these impressive increases.

To my eye, Knepp looked like a transitional landscape on its way to something else and clearly it is still on the move, but perhaps not towards continuous woodland. One thing has become clear: some areas are, unpredictably, developing differently from others. There is a continuity of process, but the outcome is unforeseen. It seems that the changing landscape has personality, is wilful. A dynamic process has been let loose by the very act of not acting; the mice have indeed come out to play.

There are many limitations to comparing this project with a truly wild ecosystem, one of which is the absence of large predators to limit the populations of introduced herbivores. You could say the estate has to accept the responsibility of apex predator and cull them. But to what level? 'Overgrazing' and 'too many' are fascinating questions in a project that claims to have no desired (or undesired) outcome. How will they react if the numbers of purple emperors or turtle doves start to go down? Hold their nerve and do nothing, I hope – whilst the rest of us will watch with interest.

Knepp's herbivores are effectively free-range and in many ways less 'wild' than the ponies on the Carneddau or the goats in Cwm Idwal. This suggests that as long as we are willing to accept the role of predator and cull herbivore populations to 'sustainable' levels, this kind of rewilding scheme could be a practical proposition in the Welsh uplands; but adjusting and readjusting stocking levels so that the vegetation remains dynamic and the animals healthy would be demanding, particularly in remote upland areas. George Monbiot quotes Scottish experience suggesting that to allow tree regeneration, a maximum stocking density of one deer or sheep per twenty hectares is required,[136] but a bald figure is rarely the answer; much depends on terrain, aspect, shelter, palatability and distribution of vegetation and so on. Every place is different. Even with careful management, what happens in the interplay between the grazing animals and the vegetation will be dynamic and unpredictable, as they have discovered at Knepp. George Monbiot has also said he 'would be surprised if there were no unintended consequences' of rewilding and that 'policies must be constantly assessed and adjusted to head off any problems that emerge'.[137] Does this imply some flexibility to the 'no intended outcome' usually enshrined in definitions of rewilding?

Knepp Castle estate has undoubtedly come up with an innovative version of rewilding suited to lowland England which will be fascinating for naturalists and ecologists to watch unfold over the years. It is already a reservoir from which wildlife can colonise the surrounding countryside and a source of inspiration and research, as well as a haven of wildness for visitors in this very crowded corner of Europe.

However, any stock such as horses or cattle released onto a rewilding site in Britain are classed as domestic animals and therefore subject to veterinary and public health regulations. This issue was highlighted recently in the Oostvaardersplassen project when a spell of freezing weather caused a significant number of their animals to starve. The sight of emaciated and dying animals provoked public outrage in the Netherlands resulting in a considerable backlash against the scheme. The veterinary regulations are less exacting in Holland so it is possible for them to treat their herbivores more like wild animals than it would be in Britain. But Oostvaardersplassen is very close to urban areas and, as they found out, allowing animals to fall sick and die is not readily tolerated in today's society. An upland rewilding scheme is less likely to be in the public gaze than Oostvaardersplassen but it may be more difficult to carry out stock management in such terrain, especially if it is wooded.

The third, and most ecologically complete, level of rewilding, which introduces both herbivores and their predators, is not a practical proposition in Wales. Leaving aside the misgivings of farmers and the public, a self-sustaining population of lynx would need a very large area of land. The hunting range of a lynx varies between 8 and 174 square miles and wolves are off the scale.[138] Experiments of that kind in Britain are only likely to be possible on large estates in northern Scotland.

Perhaps largely as a result of George Monbiot's abrasive style in *Feral*, something of a false dichotomy has grown up around rewilding and conservation management; in practice they are not always easy to tell apart. An interesting example of this is the Cambrian Wildwood / Co-etir Anian project near Machynlleth in Mid Wales, which intends to 'restore' 140 hectares of hill land at Bwlch Corog to 'mature woodland, heather moorland, blanket bog and other habitats'.[139] To this end they are planting trees, grazing the area year-round with Konik ponies and during the summer with Highland cattle 'to reduce *Molinia*': so they clearly do have some desired (and perhaps undesired) outcomes. This approach is set within a 'defining principle' in which 'outcomes are led by nature; we do not set defined targets for habitats or species. Early management interventions are to establish conditions favourable to the development of natural ecosystems. Herbivore numbers are to be managed over the long-term to allow tree cover to increase across the site'. This project is deliberately not styled as rewilding although, in a thoughtful and locally sensitive piece on this topic, they admit that 'many people are interested in Cambrian Wildwood as an example' of rewilding but they prefer to speak of 'habitat and species restoration'.[140] If you set aside the endless conceptual tangles around rewilding this seems to be a well-run and carefully thought out conservation project from which much can be learned about 'wilding' in the Welsh uplands. In essence, the Cambrian Wildwood project is indistinguishable from conservation management being delivered on upland nature reserves such as Haweswater or Llyn Efyrnwy; so perhaps ten years on from the publication of *Feral* we can give rewilding and conservation management equal weight along a continuum from which appropriate methods can be chosen. An article in *British Wildlife* in 2021 put forward a similar 'horses for courses' argument, suggesting that embracing the varied conservation management approaches our 'extraordinarily varied landscapes' have produced was the best way to cope with the environmental challenges that confront us.[141]

It can often seem to farmers that the latest fashionable ideas (like rewilding) are being foisted on them from somewhere other. Perhaps that is true of many occupations (the NHS and education come to mind) but because for farmers the attachment to place is so strong, and in this part of Wales expressed mostly through the Welsh language, the gap between here and an office in London or Cardiff can seem very wide indeed. Whilst George Monbiot's inflammatory prose style in *Feral* provided an effective and elegant polemic for those at a distance, it did much to stoke resentment here. 'Rewilding' has become a toxic brand in Welsh farming circles.

Much of George Monbiot's ire was directed towards the Cambrian Mountains, and having walked there a lot, I have some sympathy with his viewpoint, if not his style. Grazed sheepwalks and extensive conifer plantations dominate these hills. The several large reservoirs, which are too deep and cold to attract wildlife, and the wind turbines that now dominate most horizons only add to the sense of an industrialised countryside. The notion of 'self-willed ecological processes' being given their head here could seem an attractive prospect. But of course, people similar to Hywel and his forebears, who have been here for many generations, live and work in these hills. This is not a blank canvas onto which to project visions and policies, but a lived-in landscape for an indigenous population of people whose lives are deeply entwined with the land.

So far, I have considered rewilding largely from an ecological and conservation viewpoint and, interesting though that is (for those with that perspective), it can seem abstract and presumptuous to people living and working on the land. There have been strong reactions here amongst farmers around rewilding, ranging from nervous to downright hostile. Fundamental to this is the understanding that for rewilding to be fully effective it needs large areas of land and, as nearly all of Wales is farmed, that implies the displacement of farmers and their families. In short, it feels threatening.

For many Welsh farmers not only does rewilding seem to need a lot of land, it also appears to be promoted by an English-speaking urban elite who do little to try and understand the realities of their lives. Consequently, some people feel that the fate of their livelihoods and culture are being decided upon conceptually and at a distance. In 2019 Nick Fenwick, a farmer from Mid Wales, wrote an essay in which he said, 'The lust for rewilding is clearly a symptom of a sad detachment from farming, nature and the land … For those families who have farmed the uplands for millennia and understand the interdependence of farming and nature, proposals by foreigners to turn the clock back thousands of years are (equally) preposterous.'[142] In an earlier article in *The Guardian*, in response to George Monbiot's writing about rewilding, including *Feral*, Nick Fenwick also wrote:

> *Over the past half century we have witnessed the arrival of countless rat-race refugees and environmental fundamentalists, all determined to reconnect with rural life and nature, seemingly oblivious to the fact that their new-found paradise is already occupied by people whose connection with the land is deep rooted, dates back thousands of years, and is embedded in their language and culture. While many quickly recognise the reality and become genuine and welcome members of the community others hide themselves away amongst the English ex-pat community busying themselves with sorting out the world's problems, usually starting on their own doorsteps.[143]*

It feels important to say at this point that people here are generally friendly and polite rather than abrasive or confrontational, but if an afront is felt strongly enough, then strong views can be expressed – as anywhere. Also views can change and sometimes soften over time – as mine have done – especially if there is a dialogue of understanding.

Just outside Machynlleth, about thirty miles south of Craig-y-tân, is a large red noticeboard in a field, which says in both languages 'Say No to Rewilding'. A few miles further down the road is another sign: 'Conservation Yes/Rewilding No'. These reactions were provoked by a large-scale landscape/habitat restoration scheme called Summit to Sea, launched in 2018, covering 10,000 hectares of land flowing from the summit of the Cambrian Mountains down to the waters of Cardigan Bay. Summit to Sea was financed by a philanthropic organisation called the Endangered Landscapes Programme and led by Rewilding Britain. It hoped to enrich the wildlife and landscape of the area and promote the economic livelihood of the people living there.

But they got off to a bad start – largely because farmers, or at least some of them, felt strongly that they had not been consulted about proposals being made by outsiders, despite their land being within the area mapped in the publicity. There were three particularly toxic elements in this situation: outsiders, maps and rewilding. The scheme was apparently never intended to be about rewilding, but the lead involvement of the organisation Rewilding Britain was enough to arouse suspicion. Then there was the distinctly 'colonial' act of drawing a line on a map outlining the project area without consulting the people who live and work there. What is more, the people drawing the line had come from 'somewhere other'. Add into this mix that these very hills are the 'sheepwrecks' George Monbiot refers to in *Feral* and you had a pretty poisonous brew.

The reactions to the Summit to Sea proposals were very strong, like those from Nick Fenwick above; the angry opinions expressed in print as well as in person effectively caused a meltdown of the project. The people who launched it had not been sensitive to the local implications and they paid the price.

After staring into the ashes for a while, those that still cared about this proposal realised they must either abandon it or listen and understand what was really needed. And hearteningly they decided to listen. Rewilding Britain withdrew and the RSPB stepped in and has been quietly hosting the project and funding the project officer on a temporary basis. Now, after two years of meetings and listening to hundreds of people in farm kitchens and village halls, a more inclusive, locally generated way of working has evolved. They have arrived at a new 'blueprint' for which there is a sense of collective ownership and pride. There is no mention of rewilding but it is still about conservation at a landscape scale. Gone are the flashy press releases, lines on maps and talk of multi-million-pound funding and, under the patient and astute leadership of Sian Stacey, something quieter, more naturally bilingual and locally distinctive has arisen. They have a Liaison Group that includes representation from the farming unions as well as individual farmers. This new project has been named Tir Canol (Middle Ground) and they have decided not to apply to the Endangered Landscapes Programme for the big funding that had been proposed, but to go it alone. The essential vision of a landscape that is better for nature and people between the rivers Rheidol and Dyfi is the same, but the way to achieve that is radically different.

After all this careful and inclusive preparation, they now have to show that the project can deliver their vision. Goodness knows if it will work as there is much uncertainty – not least how they will dovetail with the new Sustainable Farming Scheme, assuming that becomes a reality, in the next couple of years. Perhaps Tir Canol could provide the collective, locally based expertise that has been so badly missed in the agri-environment schemes, like the one at Craig-y-tân. Whatever happens next, they listened and proceeded at the pace of trust, which has done much to heal the wounds inflicted following the publication of *Feral* and the proposals for Summit to Sea.

When reflecting on all of this it is important to understand how farmers view farming. During and after the Second World War, farmers and foresters were urged to produce more, and they responded magnificently. We now produce far more food and timber than ever before to meet the needs of a much larger population. As a result, farmers have come to think that maximised food production is the (only) proper purpose of their business. That is how they judge themselves and each other.

For a long time it was understood that part of the reason for a basic farming subsidy was to keep people on the land.[144] The EU's Common Agricultural Policy version of that was (and temporarily still is) the Basic Payment Scheme, which in effect, acted as a safety net to keep farmers solvent as markets and the weather fluctuate. Many farmers have been apprehensive about the Welsh government's post-Brexit Agriculture Bill and Sustainable Farming Scheme, (which at the time of writing – December 2022 – is in front of the Senedd, the Welsh Parliament). This proposes to shift the emphasis to include producing 'public goods' such as carbon storage or biodiversity, as well as food. Many farmers fear that without a basic area-based subsidy they could go out of business – early on I heard one source claim that thirty per cent of farmers in Wales could go bust if these proposals were adopted. Who knows if that is an accurate assessment – there is a lot of fear around. There is also concern in the wider Welsh community because farmers and their families are the backbone of rural society here; they are the continuity that ensures a particular identity associated with the Welsh language prospers from one generation to the next. A thirty per cent decrease, or anything like it, in farming families would be a disaster. The rich cultural and linguistic web within which Marged and Hywel have expressed their lives could be broken forever.

I feel both sides of this dilemma keenly. I have been a naturalist and conservationist for fifty years or more and the backdrop to that has often been depressing. Much of the drive behind rewilding arises from the distress felt by many, including me, at the continuing impoverishment of our wildlife. During my lifetime there has been a quiet draining away until many green and pleasant landscapes are now virtually empty of wildlife. Much of this remains unseen by the majority of people but, as Aldo Leopold said, 'One of the penalties of an ecological education is that one lives alone in a world of wounds.'[145] I recognise that sentiment deep in my gut. But during the last thirty-five years of living here I have also come to value the human culture and community that has shaped this land for centuries. Aspects of these seem to be amongst the finest expressions of being human. I have also learned to value the Welsh way of viewing the countryside primarily through the lens of language, community and history alongside my original science-based habitat and species approach. Consequently, it has become essential for me to consider the 'full catastrophe' and view any proposition from all these perspectives. Although I have written about Craig-y-tân mostly from a conservation viewpoint, the implications of any rewilding proposals there would fill me with foreboding – it could be part of a cultural and economic 'death by a thousand cuts'.

Chapter 13

In the End

I hadn't been to Craig-y-tân for months: a combination of a hip re-placement operation and Covid lockdown had made it impossible. But by late June in 2021 I couldn't stand it any longer and had pulled up at the farm by 7.30 a.m., on what promised to be the hottest day of the year so far. Parking someway short of the farmyard, I can see Hywel walking across the field below the house. He is carrying one grandchild and leading the other by the hand; in front of them, seven sheepdogs spin and leap, let out for their early morning exercise. Hywel stands for a while, looking down the valley and I can imagine he is talking to the children about Craig-y-tân: I know how important it is to him that they are steeped in this place. It is a tender scene, evoking the continuity of care for family and place bound together, generation upon generation. I catch up with them a bit later, under the sycamore tree by the house. Anest is pushing herself on a swing Hywel has fixed up in the tree; Eurig, a sturdy lad just past his first birthday, stands holding on to the fence regarding me solemnly. Hywel and I talk a bit of nature and a lot about family; the affection for his grandchildren shines out of him transcending anything else we speak about.

As I set off across the meadows and rough grazing, I recall Marged telling me about her father farming at Craig-y-tân. This morning I have been talking to her nephew and her great-great-niece and nephew in the very same place. Continuity and commitment like that must count for something in the 'full catastrophe' of life. The grass is wet with dew, but the streams are low after the dry weather and it is very quiet: apart from a wren belting it out and the dry, intimate calls of house martins swooping above me, there is a deep silence. It is already getting hot; the gentle breeze barely stirs the leaves. There is little evidence of 'human time' in front of me, just the unhurried rhythm of natural processes – even the sheep seem in step with that. The rocks, squat hawthorns and sheep cradled in this valley feel once again like a scene outside of time – as if nothing has ever changed or ever will; a paradoxical thought in a book about the consequences of change.

Heading uphill I scramble over the fence into the woodland (a bit of a challenge for my new hip) and everything changes, or at least intensifies. Because it is so rare for anybody to step into these woods, they have an untouched, fairy-tale atmosphere. A buzzard circling overhead starts its mewing call, a wild sound that only adds to the estrangement. The grasses and ferns are tall: patches of stately marsh hawk's-beard and valerian decorate the wetter places; delicate beech ferns grow profusely around the rocks. There are a few rowan seedlings here and there, an encouraging sign of woodland regeneration. I feel uncomfortable about crushing the vegetation as I walk, as if I am spoiling the place. Painstakingly, I clamber up the moss-covered block scree, testing each step with my stick; this is not what the doctor ordered – I am glad he is not here to see me.

I make it up to the base of the cliff and settle down with my back against a rock: I have returned to the place where I started this book. Below me I can follow the intricate cushion of woodland to the rough pastures either side of the river, and then up towards the mountains on the other side. The lower slopes are gridded with elderly stone walls and beyond that a long bare ridge stretches up to the summit of the Arenig, at nearly 3,000 feet. There probably isn't a single other human being between here and there. Around me the plant and insect life is prolific: small flies, a beetle and various spiders run over my clothing and notebook. Two spotted flycatchers 'tsskk' their soft familiar call at me; I am surprised to find them here, so far from habitation. Perhaps they have a nest in a rock crevice, the sort of place they must have used before houses and barns or even hedges existed. The air smells clean and sappy – fresh and far from harm. Once again, it seems as if nothing has changed or needs changing, but I know this is delusional: the hand of humankind continues to shape all of this.

I have been exploring and writing about Craig-y-tân for nearly seven years now and sitting here I find myself wondering what I have learned. Firstly, it is important to acknowledge the mindset that I have come at this from. I have been a naturalist since the age of ten and, more than sixty years later, the wonder and excitement of finding, watching, naming wild creatures and plants still does it for me. In my adult life I also became a conservationist – someone who is committed to caring for wildlife – so I am motivated by a sense of discovery coupled to a duty of stewardship. Surrounding all of that is an appreciation of the beauty and mystery of wild places that is essential to me. None of this can be disentangled. Craig-y-tân has fed my soul; I would wither away if I did not have contact with such experiences. This is how I look at the wild world and it has shaped this narrative. Somebody else would have done it differently.

Is Craig-y-tân farm a delightful anachronism or a beacon for a more ecologically sensitive world, in which hill farming and nature conservation are reconciled? Finding out has been a great learning. After thirteen years on the Berwyn Mountains I thought I knew a bit about hill farming, but I know a lot more now. Similarly, I brought some natural history and conservation knowledge and experience with me, but nothing beats paying close attention to one patch. When it comes down to it, the world is essentially local, and all the better for being understood that way. I can see more clearly now how this landscape works. After thirty-five years of living here I have developed an appreciation of the farming way of life and its cultural context but, largely thanks to Hywel, that has deepened and become more nuanced. Hywel has been quietly and kindly educating me into understanding his perspective, mostly by being just how he is. He is not a man to proselytise or thump the table, but he feels strongly nonetheless. His point of view has gradually seeped into me, subtly changing my perspective.

I am even more aware now than I was seven years ago of the global picture: the looming threat of environmental collapse that sometimes makes all of this seem like fiddling about on the margins. The UK is now one of the most nature-depleted countries in the world. Since 1970, we have lost half of our wildlife; 1,200 UK species are extinct or under threat of it.[146] This is happening all across the planet – the Sixth Great Extinction. There have been endless reports, conferences and statistics but still it goes on. We know it is our responsibility and yet, so far, next to nothing has been done about it.

Consequently, the long-held mantra of nature conservation to 'get the habitat management right and everything else will follow' often sounds hollow now. It is also time to own and grieve the attachment my generation of conservationists had for the pre-war British landscape. The longing for flowery meadows, chickens in the yard and the smell of wood smoke is now futile; the countryside has changed out of all recognition, even here in the Welsh hills. Today's mid-career conservationist longs for the countryside of the 1970s and 1980s, which was already impoverished.

I have also (belatedly) come to appreciate that a whole host of people appreciate nature other than naturalists: farmers, foresters, hikers, climbers, kayakers, strollers, mountain bikers, wild swimmers, environmental activists and many others. They may not be interested in studying plants or insects but take great pleasure in a buzzard arcing across the sky or the near sacred brilliance of a bluebell wood in May; they want such things to remain and be available to their children's children. Such folk might pass through Craig-y-tân, call it Paradise, and walk on. It is up to the specialists – farmers, foresters, and conservationists – to explain how it all works; we cannot afford to keep our heads down and go on counting sheep or butterflies. It is still sometimes only dimly appreciated that almost any landscape in Britain is the product of its human land use history – even in the wilds of Eryri (Snowdonia) – and that this is a live and ongoing process.

In considering whether Craig-y-tân is a success for nature I would ideally be able to present a wildlife bill of health for the farm, but, apart for a few generalisations, particularly about birds, I can't do that. As discussed in Chapter 3, we know next to nothing about the populations of most wildlife, the bulk of which is made up of relatively little-known groups such as spiders or springtails, fungi and fungus gnats. Apart from birds, butterflies and moths, information about 'how many' is patchy or absent; it is not just biodiversity that is a problem, but bio-abundance. A dot on an atlas map can tell us a species is still there but not that only one remains where there used to be ten or a hundred. I suppose assessing what wildlife is present at Craig-y-tân could be answered for some groups of organisms in a couple of years by a relatively small group of specialists: coleopterists, dipterists, bryologists, botanists, mycologists, ornithologists. Measuring the distribution, size and trend of those populations would take even more detailed surveys repeated over twenty years or more. Answering the question 'why' is off the scale. That is how complex the world on which we depend, and are embedded in, really is.

So in the absence of local information about plant and animal populations I can only offer a rough and ready assessment of the health of Craig-y-tân for wildlife, and how it is managed.

The pastures and rough grazing on the lower part of the farm still have a good range of flowering plants, although some of them do not get a chance to flower and set seed as they are grazed off too early. But the grazing levels are sufficiently light that most of the perennials are probably surviving and some of them get to flower. Some permanent losses probably occurred when the flock size was much higher twenty years ago. If Craig-y-tân were a nature reserve, I would want to remove or drastically reduce grazing in the summer on the pastures and rough grazing. But it is a farm, and this grazing land is vital for the viability of Hywel's farming system. Perhaps this could be reworked to include less grazing in spring and early summer, within the framework of public funding, but judging the tipping point between farm and nature reserve, including the wise use of public money, is an important consideration.

The riverside at Craig-y-tân is somewhat bare, with the sheep grazed pasture running right to the water's edge. I find this attractive when strolling along the riverbank, but an increase in trees, shrubs and herbaceous plants along the river would benefit wildlife: particularly bats, birds and insects. I remember the dramatic change in the riverside environment (described in Chapter 8) where it is fenced off at the bottom of the waterfall only 300 yards upstream of here: it was immediately more varied and three dimensional in its detail. For this reason fencing off riverbanks to allow natural regeneration is often suggested by agri-environment schemes, and would seem to be a good option here.

Woodlands on the western fringe of Britain are often of international importance, particularly for bryophytes and lichens, which need open conditions without tangles of bramble and vigorous tree regeneration. Ornithologists are now suggesting something similar for birds that are characteristic of these woodlands, such as pied flycatcher and wood warbler and redstart.[147] The woodlands at Craig-y-tân are probably the most valuable habitat on the farm for nature conservation at the present time, but they are beginning to move away from near ideal condition as brambles get a foothold; the light winter grazing appears to be not quite enough. Increasing the numbers of sheep in the winter might hold the brambles back; on the other hand, manual removal of brambles at this stage would be quite feasible. Perhaps the new Sustainable Farming Scheme could pay Hywel, and others like him, to cut the brambles out. Beginning to see farmers not just as food producers but as all round land managers seems critical to the way forward; they have the skills and perhaps over time many more of them will come to see management for nature as an equal first amongst their objectives.

The mountain, that wild and brutal space that takes up a major part of the farm, is in many ways the least interesting for nature conservation in its present condition. Saying this feels a bit heretical as blanket bog is so highly valued ecologically, and scenically it is magnificent here. The Craig-y-tân moorland is part of a large site of European importance for upland birds whose populations are, as elsewhere in Wales, teetering on the brink of collapse. The vegetation is dominated by even-aged heather and so lacks diversity of structure and opportunities for associated species of plants and invertebrates. Whether the re-wetting of the blanket bog has more to deliver over the long term remains to be seen. Some significant management changes would be needed to improve the bird populations and increase the variety of plants and insects: a combination of fox and crow control; heather cutting to vary the structure; followed by long-term cattle, as well as sheep, grazing would probably be required. Controlling foxes and crows just on Craig-y-tân's mountain would be next to useless as these species are so mobile that the gaps would soon be filled from elsewhere. Cooperation between neighbours is probably the only way this could be effective.

Another consideration is that, from an ecological perspective, Craig-y-tân is not a place at all; it is just a part of a very patchy continuum across all of Britain. There is a case for treating some large-scale landscape features as being ecologically relatively distinct, such as the fens in East Anglia or in this case the North Wales moors, but any one location within that is interdependent with the whole. It is also important to acknowledge that wider forces are at play than just local land use; for example the fate of wildlife at Craig-y-tân is intertwined with the sale of Welsh lamb, ninety-five per cent of which is exported from Wales and about forty per cent of that goes to Europe;[148] if tastes change there the viability of this farm could be threatened. Some people are even predicting that 'protein fabrication' (artificial meat) will soon become commercially viable, which could lead to the collapse of livestock farming altogether. Due to climate, soils and terrain rearing sheep, and occasionally cattle, is the only kind of farming that is currently feasible in these upland areas – so farmers don't have much room to manoeuvre. Beyond all of that is the looming threat of climate breakdown. If we accelerate to two or three degrees of warming above pre-industrial levels by 2050, most concerns in this book will seem very small beer.

Looking across the valley to the conifer plantations on the other side, I wonder if I have been too harsh about them. I know I carry historical baggage which may cloud my judgement; younger conservationists will help to develop the wildlife potential of these forests over time – but I do fear another wave of conifer planting on native grasslands in the uplands. Hywel's grandfather and I are of one mind on this.

Despite the day warming up, I am getting a bit stiff sitting at the top of the woods. Also I am resting against a rock draped in sponge-like sphagnum moss, which has wet my back through to the skin. Time to move – which will no doubt be a relief to the spotted flycatchers who are agitating to have the place to themselves once again.

Going down is even more hazardous than coming up, so it takes a while to get back to the boggy pasture outside the wood. Towards the river, the butterflies are now on the move in the warmth of the day: meadow browns, ringlets, a small skipper and, to my delight, several small pearl-bordered fritillaries, the first I have ever seen at Craig-y-tân. Heath spotted-orchids are just beginning to open their delicate spikes and the magenta bells of the cross-leaved heath are attracting nectar-feeding butterflies. A very small frog, alarmed by my approach, struggles to get away through thick rushes and into a ditch. Seeing all of this with fresh eyes after a few months away, I acknowledge just how abundant wildlife is on this farm.

At the riverbank I am grateful to pitch into the shade of a big haw-thorn. The river is about half full and burbling along with a lack of drama that seems to suit the day. A medium-sized trout jumps and lands back with a splash. I wait in vain for a dipper to come barrelling past, but the dragonflies keep me entertained. Two impressive golden-ringed hawkers are scrapping intermittently, wings rustling, presumably over territorial rights. Several splendid demoiselles flit elegantly above the water like Georgian dowagers with time on their hands; their electric blue does seem a little gaudy for North Wales. Looking along the river then back across the boggy pastures and up into the woods where I have been this morning, the farm seems rested, harmonious, there is no intensification or stress on the land or stock.

This raises once again whether Craig-y-tân farm is an anachronism maintained at considerable public expense, or a beacon of hope and a way forward. It is still a beautiful place and rich in wildlife, especially by current standards; it is also a viable, if subsidised, working farm in the hands of a local Welsh-speaking family committed to their community and way of life.

From the perspective of ecosystem services such as carbon storage and sequestration, water quality, flood prevention, biodiversity and public well-being, it also scores highly. Through the agri-environment scheme the current land use system has been tailored to meet nature conservation needs and, with some important caveats, is doing quite well. In Hywel we are lucky to have a farmer who is interested in the wildlife of his farm; I don't pretend he is typical. How could things change so that more farms could be like this?

The first thing to say is that something *has* to change. Outside, and sometimes inside, agricultural circles there is general agreement that much of the uplands in Britain are impoverished for wildlife and that this is largely a consequence of past and current land management.[149] There is also a consensus that the uplands could deliver much more for carbon capture and storage, flood prevention and provision of good quality drinking water. Food production in the uplands is inherently unprofitable and huge sums of public money are spent annually to enable farmers to continue living and working in the hills. The RSPB have published some figures about their upland farming enterprise at Haweswater in the Lake District which illustrate the eye-watering level of dependency hill farming has on public finance. Between 2013 and 2016, the Haweswater farm made an average profit of £97 per ewe and follower (last year's lamb) per year. Without the subsidy the corresponding figure would have been a £135 loss.[150] Other farms will have other figures, but these illustrate vividly that in this post-Brexit era something has to change; the uplands surely must deliver much more in the way of public benefits to continue receiving a similar level of support. If farmers can only make a living by being heavily subsidised but are not delivering a healthy ecosystem into the bargain, then clearly something is wrong. Delivering public goods, as well as meat, would put hill farmers in a stronger position if lab-grown meat ever threatens to make livestock rearing redundant (see Chapter 12). Adopting with enthusiasm a land management system that delivers a range of features valued by society, including high quality meat, in exchange for public money is surely better than no farming at all.

There are two pieces of recent legislation unique to Wales that have a bearing on all of this. The Environment Act (Wales) 2016 brings greater scrutiny to the health and resilience of the countryside by requiring regular 'state of natural resources reports'. Interestingly these reports, the most recent being from 2020, consider marine, woodland mountains, moorland and heath ecosystems in terms of air and water quality, land use and soils, climate change, invasive non-native species and biodiversity: so the ecosystem services approach is now formally established.

The second piece of legislation that is special to Wales is the Well-being of Future Generations Act (2015) which describes how this ground-breaking legislation came into being.[151] This has the power to ensure all public bodies carry out their duties in a way that achieves global sustainable development goals, including the restoration and enhancement of biodiversity, whilst taking equal account of social, environmental and cultural well-being. Any public funding of operations such as flood prevention or carbon storage must contribute to these well-being goals. Both of these pieces of legislation have important implications for the new framework for public funding of farming.

So what sort of framework might encourage hill farming and nature conservation to live in harmony? The Welsh government's proposed 'Sustainable Farming Scheme' is clearly intended as a step towards that. It is underpinned by the principle of 'public goods for public money' and puts forward proposals to pay farmers to deliver such things as carbon storage or biodiversity increases rather than just subsidising food production, which has mostly been the case since the Second World War. Much will depend on the nature and extent of revisions as it progresses through the Senedd in winter 2022. It is intended for publication in its final form in 2023, and all sides will be waiting anxiously to see the detail.

It is evident that right now there is a struggle going on in farming between these new ideas and the traditional system. I think one of the reasons farmers cling so tightly to food production is that it has an inherent 'dignity' in their eyes, as it has to many people. Producing food is clearly a worthwhile livelihood. Asking farmers to see carbon capture, flood prevention or wildlife enhancement as of equal importance to food production is a big stretch. Such things do not yet have the same substantiality within local communities as producing food. Anything other than 'proper farming' might seem demeaning. What I hope will arise is a cultural change whereby farmers take pride in delivering these things, rather than doing them only in order to get paid.

Ever since the huge push to feed the nation during the Second World War, farmers, along with the people who train and represent them, have seen increased food production as their *raison d'être*, and as they have intensified their operations to meet this, our wildlife has, incidentally, been obliterated. This largely unconscious mindset of increased production has become ingrained in agricultural colleges and handed down by several generations in farming families. Inevitably in that process there has been a loss of familiarity with wildlife and consequently less value placed upon it. This has been aided and abetted by mechanisation, which means farmers rarely walk round their farms anymore: they drive and therefore see and hear less.

Over the years I have spoken to many different farmers very few of whom knew, or frankly cared, about the wildlife on their land. I think there is more environmental awareness in recent years, but what is so often lacking is knowledge about nature. Farmers are not alone in this lack, but they are in charge of the land on which wildlife depends. This deficit could be addressed through the agricultural colleges; they could make biodiversity respectable again, enabling young farmers to acquire knowledge that could once again be passed down in families. Not all young farmers go to college, but their ethos is influential. The way forward is surely to persuade, educate and incentivise farmers to accept an expanded job description in which food production is not the only heading. The emphasis will inevitably vary from farm to farm. Even in this district if your farm is on lower ground, all the pastures are improved, and there are few hedges and no mountain land then, in the new framework envisioned by the Welsh government, biodiversity would be a smaller part of your brief than on a farm like Craig-y-tân. This could equally apply to carbon capture and storage, and flood prevention, so the new proposals might mean that some farmers would be paid more than others, which is a cause for anxiety. I understand there are proposals for 'baseline payments' within the Sustainable Farming Scheme which would go some way to addressing this. But as ever, much will depend on the budget being big enough to deliver on this.

Any new proposals to encourage sustainable and environmentally sensitive farming will need to be more flexible and farm-friendly than the agri-environment schemes. Not having ready access to expert advice or the flexibility to vary the management of land is understandably frustrating for farmers and has made them cynical; a lot of goodwill has been ground down by rigid bureaucracy and associated harsh penalties. Well-informed, Welsh-speaking officers who could build a relationship with farmers and their farms would go a long way to making any new scheme a success. These kinds of 'green' countryside jobs are now in high demand amongst Welsh speakers, as they enable bright young people to remain in rural Wales rather than having to move away for meaningful work.

In the light of all this, the proposals for the Sustainable Farming Scheme are very encouraging – at least on paper. It does address the 'full catastrophe': its principal aims revolve around producing food sustainably; responding to climate change; caring for ecosystems;

conserving the countryside, and fostering the Welsh language. It may be that we are on the brink of a new era in Wales in which the framework for agricultural support begins to repair the damage to wildlife and respond to climate change whilst keeping local families on the land. If this scheme gets onto the statute book more or less as envisaged and is backed up with the resources and expertise required to deliver it, then Wales could be at the cutting edge. It is very encouraging to see a small, rural country like Wales leading the way on something so ground-breaking.

It will be important for this scheme to be able to respond creatively to the differences between one farm and another and to have bilingual staff who understand the farming way of life. And as Tir Canol has demonstrated, it pays to proceed at the pace of trust. I can understand that after centuries of accumulated knowledge and experience how irritating it must be when Johnny-come-lately pitches up and says you have got it all wrong. Farmers have been shaping the land since forever, and society needs them to go on doing it – it's true we now need some different patterns for different reasons, but they are the only people who can deliver them.

Agricultural communities are the backbone of Welsh-speaking life and, along with their dependent vets, contractors, seed merchants and others, are the glue for a rich and indigenous culture and rural economy. There is still strong attachment to a 'traditional way of life'; although it must be said that way of life has been continuously changing, so it is now very different from seventy years ago, in Marged's day.

The sun is beating down now, and I decide to call it a day. Ambling back along the river my head is full of the many dimensions thrown up by taking this farm as a sounding board for the intersection of farming and wildlife conservation in the uplands of Wales. Here, at Craig-y-tân, it does seem to be working; there is harmony between the two, albeit at considerable public expense. I do think that Craig-y-tân can be seen as a beacon of hope rather than an anachronism

– this is a place to aspire to. Meeting Hywel and his grandchildren this morning has stayed with me all day. It is a reminder that although Craig-y-tân represents the struggle to retain a rich wildlife heritage in a farmed landscape it is also about family, simple pleasures, hard work and continuity. Anest and Eurig will, I hope, enjoy and remember Craig-y-tân all their lives, as perhaps their descendants will. I am just passing through – and I call it Paradise.

Notes

1   Jon Kabat-Zinn used this phrase in the title of his seminal book on mindfulness, *Full Catastrophe Living*. It is a quote from the movie *Zorba the Greek* in which Zorba describes his life as 'wife, house, kids, everything … the full catastrophe!'

2   Although I often write in the present tense to convey the vividness of my experience, the events were spread unevenly throughout that period, and I have forged them into the semblance of a single year for the sake of a coherent narrative.

3   Thoreau, Henry David, *Walden: Or, Life in the Woods* (Boston: Ticknor and Fields, 1854).

4   There is a useful account of those events in Lowe, Philip et al., *Countryside Conflicts* (Aldershot: Temple Smith Gower, 1986).

5   Hayhow, D. B. et al., *State of Nature 2016*. The State of Nature partnership.

6   According to *Farming Facts and Figures, Wales 2020 (https://www.gov. wales/sites/default/files/statistics-and-research/2020-07/farming-facts-and-figures-2020-658.pdf)*, the number of farmers, partners and directors on farm holdings in Wales in 2019 was 39,000.

7   Published posthumously in 1975 by Gwasg Gwynedd.

8   Jones, Simon, *Straeon Cwm Cynllwyd: Atgofion, Tan-y-bwlch* (Gwasg Carreg Gwalch, 1989).

9   Jefferies, Richard, *Field and Hedgerow: Last Essays* (Oxford: Oxford University Press, 1982).

10   *The London Review of Books*, Vol. 30/5 (March 2008).

11   McCarthy, Michael, *The Moth Snowstorm: Nature and Joy* (London: John Murray, 2015).

12   In his excellent book, *Wild Fell* (London: Doubleday, 2022), Lee Schofield writes painfully about a similar cultural gap that he has experienced in recent times in the Lake District working on a large-scale farming and conservation project for the RSPB at Haweswater.

13   Plantlife, *Save our Meadows* report, July 2018 (*https://www.plantlife. org.uk/uk/about-us/news/devastation-of-meadows-endangers-flower-favour- ites-like-wild-strawberry-ragged-robin-and-harebell*).

14   There is a fascinating account of this in Mid Wales in Howells, Erwyd, *Good Men and True: The Lives and Tales of the Shepherds of Mid Wales* (Aberystwyth: Erwyd Howells, 2005).

15   This is Ifan, Hywel's grandfather.

16   Bollam, George, *Wild Life in Wales* (London: Frank Palmer, 1913).

17   In the 1980s, numbers of red kites were probably less than fifty pairs in the UK, all of which were confined to the hills of Mid Wales. This was prior to the reintroduction programmes in England, Scotland, and more recently Ireland, getting established. Thanks to a dedicated and long-term effort to safeguard this precarious population they have now increased to many hundreds of pairs spread throughout Wales.

18   Brenchley, Anne et al., *The Breeding Birds of North Wales* (Liverpool: Liverpool University Press, 2013).

19   British Trust for Ornithology Breeding Bird Survey (*https://www.bto. org>projects>breeding bird survey*).

20   There is a formal UK Farmland Bird Index from which figures for Wales are available, but this includes birds that are not characteristic of hill farms, so I have not depended on it here. That index was relatively stable between 1995 and 2005 but fell by twenty-four per cent between 2006 and 2016. Bladwell, S. et al., *The State of Birds in Wales 2018* (Cardiff: RSPB Cymru, 2018).

21   This is rough, often steep land with bracken, scattered rocks and bushes amongst the native grasses. It is usually found between the better pasture lower down and the 'mountain' grazing above.

22   There is less arable land in Meirionnydd than any other county in Wales: Blackstock, T. H. et al. *Habitats of Wales* (Cardiff, University of Wales Press, 2010).

23   British Trust for Ornithology Breeding Bird Survey, Trends in Wales 1995–2020 (*https://www.bto.org>projects>breeding bird survey*).

24   Pritchard, Rhion, *Birds of Meirionnydd* (Bangor: Cambrian Bird Society, 2012).

25   Pritchard, Rhion et al., *The Birds of Wales* (Liverpool: Liverpool University Press, 2021) looked at factors that had driven the changes in populations of 127 bird species since 1950. It found that agricultural

management accounted for forty-one per cent of cited declines and was the single most significant cause of change in Wales.

26   Bollam, George, *Wild Life in Wales* (London: Frank Palmer, 1913).

27   Pritchard, Rhion et al., *The Birds of Wales*, (Liverpool: Liverpool University Press, 2021), p.115.

28   Rackham, Oliver, *Woodlands* (London: Harper Collins, 2006).

29   Woodland Trust, *Rowan (https://www.woodlandtrust.org.uk/trees-woods-and-wildlife/british-trees/a-z-of-british-trees/rowan/).*

30   Details of all ancient woodlands in the nations of the UK can be found in the appropriate Ancient Woodland Inventories. In England all woods dated from 1600 (when the first reasonable maps became available) and still extant today are listed, but in Wales, where comprehensive |mapping is more recent, the first editions of the Ordnance Survey one-inch maps published in the 1830s are used as a baseline for including woodlands in the register. Many of the woodlands listed in Wales will, of course, predate that era.

31   Source: personal comment by Nick Fenwick.

32   Rodwell, J. S. (ed.), *British Plant Communities* (Cambridge: Cambridge University Press, 1991).

33   Linnard, William, *Welsh Woods and Forests* (Llandysul: Gomer, 2000).

34   Simmons, I. G., *The Moorlands of England and Wales* (Edinburgh: Edinburgh University Press, 2019).

35   Vera, F. W. M., *Grazing Ecology and Forest History* (Egham: CABI Publishing, 2000).

36   Latham, J., 'How "natural" is woodland nature?', *Natur Cymru*, Number 10 (Spring 2004).

37   *https://gov.wales/sustainable-farming-scheme.*

38   This probably refers to a loft above the stables where the farmhand would have slept – benefitting from the warmth from the animals below.

39   Blackstock, T. H. et al., *Habitats of Wales* (Cardiff: University of Wales Press, 2010).

40   To 0.025 livestock units per hectare.

41   Source: personal comment by Andrew Graham.

42   In *Wild Fell*, Lee Schofield details an interesting high-tech approach being used by the RSPB Haweswater on open hill land whereby cattle fitted with GPS collars receive a mild electric shock if they stray over virtual boundaries. The animals soon learn to stay within the invisible boundaries,

which can be reconfigured using aerial photographs linked to the GPS system. This system enables them to mimic natural systems where grazing would be more irregular.

43 Dasgupta, P., *The Economics of Biodiversity: The Dasgupta Review* (London: HM Treasury, 2021).

44 Although carbon credits used for tree planting and peatland restoration fall under this heading.

45 Blackstock, T. H. et al., *Habitats of Wales* (Cardiff: University of Wales Press, 2010), p.125. More recent published figures are hard to clarify but this reference clearly illustrates the legacy of conifer planting.

46 There are now about 665,000 hectares of Sitka spruce in the UK, making it our most common forest tree: Kirby, Keith, *Woodland Flowers* (London: Bloomsbury, 2020).

47 Condry, William, *The Snowdonia National Park* (London: William Collins, 1966), p.188.

48 *https://ymgynghori.cyfoethnaturiol.cymru/forest-planning-cynllunio-coedwig/llanuwchllyn-forest-resource-plan/*.

49 For a well-researched discussion of this issue see Alexander, Mike et al., 'Where Next for Welsh Woodlands?', *Natur Cymru*, No. 66 (Summer 2022).

50 There are more details of this in Reynolds, Fiona, *The Fight for Beauty* (London: Oneworld, 2016).

51 From an excellent account of the Flow Country scandal in Thompson, Des et al., *Nature's Conscience – The life and legacy of Derek Ratcliffe* (King's Lynn: Langford Press, 2015).

52 Bradfer-Lawrence, T. et al., 'The potential contribution of terrestrial nature-based solutions to a national net-zero climate target', *Journal of Applied Ecology* (2021) pp.2349–60.

53 Monbiot, George, *Carbon Colonialisation* blogpost, 31 January 2022 (*https://www.monbiot.com*).

54 See Roger Lovegrove's detailed account of this widespread practice in *Silent Fields: the long decline of a nation's wildlife* (Oxford: Oxford University Press, 2007).

55 Newton, Ian, *Farming and Birds* (London: William Collins, 2017), p.39.

56 *https://www.bto.org/our-science/projects/breeding-bird-survey*.

57 Douglas et al., 'Changes in upland bird abundance show associations with moorland management', *Bird Study* Vol. 24/2, pp.242–54; and Roes et al., 'A review of predation as a limiting factor for bird populations in

mesopredator-rich landscapes: a case study of the UK', *Biological Reviews* (2018) pp.1–23.

58 UK Centre for Ecology and Hydrology Peatlands Factsheet.

59 Linnard, William, *Welsh Woods and Forests* (Llandysul: Gomer, 2000).

60 Source: personal comment by Nick Fenwick.

61 Elen and I repeated this outing the following year and to our delight saw fourteen large heaths in the same area.

62 Midgley, Mary, *Beast and Man: The Roots of Human Nature* (Abingdon: Routledge, 2002).

63 British Trust for Ornithology *News* (Spring 2018).

64 Wilson, M. W. et al., 'The breeding population of Peregrine Falcon in the United Kingdom in 2014', *Bird Study*, 65/1 (2018).

65 Williams G., *Birds in Wales 2018* 15/1 (Welsh Ornithological Society).

66 *Birds in Wales – Welsh Bird Report 2020* (Welsh Ornithological Society, 2021).

67 'Hen Harriers in Wales in 2016', *Birds in Wales* 16/1 (2019).

68 Pritchard, Rhion et al., *Birds of Wales* (Liverpool: Liverpool University Press, 2021).

69 Pritchard, Rhion, et al., *Birds of Wales* (Liverpool: Liverpool University Press, 2021)..

70 Huntley, B. et al., *A Climatic Atlas of European Breeding Birds* (Barcelona: Lynx Editions, 2007).

71 British Trust for Ornithology (Winter 2017).

72 Pritchard, Rhion et al., *The Birds of Wales* (Liverpool: Liverpool University Press, 2021).

73 Balmer, Dawn, *Bird Atlas 2011–17* (Thetford: British Trust for Ornithology, 2013).

74 Huntley, B. et al., *A Climatic Atlas of European Breeding Birds* (Barcelona: Lynx Editions, 2007).

75 Pritchard, Rhion et al., *The Birds of Wales* (Liverpool: Liverpool University Press, 2021).

76 Brenchley, Anne et al., *The Breeding Birds of North Wales* (Liverpool: Liverpool University Press, 2013).

77 British Wildlife, *Wildlife Reports: Birds* (August 2018).

78 Huntley, B. et al., *A Climatic Atlas of European Breeding Birds* (Barcelona: Lynx Editions, 2007).

79 Lovegrove, Roger et al., *Birds in Wales* (London: T. & A. D. Poyser, 1994).

80 Pritchard, Rhion et al., *Birds in Wales* (Liverpool: Liverpool University Press, 2021).

81 Baines, D. et al., 'The invertebrate diet of black grouse chicks', *Bird Study* 64/2 (2017).

82 Scridel, D. et al., 'Native woodland creation is associated with increase in a Black Grouse Lyrurus tetrix population', *Bird Study* 64/1 (2017).

83 Warren, P. and Baines, D., *Changes in the abundance and distribution of upland breeding birds in the Berwyn SPA North Wales 1983–2012* (Game and Wildlife Conservation Trust, October 2012).

84 Nature Conservancy Council unpublished survey.

85 *https://www.bto.org/our-science/projects/breeding-bird-survey*.

86 Taylor, Rachel, 'Curlew Collaboration', British Trust for Ornithology *News* (Spring 2022).

87 Franks, Samantha E. et al., 'Environmental correlates of breeding abundance and population change of Eurasian Curlew in Britain', *Bird Study* 64/3 (2017).

88 Newton, Ian, *Farming and Birds* (London: William Collins, 2017), p.496.

89 Source: Dave Smith, RSPB – personal comment.

90 Lovegrove, Roger et al., *Birds in Wales* (London: T. & A. D. Poyser, 1994).

91 Brenchley, Anne et al., *The Breeding Birds of North Wales* (Liverpool: Liverpool University Press, 2013).

92 Unpublished Nature Conservancy Council survey report by Peter Davis, 1984.

93 Taylor, Rachel, 'Curlew Collaboration', British Trust for Ornithology *News* (Spring 2022).

94 Powney, Gary et al., 'Widespread losses of pollinating insects in Britain', *Nature Communications* 10 (2019).

95 I didn't.

96 Holmes, Nigel and Raven, Paul, *Rivers* (Oxford: British Wildlife Publishing, 2014), pp.345–61.

97 *https://waterwatchwales.naturalresourceswales.gov.uk/*.

98 Brenchley, Anne et al., *The Breeding Birds of North Wales* (Liverpool: Liverpool University Press, 2013).

99 Holmes, Nigel and Raven, Paul, *Rivers* (Oxford: British Wildlife Publishing, 2014), pp.345–6.

100 Ingersoll, Robert G., 'The Christian Religion', *The North American*

Review (August 1881).

101 *State of Nature 2019 report*, Joint Nature Conservation Committee.

102 Rind, Peter, 'Britain's Contribution to Global Conservation', *British Wildlife* (December 2003).

103 *Mosses and Liverworts of Welsh Atlantic Woodland* (Plantlife, August 2015).

104 There was yet another wave of felling during World War One. Source: Nick Fenwick – personal comment.

105 Averis, A. et al., *An Illustrated Guide to British Upland Vegetation* (Peterborough: Joint Nature Conservation Committee, 2004), pp.113–4.

106 Unpublished species list and summary per Margaret Crittenden of the British Bryological Society.

107 I later found out that this was an old fence that he didn't remove when the wood was enclosed, so a sheep exclusion area arose accidentally and there is little incentive to reinstate it.

108 Personal comment from UK CCC member Rebecca Heaton in an unrecorded online forum.

109 *https://community.rspb.org.uk/getinvolved/wales/b/wales-blog/posts/a-national-forest-for-wales-1340769852.*

110 'Conservation News', *British Wildlife* (April 2022).

111 Barkham, Patrick, 'Trees on commercial UK plantations "not helping climate crisis"', *The Guardian* (10 March 2020).

112 At that time we had no certain information, only rumours.

113 Kevin Austin, Head of Agricultural Strategy and Policy Unit, Welsh Government: presentation at The Future of Upland Farming in Wales Conference, Llanrwst, March 2017, unpublished.

114 Newton, Ian, *Farming and Birds* (London: William Collins, 2017).

115 McDonald, J. et al., 'Have Welsh agri-environment schemes delivered for focal species?' *Journal of Applied Ecology* (January 2019).

116 This is unusual as in most woodlands in Glastir schemes livestock are excluded all year round. Source: Nick Fenwick – personal comment.

117 Source: Nick Fenwick – personal comment.

118 In 2018.

119 National Nature Reserves.

120 There is an interesting account of the 1980s conflict on the Berwyn in *Countryside Conflicts* by Lowe, Philip et al. (Aldershot: Temple Smith Gower, 1986).

121 Schofield, Lee, *Wild Fell* (London: Penguin, 2022).

122 Lovegrove, Roger, *Silent Fields* (Oxford: Oxford University Press, 2007) is an eye-opening account of the scale of this killing.

123 See the very instructive map from the British Trust for Ornithology at: *https://app.bto.org/wader-map/*. This clearly illustrates how marginal Wales is for breeding moorland waders these days.

124 For an overview of this aspect see: King, Sara and Oldham, Emma, 'A kaleidoscope of approaches to rewilding in Britain', *British Wildlife* (December 2021), pp.187–93.

125 Dafydd Morris-Jones, who farms in Mid Wales, wrote 'O'r Mynydd – What future on Rewilding's doorstep?' in the Cambrian Mountains Society journal in 2019.

126 Monbiot, George, *Regenesis: feeding the world without devouring the planet* (London: Penguin, 2022).

127 Monbiot, George, *Feral* (London: Allen Lane, 2013).

128 I am grateful to Aled Thomas, ex-Forestry Commission, for the story of the Ranges.

129 Williamson, Tom, 'Rewilding: a landscape history perspective', *British Wildlife* 33/6 (May 2022).

130 Williamson, Tom, 'Rewilding: a landscape history perspective', *British Wildlife* 33/6 (May 2022).

131 A seminal source around this and much more is Tree, Isabella, *Wilding* (London: Pan Macmillan, 2018).

132 Peterken, George, 'A long-term perspective on rewilding woodland', *British Wildlife* 33/8 (August 2022).

133 Williamson, Tom, 'Rewilding: a landscape history perspective', *British Wildlife* 33/6 (May 2022).

134 Alexander, Keith, 'Britain's natural landscape', *British Wildlife* 29/5 (2018).

135 Williamson, Tom, 'Rewilding: a landscape history perspective', *British Wildlife* 33/6 (May 2022).

136 Monbiot, George, *Walk on the Wild Side* blogpost 17 December 2015 (*https://www.monbiot.com*).

137 See note 136.

138 Tree, Isabella, *Wilding* (London: Picador, 2018), p.152.

139 *https://www.cambrianwildwood.org*.

140 All information on this project is from *https://www.cambrianwildwood.org*.

141 Fuller, Rob and Gilroy, James, 'Rewilding and Intervention: complementary philosophies for nature conservation in Britain', *British Wildlife* 32/4 (February 2021), p.258.

142 Woodfall, David, 'Pant Glas' in *Rewilding* (London: William Collins, 2019). Nick Fenwick also works for the Farmers' Union of Wales.

143 *www.theguardian.com/environment/blog/2013/jun/26/wales.*

144 The 1947 Agricultural Act and the 1957 Treaty of Rome have the same objectives: production of sufficient food at affordable rates with minimum volatility to supplies and prices, while providing fair incomes for farmers and farm workers. This has been the platform for agriculture for the last 70 years.

145 Leopold, Aldo, *A Sand County Almanac* (Oxford: Oxford University Press, 1949).

146 *State of Nature 2019 report*, Joint Nature Conservation Committee.

147 Mallord, John W. et al., 'Are changes in breeding habitat responsible for recent population changes of long-distance migrant birds?', *Bird Study* 63/2 (2016), pp.250–61.

148 Data per Nick Fenwick, Farmers' Union of Wales.

149 Monbiot, George, *The Hills are Dead* blogpost 4 January 2017 (*https://www.monbiot.com*).

150 Schofield, Lee et al., 'Balancing Culture and Nature in the Lake District', *British Wildlife* 31/4 (April 2020).

151 See Jane Davidson's book *#futuregen: Lessons from a Small Country* (Vermont: Chelsea Green, 2020); *#futuregen: Gwersi o Wlad Fechan* (Aberystwyth: Y Lolfa, 2022).

Further Reading

This is for those who would like to delve further into the main publications cited, plus some others that have informed and inspired me. For journal articles etc. see footnotes.

Averis, A. et al., *An Illustrated Guide to British Upland Vegetation* (Peterborough: Joint Nature Conservation Committee, 2004).

Avery, Mark, *Inglorious: Conflict in the Uplands* (London: Bloomsbury, 2015).

Avery, Mark and Leslie, Roderick, *Birds and Forestry* (London: T. & A. D. Poyser, 1990).

Blackstock, T. H. et al., *Habitats of Wales.* (Cardiff: University of Wales Press, 2010).

Bollam, George, *Wild Life in Wales* (London: Frank Palmer, 1913).

Brenchley, Anne, *The Breeding Birds of North Wales* (Liverpool: Liverpool University Press, 2013).

Cocker, Mark, *Our Place* (London: Jonathan Cape, 2018).

Condry, W. M., *The Snowdonia National Park* (London: William Collins, 1966).

Davidson, Jane, *#futuregen: Lessons from a Small Country* (Vermont: Chelsea Green, 2020).

Davidson, Jane, *#futuregen: Gwersi o Wlad Fechan* (Aberystwyth: Y Lolfa, 2022).

Forrest, H. E., The *Vertebrate Fauna of North Wales* (London: Witherby, 1907).

Fowles, A. P., *Invertebrates of Wales* (Peterborough: Joint Nature Conservation Committee, 1994).

Holmes, Nigel and Raven, Paul, *Rivers* (Oxford: British Wildlife Publishing, 2014).

Howells, Erwyd, *Good Men and True* (Aberystwyth: Erwyd Howells, 2005).

Huntley, B. et al., *A Climatic Atlas of European Breeding Birds* (Barcelona: Lynx Editions, 2007).

Kabat-Zinn, Jon, *Full Catastrophe Living* (New York: Delta, 1990).

Kirby, Keith, *Woodland Flowers* (London: Bloomsbury, 2020).

Lake, Sophie et al., *Britain's Habitats* (Woodstock: Princeton, 2015).

Laurie, Patrick, *Native* (Edinburgh: Birlinn, 2021).

Leopold, Aldo, *Sand County Almanac* (Oxford: Oxford University Press, 1949).

Linnard, William, *Welsh Woods and Forests* (Llandysul: Gomer, 2000).

Lovegrove, Roger, *Silent Fields* (Oxford: Oxford University Press, 2007).

Lovegrove, Roger et al., *Birds in Wales* (London: T. & A. D. Poyser, 1994).

Lowe, Philip et al., *Countryside Conflicts* (Aldershot: Temple Smith Gower, 1986).

Marsden, Philip, *Rising Ground* (London: Granta, 2014).

McCarthy, Michael, *The Moth Snowstorm* (London: John Murray, 2015).

Monbiot, George, *Feral* (London: Allen Lane, 2013).

Monbiot, George, *Regenesis* (London: Allen Lane, 2022).

Newton, Ian, *Farming and Birds* (London: William Collins, 2017).

Pritchard, Rhion, *Birds of Meirionnydd* (Bangor: Cambrian Ornithological Society, 2012).

Prichard, Rhion et al., *Birds of Wales* (Liverpool: Liverpool University Press, 2021).

Rackham, Oliver, *The History of the Countryside* (London: J. M. Dent, 1986).

Rackham, Oliver, *Woodlands* (London: Harper Collins, 2012).

Rebanks, James, *The Shepherd's Life* (London: Penguin, 2016).

Rebanks, James, *English Pastoral* (London: Allen Lane, 2020).

Reynolds, Fiona, *The Fight for Beauty* (London: Oneworld, 2016).

Schofield, Lee, *Wild Fell* (London: Doubleday, 2022).

Sheldrake, Merlin, *Entangled Life* (London: Bodley Head, 2020).

Simmons, I. G., *The Moorlands of England and Wales* (Edinburgh: Edinburgh University Press, 2019).

Smith, Malcolm, *Ploughing a New Furrow* (Dunbeath: Whittles, 2018).

Thompson, Des et al., *Nature's Conscience* (King's Lynn: Langford Press, 2015).

Tree, Isabella, *Wilding* (London: Picador, 2018).

Usher, M. B. and Thompson, D. B. A., *Ecological Change in the Uplands* (Oxford: Blackwell, 1988).

Vera, F. W. M., *Grazing Ecology and Forest History* (Egham: CABI Publishing, 2000).

Woodfall, David, *Rewilding* (London: William Collins, 2019).

Acknowledgements

There is nowhere else I could start other than with Hywel Jones, his son Rhys and the rest of his family. On that day I went to Hywel with an idea about a book he could have said 'no' – or more likely politely declined. And there would have been no book. But Hywel gave me free run of his farm and has been generous with his time, explaining patiently and carefully about farming at Craig-y-tân, and what it really takes to manage that obdurate and beautiful place. I have learned much from him for which I will always be grateful.

Special thanks are also due to Marged Jones, Hywel's aunt, for wonderful reminiscences about her early life, and for the warmth of her company.

Beyond *teulu* (family) Craig-y-tân there are many people who have helped me along this journey.

Foremost amongst these must be Helen Pendry, who early on and throughout gave me encouragement, read drafts and offered critical feedback. Helen was the first person to read *Shaping the Wild* in its entirety and I remember the relief of having shared it with somebody whose expertise and honesty I could trust. Helen saw potential in the early drafts of this book that I didn't know were there. She also ran a wonderful writing group in Machynlleth which inspired me to broaden my vision and keep going.

I am grateful to Christine Evans for encouragement and generous feedback at a very early stage, and for some inspiring writing conversations on Ynys Enlli (Bardsey Island) over numerous summers.

Andrew Graham has been of great help and given me much companionship, encouragement (and some provocation!) across the years.

He is probably the most knowledgeable naturalist I have ever met –
and I have met a few.

Arthur Chater kindly read some early draft chapters and has been
unfailingly encouraging throughout.

At the other end of the writing process Heather Garret, recently of
NRW, very generously read a complete late draft and brought new
and more recent thinking to areas where I might have sounded like
1980s-man. Even later in the day Nick Fenwick kindly read the entire
manuscript and, drawing on his extensive farming background,
provided new perspectives, personal observations and up-to-date
information that have significantly enhanced this story.

Awel Jones was especially helpful with translating Welsh terms and
text that were beyond Elen's reach. Awel also allowed me to draw on
her deep knowledge of local history and she supplied the historic
Farmers Weekly article that was so informative for Chapter 2.

Grateful thanks for their specialist and generous help in various
ways to: Dave Lamacraft, Mick Green, Mike Walker, Barbara Jones,
Dave Smith, Sian Stacey and Aled Thomas.

My thanks to Diane Bailey and Geoff Young of Penrallt Bookshop
in Machynlleth for providing us with the inspirational essence of good
reading. More than one aspiring writer has been nurtured there.

I am grateful to Malka and Beorn Holmes for allowing me to use an
image of one of their father's paintings on the cover of the book. I still
miss Clyde, so it means a lot to have him front me up.

I also want to thank Iolo Williams for his supportive enthusiasm for
my writing over the years, culminating in his generous foreword for
this book.

For the long process of getting this book from my computer to a
bookshop shelf I am deeply grateful to all at UWP and Calon books. In
particular Amy Feldman had faith in my work and nudged me along
with great skill and kindness. I always felt in good hands. Later in
the process Abbie Headon picked up the baton from Amy, made it all
possible when I began to wobble, and skilfully navigated us through
the later stages of publication.

Thanks also to Adam Burns and his colleagues for doing such a good job with the cover and accepting my suggestion of using Clyde's painting.

I am grateful to the Ruth Killick agency for their input into publicising this book. Theirs is a world that was new territory to me, and I was very glad of somebody who could read the map. Thanks also to Julia Crompton for some very helpful initial advice on how to approach publicity – so at least I started with the map the right way up.

At a more personal level deep thanks go to Candace Harris for her unfailing guidance and wisdom. Also to my dear friend David Cooke who has been more help than he will ever know during twenty years of walking the hills of Wales together.

Moving closer to family, how can I thank Pete Hanauer enough, not only for sixty years of deep friendship, but a superb collection of illustrations for this book. Pete and Gethin are the only two people I have taken to Craig-y-tân over all these years.

Special appreciation for my children, Owen, Megan, Gethin and Angharad, each of whom have helped and encouraged me with their enthusiasm and interest in one way or another. Without Angharad sorting out yet another of my computer panics this book would never have got written. Loath though I am to be partial, special regard must go to Gethin, not only for his companionship in the hills and endless conversations about all of this, but because this is his life – he lives and breathes it. Conservation is to him what farming is to Hywel.

Lastly, deep gratitude goes to my wife Elen, who has read and corrected drafts, translated Marged's and E. D. Rowlands' writings and, even more to the point, put up with endless absences, moaning and doubt, which she has borne in her characteristically kind and even-natured way. She as much as I will surely be glad to see this book completed. And I think I owe her a walk round Craig-y-tân.

And can you thank a place? There have been times when I have thought, 'if I fall and break my neck right here, what better place to do it.' I don't think I could pay Craig-y-tân a bigger compliment.